If You Ask Me

If You Ask Me

LIBBY GELMAN-WAXNER

Fawcett Columbine • NEW YORK

A Fawcett Columbine Book
Published by Ballantine Books

Copyright © 1994 by Libby Gelman-Waxner

All rights reserved under International and Pan-American Copyright Conventions. Published in the United States by Ballantine Books, a division of Random House, Inc., New York, and distributed in Canada by Random House of Canada Limited, Toronto.

This edition published by arrangement with St. Martin's Press, Inc.

Collection of movie reviews appearing over
a five-year period in *Premiere* magazine.

Library of Congress Catalog Card Number: 94-90790

ISBN: 0-449-90991-3

Cover design by Barbara Leff
Cover illustration by Robert deMichiell

Manufactured in the United States of America
First Ballantine Books Edition: July 1995
10 9 8 7 6 5 4 3 2 1

CONTENTS

CONTENTS

CONTENTS

vii

CONTENTS

INTRODUCTION

— — — —

When some ultrastars are interviewed, they say that they never dreamed that someday they would be worshipped by millions all over the planet and beyond. I always knew. Even as a child, my mother, the beloved Sondra Krell-Gelman, would tell me, along with all the other children on the playground, "Libby, you're more than special. You're not just gorgeous and highly intelligent, you don't just read in the third grade at a college freshman level, you're not just more gifted than any of those little eight-year-old robots who play the violin or the oboe with philharmonic orchestras. Libby—you have opinions. And someday the world will listen."

And so even then I told the other children that Disney's *101 Dalmatians* was entertaining but morally inchoate; it was as a preschooler that I first began to use words which I could neither pronounce nor understand. Yes, sometimes the other kids were jealous, especially when I began to rate their bag lunches with a five-star system (one star for wholewheat bread and an apple, five stars for anything in an individual foil-sealed freshness cup). But even as a child I realized that while the life of a critic would never be easy, I would know the unique joy of always being absolutely right.

A critic's life can be lonely; sometimes I feel like the only person who can really understand me is the Pope, because only His Holiness can know the special ache of the infallible, and only His Eminence can truly share my feelings for gold accents and brocade—when I picture the Pope's sumptuous private quarters at the Vatican, I know I would feel right at home, and I see plastic slipcovers, because even altar boys will be boys. Thank God I also have my wonderful friends and family, who have always been there to say, yes, Libby, you were right about the lambada—it is the new waltz. Still, sometimes I look at my colleagues, at Siskel and Ebert, at Kael and Sarris and Rex, and I wonder—why don't they ever return my friendly screening-room waves, or take me up on my offers of hard candy, Kleenex, and Wash 'N' Dri's? I mean, it's not for nothing that I am heralded as the glove compartment of the American cinema. And then I think again and I realize, of course, they're shy. They want to reach out, but they're afraid—after all, I'm Libby, and they're just part of the yearning multitude, awaiting my next sparkling commandments. Sometimes I want to run to them and say, Please, I'm just a person like you, only more pulled together, but I know they won't believe me. Their shining eyes and word-processor-weary fingers say, Libby, you are a goddess, and we are mortal, just look at the condition of our shoes and our sad little state school grad-student briefcases. The most we can share is an occasional moan at the new Oliver Stone trailer.

Many have asked, occasionally while pointing sharp objects in my direction, Libby—how did you come to be America's most beloved and irresponsible film critic? Or as one devoted fan put it, in a postcard I have since turned over to the authorities: Who died and made you the biggest jerk in the tri-state area? All I can say is: I love movies and sometimes I even love films, but above all, I always love watching what Kim Basinger will do with her hair so it will always get caught in her mouth; I'm telling you, I think that Kim and Ann-Margret get half of their daily protein intake from split ends. For me, cinema is about so much more than just character, structure, cinematography, and a director's searing and soaring personal vision. It's about watching Sylvester Stallone mowing down evil Asians or Arabs, while tucking his submachine gun under his arm like a clutch bag. It's about how Michelle Pfeiffer can make me love her even though her cheekbones and thighs could be grounds for a class action lawsuit by women everywhere, and it's about wondering if Woody Allen's marital problems can be traced to his obsessive use of beige, years before last summer when beige became the new denim. Movies are about Cher's wigs and Madonna's abs and how there should be high schools and bridges and highway rest stops named after Steve Martin, Bill Murray, and Tom Hanks. And mostly movies are about how much Dennis Quaid and Daniel Day-Lewis desire me on a very personal and intimate level, but that since I am happily married, they can only express their lust and adoration by removing their clothing onscreen and praying that somewhere I will be watching and clutching my armrest and my dear friend, the still tragically single Stacy Schiff, who encourages me to occasionally run down the aisle and actually whisper my fax number into Dennis or Daniel's enormous celluloid ears. I would also include my beeper number except that, frankly, I feel the only people who can justify carrying a beeper are surgeons, drug dealers, and prostitutes; anyone else with one of those things hanging off their belt is just a little too Buttafuoco for my taste, if you know what I mean and I think you do, I can tell by your fabulous Banana Republic linen separates, they're supposed to look even better wrinkled, but try telling that to my mother, or yours.

Five years ago, when *Premiere* magazine first begged me to become their in-house film critic and ultimate auteurist authority, I had to ask myself: Libby, you already have it all, what do you need this for? As my devoted readers know, I am an extremely successful assistant buyer in juniors' activewear. Every year, I help decide exactly which Calvin Klein silk charmeuse slip dress will tempt our customers into having enough surgery to be able to wear it. I also have two perfect children, my daughter Jennifer and my little Mitchell Shawn; motherhood is a 24-hour-a-day job, just ask my housekeeper and my two nannies, but let's leave the *au pair* out of this, because that navel ring is making me very nervous, even on a Wellesley girl—especially on a Wellesley girl. And of course I am also devoted to my flawless husband, Josh, who is not only a wildly sought-after Upper East Side orthodontist, whose clientele includes the children of many celebrities' attorneys, but who can also balance a Lite beer, two different bags of chips, three remote controls, the *TV Guide,* the latest John Grisham, a cellular phone, and a Master Blaster water pistol to keep the cat and the kids away from the chips, all on a single arm of his recliner. With all this in my life, plus the StairMaster, which I use backwards without holding onto the handrails, thank you very much, how could I make room to mold the filmgoing of a nation?

Why did I decide to do it, to offer my nuggets of auteuristic insight every month in the pages of a magazine which never contains enough perfume strips? The answer is—YOU. Yes, I did it for YOU, the wonderful, loving, dedicated, ignorant American Cineplex addict. I do it because I love you, every one of you, even the ones who actually pretend to enjoy French movies about the ambiguity of love at the beach, or any French movies at all, or any movies that aren't in color or in English for that matter. I do it because I can hear America crying out, saying, Please, Libby, tell us what you think, guide us, help us understand the differences between the various Baldwin brothers, heal us. I am here for America and the world, to wonder if in just a few years our preschools will be filled with toddlers named Meryl, Glenn, Macauley, Christian, and Winona. I am here to say yes, do not be ashamed, join with me, let us all gather as one and shout, Take us, Harrison Ford, and bring Tommy Lee Jones with you. Both of you, take us now!

I hope that my legions of fans will enjoy this first volume of my collected columns; someday I hope that there will be enough future collections to merit an infomercial, in which the books will be offered by Victoria Principal's personal dermatologist, along with a look-of-woodgrain display case available at no extra charge if you order now. I would also like to thank all of the wonderful people at *Premiere*, for supporting me and understanding that my family and my nails must take precedence over any deadline. I would especially like to thank the gorgeous and gifted Editor-in-Chief, Susan Lyne, and my beloved personal editor and completely edible mensch-man, Howard Karren. Major hugs, kisses, and kugel must also go to my editor at St. Martin's Press, a man who understands both myself and how to coordinate brights, a man whom many consider to be American publishing's most squeeze-tempting dreamboat, Bob Wyatt.

So, here it is—Volume One, the adventure begins. Read it, reread it, buy additional copies as gifts, carry it so my name is always visible, enjoy, laugh, love. Because remember, movies are much better than real life, because movies never sit down next to you and smell and make you want to buy a handgun. And that's just where the magic starts, if you ask me.

Libby Gelman-Waxner

April 1994

If You Ask Me

THE PERM MOTIF

▬ ▬ ▬

Hi. I'm Libby Gelman-Waxner, and I'm an assistant buyer in juniors' activewear. While I find my work both rewarding and creative, especially with the new knits coming in, I want more. And so I have decided to become a film critic. In this column, my "entry-level" effort in this challenging field, I will discuss and critique many of the finest works of today's auteurs. But I ask you, can anything top a classic like *Flashdance,* the movie that really *began* the loose perm?

Perms—I see them as a major theme, a motif even, in the work of English director Adrian Lyne, who has been influenced, I'm sure, by the oeuvre of Cher, whose Cleopatra-tepee look in *Suspect* is a shoo-in for a nomination. Remember when Cher could actually sit on her hair, on her TV show? I used to worry about all that long hair—was it ever really clean?

I enjoyed Lyne's *Fatal Attraction,* particularly for the conflict between Anne Archer's at-home shag and Glenn Close's peroxided career-gal mop-top—I swear, I took one look at that woman's roots and I wanted to scream, "Michael Douglas! Go home right now!" Now, Glenn was obviously an unstable person; why else would she call herself Glenn? I haven't trusted her since *The Big Chill.* In *Fatal Attraction,* Glenn—why not Gwen, like a normal person?—works in publishing, where there's no money unless you're Joni Evans, and look at *that* marriage. Glenn lives in a fabulous loft, but tell me this—is anyone *really* happy in a loft?

In my experience, a loft just doesn't offer closet space. A single woman in a loft is just asking for trouble, what with the freight elevators and the big paintings and the sex in the sink. My husband

Josh—we saw *Fatal Attraction* and we came home to our beautiful two-bedroom co-op with a doorman and health club privileges—we came home and Josh said to me, Libby, he said, let's have sex in the sink. And I said, Josh, you want sex in the sink? Why not in the refrigerator, in the vegetable crisper? Why not in the Cuisinart, on liquefy? I said, I know, let's have sex in the dishwasher, we'll use Cascade. Sex in the sink—it's ridiculous! Theresa, our housekeeper, she has enough trouble with rust stains.

Anyway, if Glenn Close hadn't lived in a loft, she'd be alive today. Nice people have walls, and doors, and children—my daughter Jennifer is far more attractive than the little girl in *Fatal Attraction*, who was adorable, but believe me, Jennifer is the real movie star. When I pick her up at preschool, which she attends with Dustin Hoffman's child, all the other mothers say, Jennifer is so gorgeous, like that Drew Barrymore before she got chunky. If I were Drew's mother, I would say, Drew darling, have some celery, it won't kill you; Jodie Foster was a house—now look how cute she is.

Now, Diane Keaton looked lovely in *Baby Boom*. I wanted to say, Diane, everything fits, you have a waistline, good for you. But if you ask me, I don't think she should have left that nice Harold Ramis for Sam Shepard. Harold made a good living, and their apartment was spotless; this Sam Shepard, with the funny teeth and the Jessica Lange business, I just don't know. I wanted to say, Diane, I just don't hear the word "commitment."

As for what films I would recommend this month, I would have to say the following: *Cry Freedom*, because it's about important topics and because that Kevin Kline is adorable—I loved him on Broadway, I understand he dates very young starlets, but that's his business, let the girl's mother worry. I also enjoyed *Less Than Zero*, a film set among the younger crowd in Beverly Hills, although I feel there was a subconscious message linking drugs and shopping. Let me tell you, if you shop you don't need drugs. I wanted to tell those kids, Look, you have Rodeo Drive, you have Bijan, you have the Visa, you don't need crack. If you use crack while you're shopping, who knows, you could make a terrible mistake, nothing would match, you might buy Perry when you wanted Ralph, you could walk right past the sale rack and not even know. Malibu teens, please, just say no, become a male prostitute, I don't care, just don't wear those sunglasses indoors, you'll go blind.

My number-one pick for this month, tops on Libby's Go-If-It's-Playing-on-the-East-Side-in-a-Place-Where-They-Vacuum list, my auteurist must-see is Bernardo Bertolucci's *The Last Emperor*. I never really trusted this Bertolucci person. I saw *Last Tango*, and all I thought was, If my Josh came to bed with a stick of margarine, I'd just say, Honey, it's still cholesterol, don't risk it. But this time Bernardo has made a fabulous work of cinematic achievement. He was allowed to film inside the Forbidden City and has given us the first real in-depth look at the throw pillows and dining areas of imperial China.

As I understand it, before communism and Chairman Mao, people in China could shop for days. You could pick up pagodas, thrones, peacocks, you name it. Then Mao came along and said, Stop all this shopping, let's all wear the same outfit and eat rice as an entree. What was his point?

If you ask me, browsing should be included in any nation's Bill of Rights, along with the Right to Choose a New Restaurant When You Get Tired of Cajun and the inalienable Right to Return a Bathing Suit If You Change Your Mind and Decide It's Too Revealing. If I lived in mainland China, I would just say, No thank you, Mister Mao, look at how nice Mrs. Gorbachev looks; being a Communist doesn't have to mean 28 billion cheap cotton pantsuits.

And that's why I recommend *The Last Emperor*. It satisfies the basic moviegoing urge: wanting to own something on the screen. From all those Woody Allen terraces to Molly Ringwald's hoop earrings, the American Cinema is a luscious catalogue of dreams (as I said in my senior thesis at Barnard, for which I received an A−, for lateness, and which I titled "The *Annie Hall* Look—Does It Work for Everyone?").

And I, Libby Gelman-Waxner, love the movies, even movies like *Maurice*, which inspired Josh and me to take a drive upstate and go antiquing. And I, Libby, will bring my message to America, because no other critic has truly stressed the importance of the Mercedes in the films of Paul Mazursky. And I, Libby, promise to see every movie I can, if I can get a sitter and Josh isn't too tired, and both Rex Reed *and* Bill Harris say thumbs up. Because I, Libby, think movies are an important arena of expression, as well as a wonderful excuse to drink Diet Coke. And that's how I feel—if you ask me.

THE LOVE THEME
▪ ▪ ▪

Hi, it's Libby. I would call myself a critic at large, but that might imply a weight problem, and starting first thing tomorrow morning, I'm living on nothing but Stella d'Oro bread sticks and Tab. There have been so many fine films released during this past holiday season, I felt like I was at a fabulous cinematic buffet, a real auteur nosh-fest.

Before choosing a holiday picture, my husband, Josh, and I took our daughter, Jennifer, age four, to Radio City Music Hall for "The Magnificent Christmas Spectacular," which she and her little friend Amanda enjoyed very much, and afterward we took the girls to have their ears pierced, for a treat. Josh and I wondered about taking Jennifer to sit on Santa's lap, but we decided to expose her to all religions and shopping experiences; Jennifer asked Santa for a place in Amagansett on at least half an acre—she was so adorable.

In order to expose Jennifer to the religion of her ancestors, we brought her with us to see Barbra Streisand in *Nuts*. If you ask me, Barbra only gets better and better. After *The Main Event* I remember thinking, She'll never top it, and then, boom, along comes *A Star Is Born*, where she played Esther Hoffman Howard and wore those flattering peasant tops. When Josh and I were married six years ago, in a lovely ceremony in the Golden Rajah Room of Casa Sheldon in Great Neck, we had already had our first fight: Josh had wanted the quartet to play Barbra's "Evergreen" during the vows, but I had insisted on "Let's Hear It for Me," so memorable in *Funny Lady*. If I have any problem with *Nuts*, it's only this—Barbra, where was the love theme?

In *Nuts*, Barbra plays a prostitute who must prove her sanity so she can go on trial for murdering her client Leslie Nielsen, who, if you ask me, deserved a slice of mirror in the throat for trying to make Barbra take a bath with him. Barbra's lawyer is Richard Dreyfuss, who everyone always says looks so much like my Josh they could be cousins. I always say, believe me, if God had wanted it, Josh could be the Oscar winner arrested for cocaine, and Richard Dreyfuss could be the low-six-figure orthodontist with three examining rooms on 51st and Lex (where he would be called a miracle worker; just ask the Schulman twins). In *Nuts,* Barbra's mother is Maureen Stapleton, her stepdad is Karl Malden, and her psychiatrist is Eli Wallach; I kept watching the screen, thinking, if my aunt Sylvia was in this movie, you'd have my wedding reception (which was gorgeous, by the way, even if the veal was a little dry and Aunt Sylvia's hip went out).

Another holiday film I enjoyed was *Wall Street,* a story of insider trading and why it will only give you heartache in the long run. For me, this film was an illustration of all the terrible things that can happen to a person who wants to date Daryl Hannah. All the men in America, my Josh included, they all want to date Daryl; I said, Josh, so what would the two of you talk about, you and Daryl, on your big date—her bangs? A girl like Daryl—we're not talking about a Ph.D. in comparative literature; I think we're talking about the hair in the eyes and not much in the way of lingerie, if you know what I'm saying. I told Josh, go, be my guest, go date Daryl Hannah, have fun—tell me about her pot roast.

But I'm off the track—let's talk about *Broadcast News,* another Xmas favorite. May I tell you how much I loved this film? May I tell you that, after this film was over, I wanted to give the director, that James L. Brooks, such a hug? Jim, a hug and a pinch from Libby; I'd like to call your mother, she must be very proud.

Broadcast News is the story of three people working on a television news show in Washington. The leads are Albert Brooks, so cute you could spread him on a cracker and serve him to guests, Holly Hunter, whom I could just put in my pocket and squeeze to death, and William Hurt, who is just Daryl Hannah all over again and worse; William Hurt, shame on you.

In this film, Holly Hunter is a career gal much like myself, only of course she covers global terrorism and I am an assistant buyer in juniors' activewear. But believe me, we're sisters; I'd gladly handle Qaddafi and let Holly take over my back orders of spandex unitards and 50 percent ramie linen-look leggings. Holly has to choose between Albert, a very nice boy and so bright, and William Hurt, with the blond hair and the bare bottom and the anchorwomen hanging all over him—am I making myself clear? Now, I understand Holly's dilemma all too intimately—I must confess it, just between you and me, Josh Waxner, D.D.S., has not been the only man in my life. While I was dating Josh, when I was still at Barnard, I was also seeing Chris Keebler III (not Keebler cookies, he should be so lucky).

Chris was prelaw at Columbia; he was tall and blond and his family had a stunning home in Westchester and they all drank. Chris would take me waterskiing and he would tell me all about his golden retriever, Scoots, and how sad everyone was when Scoots died in a boating accident. And I must admit, I must be frank, I fell for Chris and his crooked grin and his no deodorant and his Bass Weejuns with no socks—yes, Libby was a fool.

I know what you're thinking; you're thinking, Libby, were you crazy, were you on drugs or what? There I was, the girl who had everything—a new Toyota Corolla with the optional moon roof from my folks, serious feelers from both Bloomie's and Ann Taylor, my thighs for once under control, and Josh Waxner—250 pounds of future orthodontist who would have cut off his right arm for me if I had only said the word. And there I was, about to throw it all away for Chris, a boy with a C average, a boy who said "Gee," a boy whom my own mother called "Libby's friend from Westchester, Mister Goebbels."

But luckily, I came to my senses. Just like Holly Hunter, I realized that Chris, my own Bill Hurt, was really just a Shetland sweater and a smile, a tuxedo full of trouble. And I ran to my Josh and I said, Josh, I don't care if you're going to spend your life putting rubber bands in teenagers' mouths, I don't care if your mother still buys you underwear, I don't care if Brie gives you gas—I love you, and I'll fix you.

In *Broadcast News*, of course, Holly Hunter doesn't marry her

Josh and is therefore a tragic heroine and a lesson to us all. A career is all very nice, Holly, but tell me this—who's going to bring you an Entenmann's All Butter French Crumb when you're sick or just don't want to move? And who's going to drive out to Staten Island in a snowstorm on the day before Hanukkah to find the last ballerina Barbie with posable arms on the Eastern Seaboard? And who are you going to catch staring at you murmuring "I *love* your overbite" when he thinks you're asleep? Think about it, Holly. And the answer isn't Bill Hurt with the dimples, I'll tell you that much right now. Because, while the auteur theory is very important, there's nothing like a little security and free floss till the day you die. And that's my opinion, if you ask me.

SUCH A NICE BOY

— — — —

oody, talk to Libby—I've just seen *September,* your latest auteur work, and frankly, I'm worried. I went with my dearest friend, Stacy Schiff, a gifted marketing analyst although still unattached, and we both agreed—how could you do that to Mia?

Now, when most film critics analyze Woody's work, they make such a mistake—all they talk about is dark and light, mature comedy, and the Chekhovian palette; I, Libby, have based my study on a far more revealing criterion: the girlfriends. Whenever Woody meets a nice girl, even that Mariel Hemingway, with the breast implants, the first thing he does is put her in a film; it's not a ring, it's not even a birthstone, the girl's parents will still live in shame, but at least it's a gesture.

First there was Louise Lasser—Mary Hartman, remember, with the bangs and the pigtails? Woody put Louise in *Bananas,* one of his early, crazy movies. Louise has a beautiful speaking voice, not unlike my own: as my husband, Josh, the orthodontist, says, "Libby, in your voice I hear the maid vacuuming."

And then Woody left Louise, and it was time for Diane Keaton, a wonderful girl, even with the hair in her eyes. Now, Stacy Schiff says that Woody went after Diane because she was the only funny gentile girl he'd ever met, and Lucy was too old for him. Woody put Diane in so many films, especially the ones I like to think of as his Conran's oeuvre, the films where he really began to notice real estate: *Annie Hall, Manhattan,* and *Interiors.* All of a sudden, Woody knew about mantels and moldings, and he started dressing like a Ralph Lauren person, like someone who at any moment might play racquetball or ride something. Of course, Ralph's things are lovely, and as an assistant buyer in juniors' activewear, I appreciate the quality, but my question is this: given the Ralph influence, will Woody be turning cowpoke?

I bought Josh one of Ralph's chambray cowboy shirts with the snaps and a bottle of the Chaps cologne; Josh turned to me, he said, Libby, what do I look like, Hopalong Cassidy? Should we brand the dog?

But Diane, I'm not blaming you for the Ralph business, you were a good influence on Woody; you always looked like unmade bunk beds. Before Diane, if a girl wore a derby, a man's tie, and anklets with high heels, you'd think she was an alcoholic, a morning drinker; now, thanks to Diane, if you own it, layer it. If you ask me, Diane is a pioneer; she takes that thing that hangs in the back of your closet, the thing that you just had to have at the time, the thing that was too marked down to pass up, Diane takes that thing and she doesn't call Goodwill, she wraps it around her head a few times, pins on a Smurf brooch, and wins an Oscar.

Diane was good for Woody, but she had to move on, to Warren Beatty. Woody, you're a Brooklyn Godard and more, but Diane, I'm with you. With Woody, I'm sure it was all very stimulating, and Diane probably saw a lot of six-part documentaries and Ingmar things, but that Warren—he's the Devil, and please give him my work number, that's all I have to say. And so Woody went to Mia Farrow, a dating strategy that Stacy referred to at the time as Dueling Shiksas.

Mia is a lovely girl, she's skin and bones, but what a life: remember when she was Allison on *Peyton Place* and cut off all her hair? Remember when she married Sinatra, and then André Previn, and adopted all of those Asian children? I'm telling you, for a wispy little dandelion, that Mia has a lot of energy. And that's my worry: Woody, you've put Mia in all those movies, and in each one she gets thinner. In *Zelig* she had braids on her head, like a Swedish woman, in *Hannah* she wore smocks, and now, in *September*, she mopes around in gold-rimmed eyeglasses with her shirttail out. Woody, she's turning into Liv Ullmann, only with less makeup.

September is like *Interiors*: everyone sits around talking right next to a vase. And everyone has such problems; they're not fulfilled, they have inchoate longings, they take pills—Woody, in these films, who takes out the garbage? And everyone dresses alike, they're coordinated, as if they all called each other up and said, Today we're beige. Woody, you're a wonderful genius, but it's like two hours of oatmeal.

And now Woody and Mia have had a child; there's still a vacancy sign on Mia's left hand, but please, they're movie stars, he lives on Fifth Avenue and she lives on Central Park West, that child will know every doorman in town. I think it's good that Woody has had a child; when I had my Jennifer, who's now four, it changed my life. One day you're footloose and carefree, running off to Aruba for ten days, booking a hut at Club Med, and the next day, boom, you're interviewing Honduran women to live in. Woody, take it from Libby, having a child is a beautiful experience, it opens up entire new departments. All during my pregnancy, I was glowing; everyone said, Look at Libby, she's shopping for two now.

Maybe now that Woody has a child, he and Mia will settle down, and he'll make a fun picture again, like that *Three Men and a Baby*—what a cute film, and directed by that Leonard Nimoy, with the ears. But you know, if Woody had made that film, one of the three men would have been Mary Beth Hurt, and the baby would have been very quiet, with its little beige cardigan thrown over its shoulders. Believe me, that baby wouldn't have cried, it would have had anxiety attacks about Life and the Void; Woody, let me tell you, Life and the Void are nothing compared to getting your kid into a decent play group, one with the more creative children.

Yes, Woody is beginning a new era, with his little son, Satchel. I think I've been very well-behaved in this column—so far I haven't said a word about that poor child's name, not one word. Woody, I think it's a very nice name, I mean that sincerely; it's unusual, and I read that it was a tribute to Satchel Paige, a legendary sports figure. And Woody, I assume that some day Satchel will have a little sister, and her name will be Valise. Or Carry-on. Or Garment Bag.

Woody, please, why not David, or Scott, or Adam? Why not Michael—Michael is always good, it's Mike if he plays ball, Michael if he studies. I'm sorry, this is all none of my business, I'm such a nudge. Congratulations, Woody, Mia, and little Satchel; I can't wait to see Woody with a Snugli, or browsing for bibs on Madison Avenue. Woody, your films are one thing, but there's nothing like a pair of tiny little Top-Siders to break your heart, if you ask me.

A NOVEL APPROACH

■ ■ ■ ■

What a month it's been, don't ask. I've been having a little personal problem, and I just hope it won't interfere with this column, but listen, it's nothing really, just a sort of . . . spasm. I'm fine, I just won't think about it, I'll think about Art instead, and I'm talking Literary Cinema, so complex it's almost European—*Ironweed* and *The Unbearable Lightness of Being*.

Ironweed is based on a distinguished Pulitzer prize–winning novel that I couldn't get through. The film is set in Albany, New York, in the 1930s, and let me tell you, it's no musical romp *Dennisdennisdennis*—excuse me, I'm so embarrassed, that was one of my seizures. All this month I've been trying to experience High Culture, and then I suddenly have this vision of Dennis Quaid in bikini briefs and I black out. I asked my therapist, Dr. Arlene Cole-Natbaum, and she said, Libby, it's a common pathology, I see it every day.

Ironweed—remember years ago, when movie stars would play hobos and bums with bandannas and cute scruffy dogs, and it would be fun? Well, forget it; in *Ironweed* Jack Nicholson and Meryl Streep play The Homeless, and it's very sad, even though Jack is a little chubby for someone sleeping on the street, if you ask me, and Meryl dies of whatever killed Ali MacGraw in *Love Story*, you know; something fatal but not unattractive *Dennisdennisdennis*—let's not even talk about the scene where his sheet comes off in *Innerspace*, let's not even talk about when Cher cleaned his wound in *Suspect*, let's talk *Big Easy*.

I'm sorry, for a moment there I lost consciousness, just remembering when he took Ellen Barkin's hand and put it . . . Excuse me, I had to leave my word processor for a moment and put my head out the window and scream. My husband, Josh, asked what I was doing, and I said, Josh, a few sit-ups wouldn't kill you. And you know, my own mother, Sondra Krell-Gelman, has a Dennis Quaid problem of a similar nature. She told me, she said, Libby, I love your father, and I love my second career selling palatial homes in Great Neck, and I've got a gorgeous Tudor with a deck and three and a half baths to die from just begging for you and Josh and my beautiful grandchild, who I know would love a little brother sometime soon, I love and cherish all these things, but if Dennis called the house, any time of the day or night, well, Libby darling, just color me gone.

The Unbearable Lightness of Being is based on a multilayered novel by Czech author Milan Kundera, which I never finished. It's about this Czech surgeon who fools around every other second *DENNIS-DENNISDENNIS*—listen, if Dennis was a doctor, I'd eat germs. If you ask me, there isn't a movie anywhere that couldn't be improved by putting in Dennis: *Citizen Kane, Potemkin,* you name it. I have to tell you something, please don't repeat this, I haven't even told Dr. Cole-Natbaum, because I know she'd just ask me what *I* think.

Last night, I dreamt the following: I'm on a Carnival holiday cruise to Aruba, and I get shipwrecked on this deserted tropical island—it's like St. Bart's, only there's no duty-free shop. And I'm lying on the beach, and my clothes are in tatters, although luckily I have on my Norma Kamali swimsuit with the French rise so my thighs don't bulge. Then around from a palm tree comes Harrison Ford, with stubble, and he says, Libby, this is my dream, too. And then around from another palm tree comes Dennis, and he says, Harrison, get lost; the woman in the great Kamali with the ankle bracelet and the midriff chain and the sunglasses on top of her head is mine. And they're about to have a real brawl, they're snorting, and I stand up and I say, Guys, we're going to be on this island for years, maybe until we die. I have a wonderful husband back on East 77th who will never remarry because I would kill him. But here we are, and Dennis, Harrison—you're going to have to share. Listen, if that dream included air conditioning, Sun Block 14, and Lean Cuisine's Filet of Fish Jardiniere, I'd never wake up.

I'm sorry, I know I was supposed to discuss Auteur Art Forms, but I've just seen Dennis in his latest film, *D.O.A.*, and I'm too upset. Not once in this film, and believe me I was watching, not once does Dennis remove even his watchband, let alone a more personal garment. In this film, Dennis has been poisoned and must find his own murderer, but please—wouldn't he feel better, more refreshed and able to start a manhunt, after a nice shower?

In *D.O.A.*, Dennis's costar is Meg Ryan, whom I understand he is also seriously dating off-camera. I'm sure she's a lovely girl and a fine actress, and if Dennis is happy then I'm happy, but unfortunately I have no memory of Meg's performance, may she rot in Hell, or, as my mother says, Libby, Dennis doesn't love this Meg Ryan; Dennis didn't love his first wife, another little actress, or that Lea Thompson whom he dated. Libby, someday Dennis will wake up and find true love, with a decent woman with her own identity, and then Dennis will be able, in all deep sincerity, to finally utter those three little words that will mean so much, those three little words that can move mountains—"Libby Gelman-Quaid." And that's what I think of Milan Kundera, if you ask me.

BLOND FAITH

— — — —

When I first became a film critic several months ago, I thought only of serving the cinema and sampling the new gourmet popcorns. Little did I realize that I would also become involved in a new realm of auteur glamour; just the other day, I, Libby, was invited to attend the scintillating world premiere of *Bright Lights, Big City* in Manhattan. My husband, Josh, was tired and couldn't move, so I brought my dear friend Stacy Schiff, because I thought, Who knows, she might meet someone, stranger things have happened.

The premiere was held at the Art Greenwich Theatre in the Village, because the film depicts the madcap downtown scene. There were many photographers and television crews out front, although, to my disappointment, Leeza Gibbons of *Entertainment Tonight* was not on hand. If you ask me, Leeza is much more attractive than that Mary Hart, who dates Sly Stallone and oil sheikhs.

So Stacy and I went into the theater, and we both kept our coats, because with fully let-out silver fox you can't be too careful. Now, let me tell you, that theater was jam-packed with celebrities. It was like an episode of *Hotel*—everywhere I looked, there was Lauren Hutton. I'm positive that Carl Bernstein gave Stacy a meaningful look, but I said, Stacy, don't you dare, not after what he did to Meryl Streep in *Heartburn*. Believe me, you're better off with a back issue of *Savvy,* a Dove Bar, and a *Beauty and the Beast* rerun.

Sitting in the same row as Carl was Gloria Steinem, and, may I say, I was bowled over. Gloria is my role model—she has shown the world that you can be an A-1 feminist and still streak your hair, and from what I saw at the premiere, Gloria is now involved with backcombing as well. That Gloria; ever since she hit 50, she's been like a show girl—remember when she was in *People* magazine in a bubble bath? Gloria was sitting with a man who Stacy said might be Gloria's boyfriend, real estate mega-tycoon Mort Zuckerman. I was thrilled; all I could think was, Gloria Steinem-Zuckerman. Gloria, I love *Ms.* and I love your books, but let's talk bottom line. Lie if you have to, Gloria—tell Mort you founded *Cosmo;* after the ceremony, you can fiddle.

Then the lights went down, and the film began. *Bright Lights, Big City* is all about Michael J. Fox using cocaine because his marriage broke up and his mother passed away. I wanted to take Michael and shake him; I wanted to say, Michael, what kind of example are you setting for Kirk Cameron? Michael, drugs are never the answer; there are only three occasions on which I think narcotics are permitted: childbirth, a visit from your in-laws, including grandparents, and fitting into something for a Fourth of July party in Nags Head. Otherwise, as Mrs. Reagan says, Just Say No, or, as my mother, Sondra Krell-Gelman, says, Just Say No Thank You, I'm Full, But It All Looks Delicious.

After the premiere there was a reception at the Canal Bar, an exclusive downtown spot where Stacy says they usually won't let her in. But we were on the doorman's list, so hoo-hah; inside it was all very nice, but I must confess that I did not glimpse any depravity, except for Leslie Stahl from CBS sitting on the floor with a plate and eating with her fingers. I also saw that Tama Janowitz with the hair piled up like a crazy woman on the subway, and that handsome Jay McInerney who wrote the book *Bright Lights;* I told Stacy to go talk to him, and she said, He's very nice but he's divorced and he only dates models. I said, He'll learn; one day he'll wake up married to Christie or Cheryl, and then he'll have to make conversation—Jay, believe me, you'll learn an awful lot about Maybelline Moisture Whip.

Aside from my star-spangled premiere, the other auteur experience that puzzled me this month was *The Milagro Beanfield War.* It's directed by Robert Redford, and it's about saving the environment from developers. Bob, what's the problem? Isn't that a skiing tan? I like beans just fine, but I don't think a chair lift and a chalet-style lodge with a hot tub ever killed anyone; I'm sure that even in New Mexico, "Jill St. John in stretch pants" is not a dirty word. Bob Redford, you're such a dreamboat, whatever happened to *Barefoot in the Park* and *The Way We Were?*

It's like I told Stacy: You can never really trust a blond man, because sometimes the brain is blond, too. And that's my thinking, if you ask me (and Greer of Bon Coif on 57th does my highlights, for those of you who've been writing).

Can I tell you something? I love Alan Alda—I could just nosh on his face for days—and do you know why? Because he endorses things, and I don't just mean feminism and human caring—I'm talking about his ads for IBM. When I saw Alan's latest cinematic achievement, *A New Life*, I felt a special glow whenever anyone in the movie was near a computer screen; I'd just hug myself and think, Who knows, maybe it's an IBM machine. An Alan machine.

It's like when I watch *The Cosby Show*, and Bill Cosby's running around the Huxtable kitchen, there's always that suspense—will he eat a Jell-O Pudding Pop? Is there a Coke in the fridge, or maybe near the antiapartheid poster? When an actor endorses things, if you ask me, it gives that actor a special depth. It says, Yes, I'm a dedicated artist performing a challenging role, but I'm also an active shopper, with a Brentwood mortgage or two. It's like, I never really warmed up to Sir Laurence Olivier until he did those TV spots for Polaroid; then I said, Larry, welcome to my home.

A New Life is all about relationships and divorce and men and women, and everyone learns something; it was just like watching a *M*A*S*H* rerun, only with Ann-Margret and tall buildings. That Alan, he really has something on his mind, and it won't go away; remember him in *Same Time, Next Year* and *The Four Seasons*? Well, here he comes again.

This was a very special month for me, a month jam-packed with sensitivity and human caring; I also saw the movie of Neil Simon's *Biloxi Blues*, the story of Neil's boot camp experiences. Neil Simon—what can I say? It's like talking about Mount Rushmore or Sidney Sheldon. When I think of Neil, I think of a whole new language: "yocks," "boffola," "laff riot," all the words that make you think about laughing till you get nauseous, laughing till you get a good double migraine. And with his new autobiographical trilogy of plays, of which *Biloxi Blues* is number two, you even get a special extra something for the same price—you get depth, pounds and pounds of depth; it's like brisket for two hundred.

In all of Neil's trilogy, there's this boy, Eugene Jerome, who's cute and funny and everybody loves him—I swear, you can just see Eugene in Hollywood some day, writing *The Star-Spangled Girl* and *The Cheap Detective*. It's thrilling; it's like seeing little Eugene O'Neill, and everybody's saying, That Gene, someday he'll grow up and depress the world.

I'm dedicating this column to my uncle Morty, who reminds me of Neil and Alan, and not just because Aunt Frieda, Uncle Morty's ex-wife, can't stand the three of them. Uncle Morty runs Gelman's Fine Vinyl Upholstery and TrimCo, and he always tells me, Lib, you can learn a lot from a Hallmark Card. Whoever makes them, this Hallmark person, he's a marketing genius.

I thought of Uncle Morty at another recent film, *Dominick and Eugene,* which is the story of two brothers. One is a medical student and the other is mentally handicapped; you can tell the one who's handicapped because he wears a baseball cap and his pants are pulled high—that's always a dead giveaway. Tom Hulce plays the handicapped brother, and he's a very fine actor, which is obvious because he uses a lot of saliva; at one point he runs right at the camera, just schpritzing to beat the band—I said to myself, Libby, I smell a Best Supporting.

Dominick and Eugene is loaded with human depth, and it asks a big moral question: What would you do if you had to choose between getting an internship at Stanford or taking care of Tom Hulce? I swear, the film was so moving it almost had Jane Alexander in it, as a kindly therapist. *Dominick and Eugene* reminded me of other sensitive dramas that covered universal human dilemmas, such as, What if you were a blind figure skater? or What if you met the Elephant Man? or What if you had to harvest a whole cotton crop in your print housedress?

I think about human dilemmas often, when I'm at a cinematic

viewing or just at home on East 77th, doing *Hooperman* or *Donahue* or *thirtysomething,* a show I just love because whenever there's a crisis, one of the main woman characters puts her hair in a ponytail. There's a lot to be said for sensitivity and human caring; it's like Diana Ross used to sing, before she married that Norwegian millionaire: Just reach out and touch. I think we can all learn a lot from Diana Ross about priorities; and God bless Geraldo, if you ask me.

BIG BUCKS

▬ ▬ ▬ ▬

A brand-new movie is all well and good, but frankly, I prefer a sequel. With a sequel, a *Book V* or an *Adventure Continues,* there are no unpleasant surprises—you know that Leonard Nimoy won't die and that the film always costs more than the original; if you ask me, that's quality. This month I saw *Rambo III, "Crocodile" Dundee II,* and *Willow;* even though *Willow* isn't technically a sequel, it was produced by George Lucas and there's a princess in it, so good enough.

I must confess: I know I'm not supposed to, but I enjoy the Rambo pictures, and for a simple reason—I like to watch people getting blown to bits. It's silly, but when Sylvester Stallone hangs a hand grenade around someone's neck and pulls the pin out, I always think, Why can't Sly do that to my dry cleaner, who always loses a button or a matching belt? In *Rambo III,* Sly is fighting the Russians in Afghanistan, but in my mind, he is taking on my husband's entire family. Josh, my husband, says his mother has allergies, and that's why she spit out my lemon quiche—Sly, get the flamethrower, and while you're at it, use the crossbow with the detonating arrows on Cousin Leslie, with the adorable two-year-old who chews slipcovers. Basically, I identify with Rambo completely—if it talks back, ram it with a tank. My therapist, Dr. Arlene Cole-Natbaum, says that violent fantasies are never the answer; Sly, her office is on East 81st, get the Uzi.

Paul Hogan, as "Crocodile" Dundee, is another story entirely; he's low-key and charming, and his face is all tan and craggy. He reminds me of Roy Scheider—you know, sun damage and a smile. Hogan never kills people, although he carries a big knife, and he wears a snakeskin jacket and a necklace made of crocodile teeth.

My only problem with this Dundee person is that he's Australian. Now, is it just me, or is Australia the Iowa City of continents? Think about it: Olivia Newton-John, Helen Reddy, Paul Hogan— it's like a slow day on *Oprah*. Dundee is in love with a glamorous blond reporter, played by Linda Kozlowski. Linda, do you really want a man who dresses like a pimp on a *Mod Squad* rerun?

I admire Linda Kozlowski for not changing her name or her facial expression; even when she has a gun to her neck, she is very sweet and calm, like Jaclyn Smith when she's in trouble. And when Linda is out in the bush, she wears a nice, long gauze skirt and a cute floppy hat—even if she's in the middle of a swamp, an actress can still swear by separates. My husband, Josh, has started calling himself "Crocodile" Waxner, the outback orthodontist; I said, Josh, fine, just call me "Alligator" Bag.

I took my four-year-old, Jennifer, to see *Willow*, even though I had heard that it was violent; after all, Jennifer's favorite cassette is *The Terminator*. *Willow* is just like *Star Wars*, only everyone has dirty hair because it's medieval, and the evil queen Bavmorda, played by Jean Marsh, is Darth Vader. Bavmorda did frighten Jennifer, who has always been terrified of Jean Marsh, even on *Upstairs, Downstairs*. In fact, whenever Jennifer acts up, this comes in handy: all I have to say is, Young lady, if you don't finish your stir-fried vegetables, I'm calling Jean Marsh—and bingo, the plate is clean.

Willow tells an inspirational story about dwarfs and heroes and sorceresses and believing in yourself, but what I enjoyed most about this film was the budget. When I see a film made on a shoestring, an Ingmar Bergman work or a Japanese thing, I always think the filmmaker just didn't care enough; he didn't spend the $50 million. I knew that my father loved me because my bat mitzvah cost $20,000, not including centerpieces or monogrammed matchbooks and cocktail napkins. When I saw *Willow*, I thought, George Lucas, good for you. Some people say, Gee, with the $55 million they spent on *Rambo III*, or with the $51 million for *The Cotton Club*, or with the $36 million for *Heaven's Gate*, you could feed a lot of starving people. Well, I, Libby, say: Let's ask those starving people which they would rather have, some day-old pumpernickel and watery soup, or *Howard the Duck*? Some canned peas on a paper plate, or *Labyrinth*? A bowl of rice, which is starchy and low in protein, or the last ten Burt Reynolds pictures?

I think the answer is obvious. And what's more, if you feed a hungry person, the next day he's hungry all over again. But if you make a movie with the word "star" or "heat" or "cop" in the title, you can double your money with a cable sale. It's like I told Jennifer when we were walking home from the Cineplex and we passed a homeless person, I said, Jennifer, being homeless is a terrible thing, but don't blame Steven Spielberg. Jennifer asked if, when it opens, we could take the homeless person to the third Indiana Jones picture—let me tell you, I felt so proud. I said, Jennifer, of course we can, especially if the homeless person learns to use a Kleenex. And I explained to Jennifer that in seven months, she's going to have her very own sequel, *Jennifer II: The Gelman-Waxner Family Continues*. And that's why I'm glad to be an American, a film critic, and a mom, if you ask me.

BIGGER BUSINESS

▬ ▬ ▬ ▬

I n *Vanity Fair* magazine, which is my bible, Arsenio Hall discusses how impressed Eddie Murphy's girlfriend is with the size of Eddie's penis. Now, Arsenio costars with Eddie in *Coming to America*, so Arsenio has many reasons to be nice to Eddie. But still, is such a comment truly necessary? I, Libby, could only think: Meryl Streep has worked with Jack Nicholson in *Heartburn* and *Ironweed*, and as far as I know, she's never said a word about his penis. Walter Matthau and Jack Lemmon, ditto. Ginger Rogers never said, Sure, Fred can tap, but you should see him in the locker room, *mamma mia*.

In *Coming to America*, Eddie is very funny, and for the most part, he keeps his pants on. Eddie plays an African prince who flies to the United States incognito to find a bride who will love him for himself and not for his money or his royal position. I wanted to say, Eddie, what's the problem? Being a rich prince is nothing to be ashamed of, it's a helpful asset, like a nice singing voice or a cleft chin. As my beloved mother, Sondra Krell-Gelman, has always told me from the time I was six months old, Libby, a man should have a pleasing personality, but real love means flatware.

This month I also went to see *Big*, which I imagine is what Eddie Murphy originally wanted to call his movie. *Big* is about how a twelve-year-old boy makes a wish to be a grown-up and, boom, the next morning he's Tom Hanks. Tom falls in love with Elizabeth Perkins, who's a high-powered corporate executive; she loves Tom because he acts just like a little boy. Can I say something? Does anyone really want to hang around with twelve-year-olds? Believe me, twelve-year-olds are not sweet and innocent; when my older brother, Lance, was twelve, he was cranky and snotty, and he liked to rub boogers on my legs and tell me that dog biscuits were cookies; he wasn't what I'd call a dream date.

There have been so many movies lately where an older person and a child switch bodies, such as *Like Father Like Son* and *Vice Versa* and *18 Again!* and what-have-you. I looked at my four-year-old daughter, Jennifer, the other day, and I thought, Should we switch bodies? Do I really want to wear a retainer all over again? Do I really want to take *Mademoiselle* seriously? Maybe I could switch bodies with Eddie Murphy, just to confirm things; as I'm currently almost four months pregnant, I'd like to switch bodies with anyone who doesn't vomit twice a day.

I'm telling you, any woman who is pregnant during the summer months should be subsidized by the federal government. My husband, Josh, keeps telling me I look radiant; if he says it one more time, I'll make him watch the birth. Before Jennifer was born, Josh asked me if he should stay with me in the delivery room. I said, Who cares, *I'm* going to be unconscious. The women at my health club, they're always saying that natural childbirth is a wonderful thing; I tell them, So why don't you Lamaze your way through a root canal? One of these women actually had the birth of her child videotaped; I told her, Listen, I won't let Josh take my picture when I'm in a bathing suit; when I have my appendix out, I'll call Warner Bros. It's like my mother says, If childbirth were such a beautiful experience, it would be catered.

To keep my mind off the heat and my condition, I keep going to film comedies. I saw *Who Framed Roger Rabbit?*, which I enjoyed very much, although at this point anything with air conditioning is a masterpiece. *Roger Rabbit* is all about Bob Hoskins, who's a private detective representing a cartoon character in a murder case; half the characters in the movie are Toons—all sorts of animated creatures. During this movie I began to hallucinate just a little bit, from the cold and the sugar rush from my Raisinets; I began to think that maybe I would give birth to a Toon, to a talking bunny or a zany duck. It would be my child, I thought, so I would be proud, although as a mother, I would worry.

What would it be like to say, Here he is, my son the dancing pig? Or, Welcome to my home, this is our youngest, the flying dachshund? I mentioned this to my mother, who said, Libby, better you should have Elmer Fudd than a boy like the Berman child, who had to go to medical school in the Bahamas. When I talk to my mother, everything makes sense. This month alone, she's given me many important words of wisdom. She told me, Libby, when you're pregnant there are three rules: sit down whenever possible, eat plenty of ice cream so the baby will be sweet, and don't go see *Arthur 2: On the Rocks,* because who needs the aggravation.

I took my mom to see *Big Business,* which stars Bette Midler and Lily Tomlin, both in double roles as twins. She loved the film, although she said that in real life twins are a punishment from God, a laundry curse. My mother especially loved Bette and Lily. She said, Libby, those are two terrific women; they're funny, and they know what's going on in the world. And I must say that I agree—Eddie and Arsenio, pay attention. Put away the yardstick and pull yourselves together. And if everyone will excuse me, I have to take a nap; I just did my Jane Fonda exercises for expectant mothers, and I'm exhausted. Jane, whose idea was this workout? Who said, First let's make women fat, and then let's make them roll around? It's cruel, Jane—why don't you just shoot at my feet? And has anyone noticed that on the cover of the Jane Fonda tape, skinny Jane's in a black leotard and the pregnant woman is in horizontal stripes? Rot in hell, Jane. And that's my overview of world cinema for the month, if you ask me.

Maybe I'm saying this just because I am seven months pregnant, but if you ask me, everything that's bad in the world can be blamed on men. It seemed like every movie I saw this month was about rifles or cars or baseball; frankly, morning sickness was more entertaining.

Let's talk about *Young Guns,* a movie starring all of those boys they call the Brat Pack. I'm very sorry, I know I'm not supposed to call them the Brat Pack, because it degrades their work in teen-vampire movies. Anyway, in this movie they're all gunslingers in the Old West, and they shoot people right and left. It's just like that movie *Top Gun,* only the boys are even shorter. That little Emilio Estevez plays Billy the Kid, and Emilio's brother Charlie Sheen is in the movie as well. What is all this— why is one Sheen and the other Estevez? Why aren't they in college? I know that their father, Martin Sheen, is always very good when he plays a Kennedy in a miniseries; why doesn't he talk to his boys?

Young Guns was very silly, if you ask me. All those actors, like that nice boy from *La Bamba* and that other one, Donald Sutherland's child, they wore holsters and cowboy hats and bandannas. They wanted to look very tough, but all I could think was, So what are they going to steal? Their fathers' Visa cards? It all looked like a production of *Oklahoma!* at Beverly Hills High School. And what kind of name is Lou Diamond Phillips—what is he, an engagement ring? And what about everyone's fancy haircuts? Who was the leader of this gang—Vidal Sassoon?

Some of the Brat Pack boys are also in a movie called *Eight Men Out,* which is about a World Series scandal back in 1919. Instead of shooting people, Charlie Sheen and his friends play baseball and become corrupted. What is this with baseball? At least in *Bull Durham* there was kissing; as an interesting subject for movies, baseball is right up there with nonabrasive cleansers and French people spending time at the seashore. All the men on baseball teams look alike in their matching hats and uniforms; it's like watching an ant farm. I asked my husband, Josh, Why do men like baseball? And Josh said, Libby, it's all Freudian: the bat is the penis and home plate is the vagina. I said, Josh, thank God you're an orthodontist so you don't need a brain. Although, come to think of it, maybe baseball *is* like sex—it's something to do when all the stores are closed.

Then I asked Josh, If baseball is sex, what are cars? Josh said that for men, cars are religion. Well, I saw this movie *Tucker,* and let me tell you, I'd rather watch Mormons. *Tucker* is about this man, played by Jeff Bridges, who invented a revolutionary new car called the Tucker Torpedo; it has seat belts and a big headlight in the middle. I can't wait for the sequels, *Edsel* and *Chevy Nova: The Man and the Dream.*

In *Tucker,* everyone is mean to Jeff Bridges because his car is so terrific; the film is set in the '40s, so everyone looks orange. *Tucker* reminded me of a Disney movie, because all the people in it are so happy and American—it's like *The Love Bug,* the movie about a Volkswagen that thinks. Jeff Bridges is like Dean Jones, or maybe John Davidson in *The Happiest Millionaire.* I read in a magazine that *Tucker* is secretly all about the movie's director, Francis Ford Coppola, and his troubles in the movie business; I said, Josh, next year let's buy a four-door Coppola hatchback.

This month I also saw a movie called *Cocktail,* starring Tom Cruise, who is so cute that you could smack him. In *Cocktail,* Tom plays a boy who leaves college to become a bartender—already, if you ask me, it's like Greek tragedy. So Tom becomes a swinging bartender, and all he does is wiggle his hips and flip the bottles around; all I can say is, Not in my house. Tom, you're a cutie pie, but have you ever tried to get Chablis out of wall-to-wall? Then Tom has an affair with a rich lady who buys him fancy bathrobes; finally his best friend dies, and Tom learns his lesson and marries a nice girl and settles down, although he's still a bartender. I played the soundtrack album from this film, and when I listened carefully, I could actually hear Tom's mother weeping. Tom, you've played a daredevil pilot, a pool player, and now a bartender; would it kill you to play a professional man?

Josh loved *Cocktail.* He said that if he weren't an orthodontist, he would be either a bartender or a race-car driver. I thought to myself, Libby, maybe it's time to become a lesbian. As far as I can tell, a man's idea of fun is throwing something, killing something, or steering something, and then having a Budweiser and a nice big burp. Basically, the only difference between a man and a pig is that a pig never says, "Nice one!" or wears a hat that can hold a six-pack. How come, in these movies about men, they never mention the real male issues—being under five feet five, losing your hair, and wearing the same Jockey shorts six days in a row?

To get away from all these macho films, I went to see Pee-wee Herman in *Big Top Pee-wee.* This was a terrible mistake—Pee-wee has decided to act like a guy. Personally, I always loved Pee-wee; he was always neatly dressed, he didn't play sports, and he had lovely table manners. But in this movie Pee-wee discovers girls, mostly by jumping on them. If you ask me, it was all a little strange; Pee-wee and girls, it doesn't seem necessary. It's just not Pee-wee—what is he going to do in his next film, play a bartender?

Pee-wee, listen to Libby: Men are scum. Given half a chance, they'll sit on the couch all weekend and watch golf on TV. They'll pretend an electric toothbrush is a laser sword, and they'll have duels with the towel rack. They'll make machine-gun noises with the pepper mill. They'll show you nude pictures of Brigitte Nielsen and ask you if you think she had surgery. Pee-wee, I know why God won't let men get pregnant: because they would keep daring people to punch them in the stomach. Please, no more movies about men and their toys; let them watch *Miami Vice* and play air guitar during the credits, if you ask me.

A SPECIAL GUEST

S o hello, and it's very nice to be here. My name is Sondra Krell-Gelman, and I'm Libby's mother. This month, while my beautiful daughter is in Beth Trauma Hospital giving birth, I will be writing her column of important film criticism. During the day I sell real estate for Lovely Spaces Realty in Great Neck, Long Island, but when Libby asked me to do the column, what could I say? You *make* the time.

My beautiful Libby went into labor just four hours ago, in the housewares department of Bloomingdale's, and I am proud to say that before she went to the hospital, she charged three Ralph Lauren top sheets and a handy wicker Kleenex caddy, all at 30 percent off. I met Libby at the hospital, and as the nurse wheeled her away, she had only two requests. Mom, she said between contractions, please do the column and then go back to Bloomie's and buy two more Lauren washcloths in plum. And so here I am, in the waiting room with Libby's extremely successful husband, Josh, who, if you ask me, is not just an orthodontist but an artist; you should see what he did with that Greenbaum girl—I'm telling you, she used to look like a can opener.

So let's talk cinema, even while my Libby is undergoing the miracle of childbirth; thank God she took an epidural and won't feel a thing. This month I went to see a film called *Gorillas in the Mist*; it's based on a true story about a woman who spent most of her life in Africa with all these gorillas. Sigourney Weaver plays the woman, and she's terrific, but I wanted to ask her, Sigourney, with those big monkeys, wasn't there an aroma? I could never live in the jungle, for a basic reason: no outlets. The hair dryer, the dishwasher, the vacuum; Sigourney, a travel iron is all well and good, but how long can it last? I love plants—I have a fern hanging in my kitchen—but if you want to rough it, why not Acapulco off-season?

This month I also saw *Running on Empty,* which is about two '60s radicals who blew up a napalm lab in 1971 and then went underground; now they have a seventeen-year-old son who wants to go to Juilliard. Believe me, I remember the '60s; my Libby, she was only a child, but she was very radical. Her room was covered with posters: Ali MacGraw, Cher, Lucie Arnaz, any kook with straight hair and hoop earrings. For one full week, Libby played Partridge Family records on her stereo and wore dark tights; she said she was protesting because we wouldn't buy her Barbie's Malibu Sundeck.

The nurse just came in; she says that Libby is still in labor and that she's doing just fine and that she's got plenty of moisturizer. Libby told me only last week, Mom, just because I'm giving birth, that's no reason to let myself go. She's right; I may be prejudiced, but believe me, every woman who gives birth should get the Nobel prize. All children, every day of their lives, they should call their mothers and say, Mom, I'm sorry for what I put you through, please come for the weekend, and I'll make a nice kugel and maybe a pound cake, it's no bother. I hope that Martin Scorsese calls his mother twice a day; I just saw his movie *The Last Temptation of Christ,* and all I can say is, Holy moley.

This movie is about Jesus, or, as my aunt Sylvia would say, You know, Him. I had a problem with this film, the same problem I have with most films: Where is the mother? Mary gave birth to the Son of God, you'd think it would entitle her to a little consideration; maybe they could cast Liz Taylor, but oh, no—in *The Last Temptation,* Mary is onscreen for about one minute flat, wearing a gray rag. But what did I expect—where was Gandhi's mom, where was Patton's mom, where was Mrs. Vader, Darth's mom?

And this Mary Magdalene—did Jesus ever bring her home? And all those apostles—sure, have a party, invite your pals, but whose tablecloth do you think they used? Now, I am not of the Christian faith, but I know what's right—if my son went out to wander in the desert, I'd make sure he had a sandwich and a sweater. I'm sure that Mary was a wonderful mom, but Mr. Scorsese, where is she, at the pool? Enough with the Jesus business, what about Mary's heart-ache—no grandchildren?

All of those protesters, those religious people who picketed *The Last Temptation*, let me ask you this: Where were you when we needed you? Where were the pickets for *Psycho*, in which a mother was killed, or for *Throw Momma from the Train*? I'm telling you, someone should write a book—*Moms on Film: Hollywood, Go to Your Room*.

Anyway, in *The Last Temptation*, Willem Dafoe plays Jesus, and he looks just like Him—it's like watching one of those place mats where the eyes move. When Willem is crucified, however, he's naked, and I must say, that's not how I remember Jeffrey Hunter in *King of Kings*. Personally, I prefer a little more De Mille in my religious epics; I like to see a gladiator or two, and maybe Shelley Winters as the pharaoh's wife. Also, at the end of *The Last Temptation*, there's a part where Jesus imagines what it would be like to be human rather than divine; He thinks about growing old, having kids, and doing a lot of kissing with Barbara Hershey. But Mr. Scorsese, why not show some genuine temptations? You know what I'm talking about: January white sales, real butter, éclairs, half-price fares to Europe, maybe even a stunning mink bolero. Kissing I might give up, but my cleaning lady twice a week—that I'd have to think about.

I saw one other film this month, called *Crossing Delancey*. This film is about a young single Jewish girl in New York City who works in a fancy bookstore uptown. She has a crush on a sexy Dutch novelist, but the movie says she should marry a nice man from the Lower East Side who sells pickles. Excuse me—does anyone buy this?

Crossing Delancey is very phony, and here's how you can tell. The main girl is played by Amy Irving, who's very good, but let's ask Amy's mom: If your daughter could marry Steven Spielberg—Mister *E.T.*—or a pickle man, whom should she choose? Of course, Amy should follow her heart, but with a career like Spielberg's, what's not to love? *Crossing Delancey* is about how cute and funny the Jews are; I'm Jewish, and believe me, I'm adorable, but I could live without this film.

The nurse just came back in; she says that Libby is still fine, only she keeps crying out for me, her husband, and Weight Watcher's Chocolate Mousse on a Stick. So please excuse me, I've got to go. My Libby will be back next month, once the nanny starts fulltime; being a film critic is all very nice, but live-in help that doesn't drink or worship Satan is the secret of life, if you ask me, or anyone else for that matter.

—Sondra Krell-Gelman

BE MY BABY

━━━━

ast month I gave birth to a beautiful baby boy and saw *Dead Ringers*, a movie about twin gynecologist drug addicts who go mad. I'm telling you, I'm glad I had the baby first, otherwise I wouldn't have let a doctor near me. When my gorgeous four-year-old daughter, Jennifer, was born, I composed a little poem so that she could read it someday when she's all grown up. I have now written a new poem, which I'd like to share, entitled "Ode to My New Son."

> Welcome to the planet,
> My own sweet baby boy.
> If you promise to stop crying,
> I'll give you a toy.
>
> Your birth was a pain,
> You could've come faster,
> But you're here and I love you,
> Mitchell Shawn Gelman-Waxner.

My husband wanted to name the baby something biblical, like Max or Ben, but I said no, because then the baby would grow up to be a divorce lawyer. Mitchell Shawn is a wonderful baby—he already sleeps through the night, so the nanny can get some rest. Jennifer is adapting well; she says that Mitchell is better than her Cabbage Patch doll, because when she hides the doll in a drawer no one cares. I made an appointment for Jennifer with my therapist, Dr. Arlene Cole-Natbaum. Let me tell you, I had tears in my eyes, and my husband, Josh, took a Polaroid; it's a special moment when your own little pumpkin has her very first session with the shrink. Like Dr. Cole-Natbaum says, One day it's pigtails and acting out, and the next it's first dates, bulimia, and henna.

Thank God I go to a woman gynecologist, Dr. Shanna Tetra-Rosen, who is very sensitive and has lovely floral watercolors in her office, as well as all the back issues of *Elle*. Of course, since seeing *Dead Ringers*, I have wondered if Shanna has a twin; this movie was very upsetting. Jeremy Irons plays twin doctors, both of whom have sex with Geneviève Bujold, who doesn't know there are two of them; one of the Jeremys falls in love with Geneviève, and then both Jeremys start popping pills and wearing filthy bathrobes. The movie reminded me of the Kloper twins, Brian and Bruce, whom I went to high school with. I dated Brian, who said that since he was a minute older than Bruce, he was the mature one. Until I saw *Dead Ringers*, I thought it might have been a good idea to marry a twin: you'd have a husband and a spare.

This month I also saw movies written and directed by two Pulitzer prize winners—*Things Change*, by David Mamet, and *Far North*, by Sam Shepard. Mr. Pulitzer, if you want high drama, maybe this year you can give the prize to my AT&T bill. The Mamet film is about adorable gangsters in Lake Tahoe, and the Shepard movie is about horses and people in the Midwest. If you ask me, David Mamet and Sam Shepard are the Ralph Lauren and Calvin Klein of American literature. David is like Ralph—he's short and he tries very hard; Sam is like Calvin—he's tall and cute. Personally, I could live without seeing any more movies about funny mobsters or people who have to sell the farm; just sell it and put up condos, you'll make a fortune and get a place at the beach. Why do people want to live on farms anyway? If you ask me, chickens belong in buckets, not coops, and milk is better fresh from the carton.

Another movie I saw was *Clara's Heart*, in which Whoopi Goldberg plays a Jamaican housekeeper. What's next, Eddie Murphy in *The Rochester Story*? Whoopi is a dream come true: not only does she cook and clean, but when the couple she works for get a divorce, she acts as a surrogate mom for their little boy. It's like *Mary Poppins*, only with reggae. My Honduran housekeeper, Mrs. Alejandro, also went to see *Clara's Heart*; she told me that Whoopi deserved a raise, two afternoons off, a color portable in her room, and a nicer bedspread. Mrs. Alejandro is a gem; last week she put a curse on our building's superintendent, and the next day his sauna broke down. I wonder if Mrs. Alejandro has a twin.

The last movie I saw this month was Woody Allen's latest, *Another Woman*. Hoo boy. Let me put it this way: everyone's in beige again; it's another oatmeal-and-khaki festival. In one scene, all the characters are wearing tweed blazers, even the women—it's like *Goodbye, Mr. Chips. Another Woman* is about Gena Rowlands, who's this esteemed philosophy professor and author. She says things like, I remember my mother taking her favorite volume of Rilke off the shelf. Gena, I remember my mom hauling down Herman Wouk.

Everybody in this movie is cheating on somebody or writing a novel or committing suicide; it's like an episode of *Knots Landing*, only set on the Upper West Side. Gena is very upset because she's turning fifty and she's emotionally empty—Woody, she has two rent-controlled apartments, it's enough. Everyone is in this movie: Gene Hackman, Blythe Danner, you name it, and they all wear turtlenecks and have a secret that gets revealed; let me tell you, this film is a four-Nuprin experience.

Woody, you have to perk up; everyone can't mope around to classical music and have great lamps. Maybe it's your diet, maybe you're not getting enough fresh air; Mia, help Woody out. Take him to a musical, buy him a bright red shirt, burn his library card. Woody and Mia, you have a new baby, and now I have a new baby. How about a movie about trying to get a stroller out of a cab in midtown? Or going to the supermarket with two children and no handcuffs? Woody, it's only a suggestion, but Mitchell Shawn is extremely photogenic—he looks like Dustin Hoffman, only he's bald and he spits up. Now, there's a box office bonanza, if you ask me.

MEN TALK

I have decided to give up my career and family and become Michelle Pfeiffer. I just saw *Tequila Sunrise,* and not only does Michelle look gorgeous and wear tight linen skirts that never show creases across the lap, but she also gets to choose between Mel Gibson and Kurt Russell. It's very strange, because the film treats this as if it were a problem. Getting your husband to unload the dishwasher is a problem; choosing between Mel and Kurt is like dealing with the truffles and the layer cake on the dessert cart.

In this film Mel plays a drug dealer, only he's retiring in order to look after his little boy. Kurt is Mel's friend and a police officer, so there's a conflict. Michelle owns a fabulous restaurant with flattering lighting, but here's my question: Michelle, how can you work around food day and night and still be such a toothpick? I swear, Cher's plastic surgeon must use a photo of Michelle as a game plan.

I saw this film with my dear friend Stacy Schiff, the gifted marketing analyst, who is still unattached even though she reads *Self* magazine every month and is willing to date outside the professions. *Tequila Sunrise* depressed Stacy. She says that in real life Mel is married to an Australian woman and has five kids and that Kurt lives with Goldie Hawn and their baby. Stacy says that watching this movie is like going through the Neiman Marcus catalog, only everything you want has been discontinued. She says that after seeing Mel's naked tush in *Lethal Weapon,* she took out her first personal ad. After seeing him in the hot tub in *Tequila Sunrise,* she's ready to become a surrogate mother, if the experience would include dinner.

Stacy and I also saw *Everybody's All-American,* starring the man I consider my spiritual fiancé, Dennis Quaid. Although I love my husband and children, they know very well that Dennis comes first, especially when he wears just his jockstrap and I rip the armrests right off my seat. In this film Dennis plays a college football hero who marries the campus Magnolia Queen, Jessica Lange. The movie follows the couple for about thirty years, so there are a lot of wigs involved. Dennis plays pro football and then retires, and Jessica grows strong and runs a chain of fast-food restaurants. Throughout this film all I could think was, Why isn't this movie about me and my husband, Josh? Believe me, there'd be a lot more thrills.

Picture it—Jessica as Libby, film critic, successful buyer of juniors' activewear, and modern mom. Dennis as Josh, adoring husband, father of two, and creative orthodontist. I can see Jessica experimenting with Donna Karan cashmere, and Dennis slaving tirelessly over crooked teenage mouths, battered by rubber bands, forcing the Garber boy to wear his retainer. I'm telling you, the movie company could make a fortune. In *Everybody's All-American,* Jessica and Dennis have a wedding night that's all soft-focus and champagne glasses. I spent my wedding night on a 747 to Oahu; thank God I remembered the Dramamine and the new Judith Krantz. Once we got to the hotel, Josh and I had a wonderful time. Josh loosened his belt, and we both took off our shoes and ordered up a gallon of Rocky Road. Forget slow motion and violins; there's nothing like sex with a complimentary tennis lesson the next day.

I also saw *The Good Mother* this month; it's about Diane Keaton, who gets divorced but has custody of her little daughter. Diane has been repressed, but she meets a cute Welsh artist and has orgasms. Then Diane loses custody, because she and the artist have sex while the daughter is asleep on the bed, and because the artist lets the daughter touch his genitals when she's curious. The film is about how no one likes to think of mothers as sexual beings.

I remember when I was little and I first overheard my parents having sex. My mother was screaming so loud that I thought either something was on sale or someone had taken the plastic slipcovers off the living room couches. Afterward, my mother explained to me that sex is a beautiful and tender thing, especially with a man who has a Ph.D. She said that sex was even better with a fellow who owns a business, such as my father, Sy "The Living Doll" Gelman, founder and president of Gelman Fine Vinyl Handbags and Related Accessories, Inc.

My daughter, Jennifer, is five years old, and I know that very soon she'll be asking about the facts of life. I don't know if I should tell her about sex, which is terrific, or about sex with Dennis, which, I imagine, could change your hair color and unclog your pores without the benefit of a scruffing lotion. Maybe I'll just tell her to think about buying shoes and then picture something even better, at least sometimes. Actually, I'm not so concerned about my kids' touching genitals, but if they go near a guest towel or the hors d'oeuvres, they're dead in the water.

Stacy and I also went to see *U2 Rattle and Hum,* which is a documentary about the rock group U2. Is it my imagination, or did rock stars used to be sexy? The lead singer of U2 is named Bono, which is not pronounced like Sonny Bono, although believe me, there is a physical resemblance. Bono is very glum and sings about Northern Ireland and international strife, all of which would be fine except that he has incredibly greasy hair. Stacy and I decided that the real trouble in Belfast must be a lack of Pantene products. Bono also wears a leather vest with no shirt, and he sweats a lot, and he's not exactly Mel. It's very hard to clean leather—think about it.

Life can be a struggle, and sometimes all a woman can do is try and decide who's a better kisser: Mel or Kurt. Stacy and I have discussed this. We voted for Kurt, because his kisses look deeper and more meaningful. Mel's kisses are great, but they are not, as Stacy puts it, all-devouring. Mel, Stacy says, is the man you dream about, and Kurt is the man you cheat on your husband with because he makes eyes at you on the lox line at Zabar's. Mel is so cute he's not human, and Kurt is so cute he's evil, which is more fun, although, of course, it's a very fine distinction. Stacy says that at this point she'd settle for Patrick Swayze, but I said, Stacy, hold out for a neurosurgeon. Blue eyes and great kisses are well and good, but free X-rays and unlimited prescriptions are forever. And those are the real facts of life and movies, if you ask me.

BOY MEETS BOY

■ ■ ■

Transvestites, autistic adults, and Danny DeVito with his shirt off—it's been quite a month. First I went to see *Torch Song Trilogy*, and I brought my wonderful cousin, Andrew Gelman. Andrew is an art director at a Madison Avenue ad agency, and he's so incredibly creative that, as my mother says, no one's holding their breath for grandchildren. Andrew lives in Greenwich Village with his friend, Robert, who is also an art director, so you can just imagine their apartment. The imported champagne flutes alone give me goose bumps, and the plants accept only Evian.

Torch Song is all about Harvey Fierstein, who is delightful and reminds me of Eddie Cantor in heels. In the movie, Harvey has one boyfriend who's bisexual and another who dies: Andrew says it's Harvey as Susan Hayward. Matthew Broderick plays one of the boyfriends, and he looks very nervous. As Andrew put it, Oh, Matthew, just calm down.

Anne Bancroft is Harvey's mom, and she seems to be playing all major ethnic groups combined, or at least Jewish, Italian, and Orthodox Flamenco. Anne, let me give you some advice: Jewish mothers don't wave their hands so much, because they might break a vase. Anne doesn't approve of Harvey's lifestyle, because he makes his living as a drag queen. I asked myself, How would I feel if my son grew up and wanted to wear an evening gown? I decided it would be fine, as long as we're talking Bill Blass or De la Renta. But if I caught him in a poly blend or something mother-of-the-bride, he'd be history.

Next, Andrew and I went to see *Twins*, another film about a male couple. Danny DeVito and Arnold Schwarzenegger are supposed to be twins separated at birth. I had hoped to live my entire life without seeing Danny DeVito bare-chested, but no such luck. Arnold is cute, but Andrew says that in real life he's a Republican, so we shouldn't swoon too much. Danny and Arnold clown around like they're on a talk show together, and I wanted someone to slap them. I've never really enjoyed stories about twins all that much, although I thought the girl who played Cathy on *The Patty Duke Show* was very talented—whatever happened to her?

After seeing *Twins*, Andrew and I were so exhausted that we stopped for swordfish in SoHo and talked about whether Andrew should let his hair grow. Andrew says that men with ponytails look silly, as if they should accessorize with bobby socks and angora sweaters. Andrew, like any decent human being, takes his hair very seriously, and we agreed that he might experiment with bangs. Andrew said he liked my streaks, but he warned me about going too far. He said that some women overdo the peroxide and look as if they went to Mister Ivan of Chernobyl.

We gathered our strength and went to see *Rain Man*, which stars Tom Cruise and Dustin Hoffman. Tom plays a sharpster Lamborghini dealer, and Dustin is his autistic savant older brother, who inherits $3 million, so Tom kidnaps him. At first, all I could think about was their poor mother, who waited 25 years between babies. At least Tom and Dustin aren't supposed to be twins.

Tom and Dustin go on a car trip that is just like the one in *Midnight Run*, or any movie with two big stars in a convertible. Dustin is very good at being autistic. It's like watching someone play Helen Keller or the Elephant Man: you know they'll get at least a nomination. Tom is adorable and grins a lot; in the future, all the Tom Cruise Film Festivals will be divided into halves: the movies with sunglasses and the ones without. Tom's girlfriend is played by an Italian actress who wears very little clothing and sounds just like Topo Gigio, the puppet on *The Ed Sullivan Show*.

Eventually, Tom teaches Dustin how to waltz, and the Italian girl gives Dustin his first French kiss. According to Andrew, the next step would be tap lessons and a vibrating waterbed. Maybe, for just a little while, the movie industry could outlaw the following: scenes in which someone without a license drives a car, scenes in which two characters try on matching Italian sportswear, scenes in which the characters watch *Wheel of Fortune,* and anything set in Las Vegas. While we're at it, maybe no movie should be allowed to star two men and a girl with too much hair and a great behind. As Andrew says, Please, Mr. Studio President, it's enough already.

The last film that Andrew and I saw was *A Cry in the Dark,* with Meryl Streep. This film is based on a true story about an Australian woman whose baby was eaten by a dingo, which is a wild Australian dog. Everyone thinks the woman killed her baby, and she's put in prison until the truth comes out. This film is very upsetting, and it sure doesn't make you want to visit Sydney. As Andrew said, from now on, he won't even trust Snoopy.

Meryl is terrific as the woman, and she wears a Buster Brown wig and sneakers and speaks with an Aussie accent. When Meryl wakes up in the morning, how does she sound? How do her children know which country they live in?

Meryl is a dream, though, and so far she's never gone on a wacky car trip to Vegas. Andrew says he's not so sure that it's really Harvey Fierstein in *Torch Song;* he says the movie just may be Meryl's next Oscar. She's a big winner, if you ask me, or, as Andrew says, If you ask me, darling.

IT'S AN HONOR

▬ ▬ ▬

Every year, I watch the Kennedy Center Honors, the
Golden Globes, the People's Choice Awards, and the Oscars, and I don't know which ceremony is most impressive. In each case, the winners receive America's highest
accolade—a prime-time special featuring a medley sung
by Leslie Uggams and Barbara Mandrell. If you ask me,
just sharing a stage with Helen Hayes and Chevy Chase
would be honor enough. It is in this golden-toned-statuette spirit
that I hereby present my first annual Libby Gelman-Waxner
Awards for Achievement in Cinematic Auteurism and Tasteful
Grooming—the Libbys. Each winner will receive a nice note on
my embossed note cards and one of my many duplicate wedding
gifts, which are still sitting in the hall closet after nine years.

The Wig Addiction Libby goes to John Malkovich, who in *Dangerous Liaisons* seems to be wearing two wigs simultaneously, one brunet and one powdered white, for a piggyback, wig-on-wig effect.
Throughout his career, John has worn so many wigs, falls, and hairpieces that he really should market them, following the example of
Eva Gabor and her Elegant Lady collection (my cousin Elaine
swore by Eva's Mitzi model after her hair fell out from doing liquid
protein). All I can say is, wigs are to John what accents are to Meryl.
John will receive an Ultra-Max Curling Wand, the gift of my first
cousin Lynette and her husband, Gus. Gus can't even hold a job in
his father's carpet warehouse, which explains why Gus and Lynette
consider a $15.98 item to be an appropriate token of affection.

The Back to Television While You Can Still Get a Pilot Libby is shared
by Alan Alda and Sally Field. Alan, in *A New Life*, and Sally, in
Punchline, both proved that they are far more appealing when sand-

wiched between Toyota ads and Stephanie Zimbalist movies of the week. Alan is wise, wry, and charming, which always turns me off, and Sally, well, I'm always afraid that Sally will climb right off the screen and ask me for a hug. In interviews Sally always acts as if being on *The Flying Nun* was a horrible tragedy, like a brain tumor; Sally, maybe it's time for a reunion special. Alan and Sally will each receive a set of Indonesian hand-carved teak salad tongs, which can be used at the table or hung on the kitchen wall as a decorative accent.

The Mrs. Kaslow Humanitarian Libby is split between *A World Apart* and *Mississippi Burning*, for illustrating the evils of racism as battled by cute white movie stars. Barbara Hershey fought apartheid while Gene Hackman and Willem Dafoe handled the civil-rights struggle. What's next—Rob Lowe as Malcolm X's secret pen pal? This award is named after Mrs. Ruth Kaslow, my third-grade teacher, who always said that all races could live in harmony if everyone just remembered to say "please" and "thank you" and didn't push and shove on the cafeteria lunch line. The winning films' producers will each receive a quarter wrapped in tinfoil, courtesy of my great-aunt Pearl.

The Lifetime Achievement Libby goes to Tom Cruise. In almost all his films, Tom has played a charming rebel who grins and learns an important lesson that helps him grow up, if not actually become taller. He always wears sunglasses, removes most of his clothing, and learns a new skill that only boys in a high school shop class would find attractive, like being a fighter pilot in peacetime, selling Lamborghinis, or playing pool. Tom will receive a three-speed blender, in honor of his work in *Cocktail*, a film in which he expressed emotional torment through banana daiquiris and grasshoppers.

The Libby, Book Two: The Return Award is given to the year's finest sequel, and this year's nominees included *Rambo III, Short Circuit 2, Arthur 2: On the Rocks, Police Academy 5, "Crocodile" Dundee II,* and the clear winner, *Cocoon: The Return*. If you ask me, a successful sequel depends on one magical element: Steve Guttenberg. Steve is in both *Cocoons* and four of the *Police Academys*, and he's slated for the

Three Men and a Baby sequel. The ideal cast for a sequel would be Steve, Linda Kozlowski, Chuck Norris, and Freddy Krueger—these are all people whose price probably doesn't go up a whole lot from film to film. The producers of *Cocoon: The Return* will receive my aunt Becky's humidifier, which she says does wonders for both the complexion and any hanging plants.

The Don't They Have Parents Libby, for gratuitous nudity, was another hotly contested race. Nominated were Willem Dafoe, for dangling naked on the cross in *The Last Temptation of Christ;* John Cleese, for wearing only a framed photo in *A Fish Called Wanda;* and the winner, Melanie Griffith, for vacuuming topless in *Working Girl.* My husband, Josh, disputes this award; he says that Melanie didn't want to get her clothes grimy and that he found the scene both appropriate and tasteful. Then he asked me to use the Dustbuster while wearing only my panties. I said fine, if he would regrout the bathroom tiles in just his socks. Mike Nichols, who directed *Working Girl,* will receive a Mr. Coffee, which can be operated by his wife, Diane Sawyer, wearing just her *60 Minutes* blazer.

Das Libby is the award for Best Foreign Film. I'm not crazy about subtitles, so this Libby goes to the foreign film I would have liked best if I could have forced myself to sit through it. *Pelle the Conqueror* is about Swedish farm laborers, so forget it; *Red Sorghum* is about Chinese farm laborers, so no dice; and even in 1987, *Jean de Florette* and *Manon of the Spring* were about French farm laborers, so it's enough already with the hauling water and everyone living in a one-room hut. This year's Das Libby goes to *Women on the Verge of a Nervous Breakdown,* which is in Spanish, but I hear it's a delightful film in which no one has a dirt floor or problems with locusts. The film's director, Pedro Almodóvar, will receive a lovely three-foot-tall mahogany pepper mill, which he is welcome to use or pass along.

The Sondra Krell-Gelman Public Service Medallion, named in honor of my mother, goes to the antidrug films *Clean and Sober, The Boost,* and *Bright Lights, Big City.* As my mother says, If teenagers would go see these works, they'll never want to abuse drugs or go to the movies again. Watching a movie star kick cocaine is always a highly believable experience; *The Boost*'s Sean Young and James Woods are particularly effective role models for our youth. As Sondra says, Cold sweats, dry heaves, and a great soundtrack—that's entertainment. Sean and James will receive a good talking-to from Sondra herself, and not a moment too soon, if you ask me.

A NEW SCOURGE

- - - -

World literature—I love it, but with a career, two kids, and my roots staring me in the face, who has the time? I haven't even finished the last Jackie Collins, and my husband, Josh, hasn't opened the Tom Clancy I got him for Christmas. Maybe it's for the best. As I told Josh, At least our kids won't see us reading trash. Thank God for movie adaptations. I felt so proud when I told the sitter I was going to see *The Accidental Tourist.* She knew I wasn't going out just to have fun.

The Accidental Tourist is based on the novel by Anne Tyler. Anne, I'm sure it's a swell book, but seeing the film put me into a coma—I'm not kidding you. All I remember is watching William Hurt sitting in an armchair, blinking his little pink eyes, and the next thing I knew the usher was shaking me awake because the film was over. The usher said that many people have had similar reactions to *The Accidental Tourist;* he said that even crying babies nod right off. That night I had a dream about the movie. In my dream, William Hurt came to my apartment, and he said that if I didn't give him my baby son, Mitchell, he would make me watch *The Accidental Tourist* two more times. Even in my dream, William Hurt was the most Caucasian person I have ever seen; he was like this enormous slice of Tip-Top bread in chinos and wire-rimmed eyeglasses. His hair reminded me of mayonnaise, and he spoke very slowly, like a Mormon on Quaaludes. He was like a huge rubber eraser, an albino Gumby, and he terrified me. William Hurt underplaying is much scarier than Shelley Winters at full blast, let me tell you. Just as I was about to head for the baby's room, I woke up screaming. I told my husband about the dream, and he agreed with me: We can always have more children.

After this experience, I went to see the film version of Tama Janowitz's collection of stories, *Slaves of New York*. This movie is about New Wave artists living in New York's trendy East Village, so I thought it would be lively. But the strangest thing happened. All I remember is someone on the screen saying "Come up to my loft," and then the usher was yanking my shoulder. That night I had another dream. Tama Janowitz, this woman with a wild, teased hairdo, came to my apartment wearing a rubber miniskirt and a $2,000 silver lamé motorcycle jacket. She was very sweet, but she started to tell me about her troubles with her sadistic artist boyfriend, and how she has low self-esteem, and how hard it is to finance a halfway decent co-op. And I started to think, Maybe some people *should* have low self-esteem. And then Tama said that if I didn't hand over my husband, she would tell me all about her girlfriend's problems in finding a gallery in which to show her voodoo sculpture and trying to get a man who isn't on cocaine to say "I love you." And just as I was tying Josh's wrists with an old pair of panty hose, I woke up in a cold sweat. I decided not to tell him about my dream, even though I knew he would have understood, especially if he had seen Tama's eyeliner.

The next day, I went to see my therapist, Dr. Arlene Cole-Natbaum, and I told her about my conking out at the movies and my nightmares, and about Tama's earrings. Dr. Cole-Natbaum said that I was suffering from a common condition known as movie-lepsy. Movie-lepsy, it seems, is somewhere between epilepsy and narcolepsy, and it is referred to in certain medical textbooks as Merchant Ivory syndrome. The movie-leptic's chronic napping, Dr. Cole-Natbaum explained, can be triggered by any number of cinematic images: William Hurt repressing his emotions, Robert Duvall in a cowboy hat, anything involving a child who has been mute since a parent or pet died, and any pair of zanily mismatched detectives or bank robbers. Dr. Cole-Natbaum said the origins of movie-lepsy had been traced to several TV movies in which illiterate adults learn to read.

Dr. Cole-Natbaum gave me a remedy for my movie-lepsy. She said that when I start to feel drowsy, that whenever Sissy Spacek opens a screen door, I should practice two visualizations. First, I should think about Barbara Hershey's lips. Barbara had collagen injections in her lips to make them fuller and more pouty, which I first noticed in the film *Beaches*. I've also read about a woman who used a chunk of fat from her own thigh to plump out her upper lip. This struck me as very dangerous: what if the fat decided it had merely headed upstream to spawn? My dear friend Stacy Schiff is considering liposuction in order to combat a saddlebag problem. Stacy says that the procedure sounds very satisfying, that it's what she's always dreamed of—removing her cellulite with a penknife.

If Barbara Hershey's lips don't do the trick, Dr. Cole-Natbaum said I might also think about director Peter Bogdanovich's marriage to Dorothy Stratten's younger sister. Peter loved Dorothy, but she was murdered; Peter also paid for the younger sister's plastic surgery. Dr. Cole-Natbaum is such a fine therapist; last week she cured a manic-depressive by prescribing Mallomars eaten in bed and a subscription to *US* magazine. Thanks to Dr. Cole-Natbaum, my movie-lepsy is under control; as a test, I watched an episode of *The Wonder Years*, a sitcom set in the '60s that has sensitive voice-over narration. I am pleased to report that I didn't drop off even once, and Dr. Cole-Natbaum says that any dry cracker will control the retching.

Movie-lepsy can be very serious, and it is not caused only by films adapted from acclaimed novels or plays. Still, it is a good idea to watch out for that kind of thing; remember, if you snooze off while reading a book, at least no one steals your purse or sees you with your mouth open. I would like there to be a Prevent Movie-lepsy Telethon, maybe hosted by Bill Hurt, in which funds could be raised to fight movies set in the Midwest, the outback, or London during the Blitz. I, Libby, am a movie-leptic. I only hope that my frank confession will stop the shame and encourage others to seek counseling, especially those who haven't regained consciousness since watching *Maurice* or any film in which people take tea with their maiden aunts. Helping people is what I'm here for, if you ask me.

L'AMOUR DU CINÉMA

■ ■ ■ ■

P
lease don't tell a soul. I'm only sharing this with you, my
devoted readership, and my dear friend Stacy Schiff: this
month I've been on the verge of an affair. I blame the
whole thing on the movie *Cousins* and adult braces. My
husband, Josh, is an extremely successful orthodontist, but
he wants more. He says that working only with adoles-
cents limits his creativity, so he's started doing adult
braces, the almost invisible plastic kind that hook on from behind
the teeth. All of a sudden Josh has patients who are models and actresses, and, especially, there is this one woman corporate attorney,
Elaine Blatt-Markle.

I admit it, Elaine's mouth was a disaster area, with big spaces between her teeth, as if her gums were a cemetery. But Elaine is otherwise an attractive if overly confident woman—you know, the
kind with the quilted Chanel bag and no hips and hair that swings
when she walks. She's married to Dr. Stanley Markle, a plastic surgeon, so she's always treated Josh and me like second-class citizens,
just because Josh fixes teeth instead of doing silicone implants and,
if you ask me, Elaine's own nose. I went to Camp Pocahontas with
Elaine years ago, and I distinctly recall a bump. But when Josh
started doing adult braces, Elaine changed her tune; suddenly she
and Josh were best buddies, having consultations over white-wine
spritzers at the Carlyle. One night I said, So, Josh, how come you
never take the Tishman boy, with the infected jaw and the
blemishes, to the Carlyle?

Then I went to see the movie *Cousins* with Stacy. This film is all
about how Ted Danson's ditzy wife, Sean Young, is having an affair
with Isabella Rossellini's nasty Subaru-salesman husband, William

Petersen. Everyone meets at a wedding, and eventually Ted and Isabella run off together. All the people in the movie are zany and warm and wear great all-cotton sportswear, and Stacy and I agreed that it was like one of those magazine ads "for people who like to smoke." You know, the ones where the surgeon general's warning about low birth weight and fetal injury is tucked right beside the restored Victorian mantelpiece in the glamorous couple's loft.

Anyway, right after I saw *Cousins,* I went to the reception for my cousin Larry's bar mitzvah, which was held at the Cloisters, a beautiful gothic site in Manhattan that Larry's parents had rented for the occasion. No one seemed to mind that the Cloisters is a monastic setting, because the high altar made a lovely buffet, and the florists had hidden all the crucifixes behind gladiolas and baby's breath. Larry wore his prayer shawl over a stunning Versace sport coat and a black silk T-shirt; he made a touching speech, thanking his parents for their love and patience and for posting bail when he was arrested for dealing cocaine on his computer. And who should Josh and I run into during this speech but Stan and Elaine. Elaine and Josh immediately ran off to a corner to discuss which of the hors d'oeuvres wouldn't get caught in Elaine's braces. That was when I noticed that Stan Markle is really a very attractive man, even when wearing a hot pink yarmulke with Larry's initials embossed on it in gold.

Stan brought me some champagne and asked who had done my nose, because it was holding up so well. We wandered toward the temporary dance floor that the caterers had set up, and the Stu Golden Trio began to play Debbie Gibson's "Lost in Your Eyes." As Stan and I danced I began to feel like I was Isabella Rossellini. My skin glowed, just like Isabella's does in her Lancôme ads, and I began to speak with an unidentifiable Swedish-Italian accent. I saw my beloved mother, Sondra Krell-Gelman, across the room, taking one of the floral centerpieces out to her Buick; suddenly, she looked like Ingrid Bergman—especially the way Ingrid looked in the TV movie *A Woman Called Golda.*

I gazed into Stan's eyes, and he looked just like Ted Danson, although of course I was gazing downward, because Stan is two inches shorter than I. I could see the line from where Stan had worn protective goggles at the tanning salon, but it didn't matter. "How deep is *your* love?" Stan whispered in my ear as the trio began a Bee Gees medley. We danced behind the coatracks, and Stan kissed me. I have to confess I felt excited; I'm a pushover for the taste of Wintergreen Certs with NutraSweet. We arranged to meet later in the week at Stan's office, after hours.

All week long I was in a state. Should I go? Shouldn't I go? Was Oprah's program about how adultery can strengthen a marriage a good omen? I asked my therapist, Dr. Arlene Cole-Natbaum, and she said that if it was a choice between cheating on Josh and a cheesecake binge, at least the cheating wouldn't haunt me. Stacy was upset. She said I was hoarding all the cute specialists. I was going to ask my mother what I should do, but I was afraid that she would want to come along. Finally, I consulted the ultimate authority, my horoscope in the *New York Post,* which said that it was a bad day for ocean travel, so I took that as a yes for the Upper East Side.

When Ted and Isabella ran off together, they drove to a secluded lakefront cabin on Ted's motorcycle, without helmets on so their hair would blow. I took two different cabs to Stan's office on East 82nd, in case anyone was following me; I was dressed like Isabella, in flowing cream linen, which got all creased in the cabs, but Stacy says it's supposed to look that way. Although there was no one in the office but Stan, he was still wearing his white nylon lab coat. He took me in his arms and said, Welcome to the Land of a Better You.

We went into Stan's private office, and he showed me his new video imaging equipment. He turned on his new camera, and my face appeared on a television screen. Look at Libby, he said, she's so beautiful. I'm telling you, I was shameless; I forgot all about Josh and my two kids and even whether the dress shields in my silk blouse were holding up. I told Stan that in *Cousins,* when Ted and Isabella are driving through a meadow on the motorcycle, they scream to show how free and happy they are. Stan and I screamed and the cleaning lady from the next office banged on the door to see if Stan was snipping earlobes without using an anesthetic again. Stan told her that we were screaming for happiness, and she mumbled something in Spanish and went back to emptying waste-baskets.

Stan shut the door and held me. He said, Libby, it's a big step. He said, This could change both our lives. He said, Libby, I want to do this more than anything. My head was spinning; all I could think about was how radiant Isabella had looked in bed with Ted, under a pile of handmade Amish quilts, and how in real life Isabella has been divorced twice and seems fine. I kissed Stan, hoping that my lips would give him my answer. He pulled away and pushed a button on his remote control. Libby, my darling, he said as he used the remote to alter my face on the TV screen, I can give you a whole new chin.

Well, let me tell you, I smacked him so hard that most of his hair transplants popped out. I screamed, I have a great chin! Josh loves my chin! In the cab on the way home, all I could think about was how Ted had never said a word about Isabella's chin, and how he took her sailing and not to an office with before-and-after photos of his wife's tummy tuck on the wall. I got back to the apartment, and Josh had just put the kids to bed. I said, Josh, do you love me as much as Ted loved Isabella? And he said that he loved me even more, as much as Ted loved Shelley Long on *Cheers*. And I said, But Shelley left the series. And Josh said, Libby, shut up. And then he told me how he'd removed Elaine's braces that afternoon and how she'd had a fit and decided that what she really needed was dental bonding. Josh even told me that Elaine had plaque, and that he could never love a woman who was careless about tartar buildup.

I have been considering writing Isabella a letter to ask her about all of this. I have decided that you can only have an affair if you have really great lighting and a sympathetic cameraman. Love, remakes of French films, and bar mitzvahs are a dangerous cocktail, if you ask me.

LETTERS TO LIBBY

— ■ ■ ■

Over the past year or so, I have received so many letters from you, my devoted readership and fellow students of cinematic auteurism (which is not what Dustin Hoffman suffered from in *Rain Man*). Tricia Herne of Sierra Vista, Arizona, was upset by my review of *Rain Man;* about Dustin, she asks, "He didn't touch your heart at all?" Joshua Klein of West Chester, Pennsylvania, wonders if I was "dragged into the theater to see *Rain Man.*" Please, everyone, calm down. Dustin won the Oscar, which, after all, was the whole point of *Rain Man.* The Oscar ceremony in general seemed like Dustin's bar mitzvah, because he thanked his invalid father for being such a fan. Believe me, it was all very touching; it was as if *Ishtar* had never even happened.

Personally, I most enjoyed the Oscar production number featuring Hollywood youth, such as the daughters of Connie Stevens and Eddie Fisher, a family whom I consider the American Redgraves. I was wondering if next year the show might salute the Hollywood kids who've been through rehab; there could be a chorus line with Drew Barrymore, Kristy McNichol, Carrie Hamilton, and Griffin O'Neal. I'm worried about that little thirteen-year-old Drew; I think that, tabloidwise, she may have peaked too early. When your preteen cocaine problems hit the cover of *People* magazine, what's left except stabbing your mom's boyfriend, becoming manic-depressive, or gaining weight?

Christopher Baratta of London, Ontario, writes that "Libby Gelman-Waxner is hooked on violent movies. . . . This is very abnormal behavior." Christopher is concerned that I enjoyed *Rambo III* and that I allowed my four-year-old daughter, Jennifer, to watch

The Terminator. Christopher, I agree that violence is never the answer, unless of course it's pouring rain and a taxicab drives by with its OFF DUTY light on. As I have told Jennifer, When this happens, you are allowed to take a human life at random, but only one. I asked Jennifer if she thought the violence in movies was real, and she said, Mom, get a life. Her new favorite movie is *Heathers,* a comedy in which the most popular girl and two jocks in a suburban high school are killed. I also enjoyed this film, but I explained to Jennifer that just because someone is blond and cute and popular, that's no reason to murder them. The best thing to do is wait twenty years until those girls become Connecticut divorcées with secret drinking problems and children in ashrams, and then you can run into them at reunions and sympathize.

Another big concern of my readers was my critique of Bono, the lead singer of the rock band U2, who appeared in the film *U2 Rattle and Hum*. Tarita Holm and Erin Jensen, both of California, write that they do not "appreciate" my remarks "about Bono's personal cleanliness and the comparison of him and Sonny Bono." Dani Kelly and Storm Sommer of Nashville claim that "Bono onstage exudes a raw, unaffected, and striking sexuality, which obviously escapes Ms. Gelman-Waxner." Laurie Lewis of San Diego says that "U2 is not dedicated to pleasing the eye of every love-starved woman who watches them." Jennifer McKinnon of Las Vegas tells Libby to "unglue her eyes from Mel Gibson's tush and face reality."

Girls, what is all this? Tarita, Erin, Dani, Storm, Laurie, and Jennifer—I admire your convictions, but I still have a serious problem with this Bono person and what he exudes. If he is so special, why doesn't he have a Diet Coke or Diet Pepsi ad? It's all well and good to sing about political strife and the ecosystem, but what about our inner thighs and wobbly upper arms? I also find it very difficult to take such musical personages as Tracy Chapman and Suzanne Vega seriously. Tracy never smiles, and she always wears a black cotton turtleneck—is it the same one, Tracy, or do you have hundreds? Is it just me, or is having a top-ten hit about being on welfare a little weird, like being both politically correct and catchy? As for Suzanne, well, I took one look and I thought, Here is a girl with at least one black leotard, a thrift-shop fedora, and a serious patchouli habit—I mean, we're talking herbal tea and cat hairs, if you ask me. Suzanne's hit song, "Luka," was about a battered child with a great name. When I watched the news and I saw volunteers scrubbing the oil spill off those Alaskan otters, I swear I could hear Suzanne tuning up that acoustic guitar and choosing a scarf.

Some of my devoted readers claim that I do not care about serious topics. Pat Piper of Lincoln, Nebraska, writes that all I'm interested in are my "junior-high-school crushes on such actors as Harrison Ford and Dennis Quaid. . . . You can't base a movie on what gets your hormones tingling, Libby." Oh, Pat, of course you can. Tingling hormones are the basis of all fine auteur works and any truly in-depth film criticism. A book can make you think, music can make you dance, and television can make you buy a nonabrasive cleanser, but only a movie can give you someone to think about when you're kissing your husband. I'm just kidding, Josh, my hubby, my dearest love—and I've forgotten all about that time, right after they reran *Body Heat* on Channel 11, when you looked deep into my eyes, caressed me, and said, "I love you, Kathleen."

There are nonhormonal reasons to appreciate a film, I'll admit—I went to see *Chances Are*, for example, to find out if Cybill Shepherd got her figure back after having twins. I attended *Fletch Lives* because I was worried about Julianne Phillips's emotional state after her divorce from Bruce Springsteen. Films can be educational: I learned about how awful Mrs. Thatcher is from reading the reviews of the low-budget English political film *High Hopes*. And, of course, films can be deeply moving emotional documents—such as any movie in which Dennis Quaid removes so much as a sock.

Lori Ann Johnson of Jamestown, New York, has written to warn me: She claims that Dennis is *her* spiritual fiancé, not mine. She says that she has just broken off her "spiritual engagement with Kevin Costner." Lori Ann says that she's certain I will "learn to love again." Lori Ann, let's try and be mature about this—we can share. I have just seen the trailer for Dennis as Jerry Lee Lewis in *Great Balls of Fire*, and . . . excuse me, I've just had another of my blackouts. I was thinking about Dennis in that trailer. . . .DENNISDENNIS-

DENNIS. . . . I'm sorry; I'm fine now. I just had to leave my type-writer for a moment and bite down hard on a rubber spatula. Anyway, I hope I've put all this tingling-hormone nonsense to rest.

I do appreciate the gentle and constructive criticism of my devoted readership (such as Josh Klein's feeling that "if you ask me, Libby Gelman-Waxner can go to hell"—and isn't that nice talk from a boy with such an appealing name). But even more, I enjoy the many letters of glowing praise and pleasure that have come my way. John Harris of Los Angeles says that "the yenta perspective on film has been sadly neglected for far too long. . . . Libby, I love you!" John, I could eat you alive and come back for seconds. Christine Pedi of Eastchester, New York, writes that "if you ask me, Libby is more exciting than a half-price sale at Loehmann's." Christine has also, after some bitter experiences, vowed to "do the Libby thing" and never visit a theater where they don't vacuum. Christine, you're an absolute doll, and I feel awful about the recent theft of your Lancôme weekend travel tote that contained *all* your Clinique makeup. I see the entire experience as an Oliver Stone film—an American tragedy, with cute guys.

Margaret Chaisson of Foxborough, Massachusetts, also warmed my heart with her simple letter, reprinted here in its entirety: "I have only two words to say: Libby Gelman-Waxner!!!!" To Margaret, John, Christine, and all of the others who have written—thank you, and here's a big, wet smooch. You all have my permission to buy *both* the family-size tub of buttered popcorn and the large Sno-Caps. Remember, if God had wanted us to go to the opera, they'd sell Raisinets and Goobers at *Aida*. Most films may be empty calories, but aren't those the best kind? Sugar and spice, that's what cinematic achievement is all about, if you ask me, or Christine.

THREE STRIKES
■ ■ ■

I s it just me, or is baseball about as interesting a subject for movies as that kind of Jell-O that makes three layers? I know that a lot of men are obsessed with baseball, but a lot of women are obsessed with crash diets, and nobody makes movies about living on popcorn and Tab or uses Sweet 'n Low as a metaphor for life. This month I saw *Field of Dreams,* and all you really need to know about this film is that it was written and directed by a guy named Phil Alden Robinson. I don't know which is worse, the Phil or the Alden—one is cutesy and the other is gooey, so I guess it's a toss-up.

Of course, some will say, How dare a Libby Gelman-Waxner get high and mighty about a Phil Alden Robinson? Let me clear this up. I use my maiden name, Gelman, because I am a feminist and no one's chattel; I use Waxner so that people will know, just for their information, that I'm married to Josh Waxner, an extremely successful orthodontist, who has recently been asked to speak about "Sugarless Gum: Fact and Fantasy" before the American Dental Association. I don't think that Phil Alden Robinson can make these claims. Who was Phil's dad—Sugar Ray Robinson? Swiss Family Robinson?

Anyway, *Field of Dreams* is about this farmer, Kevin Costner, who's a '60s-type person living in Iowa. One day a voice tells Kevin, "If You Build It, He Will Come." Somehow Kevin decides that this means he should turn some of his land into a baseball diamond so that "Shoeless Joe" Jackson, a dead baseball hero, can come and play. How did Kevin know that the voice wanted a baseball field? Why not a mall? Maybe if he built a casino, Donald

Trump would come. Believe me, if he built a clean ladies' room, everyone would show up.

So Kevin plows, and Shoeless Joe arrives from heaven along with some other Black Sox ballplayers from 1919. Then Kevin gets another message—"Ease His Pain." Kevin doesn't think about Extra-Strength Tylenol or Mylanta II; oh, no, he drives to Boston and kidnaps James Earl Jones, a reclusive '60s activist, and drags James Earl back to Iowa to watch baseball. James Earl, if you ask me, is allowed to have three names because his voice is so deep and because "Jimmy Jones" sounds like one of Archie and Jughead's friends. James Earl loves watching the 1919 Black Sox play, and he makes a big speech about how, back then, America was great and noble. And all I could think was, But James Earl, in 1919 baseball was segregated—so what was so swell?

Eventually Kevin hauls Burt Lancaster into all of this and almost loses the farm, and then Kevin's father, who's also dead, shows up, too. God forbid Kevin should bring back Einstein or Gandhi, or even Cary Grant; maybe if I built a K mart in my living room, my late aunt Essie would come back and buy girdles and dusting powder. Everyone in *Field of Dreams* loves watching baseball for hours on end; Kevin says that the game "reminds us of all that once was good and can be again." If you ask me, this is the same kind of thing that put the Alden in plain old Phil Robinson.

Frankly, I'm surprised it's not Kevin Alden Costner; I just read an interview with Kevin in *Vanity Fair,* and he's gone a little loony. Of course, *Vanity Fair* is my bible, because all the articles are about rich people either having S&M sex or fighting over inheritances, both of which are heaps more fun than baseball. Kevin told *Vanity Fair* that when he was little he learned about life from watching Jimmy Stewart and *Jim Thorpe—All American;* he says that *Field of Dreams* may be "our generation's *It's a Wonderful Life.*" I think Kevin wants to win one for the Gipper. I mean, I learned about life from Hayley Mills and *Bye Bye Birdie,* and I think that's much healthier, or at least less Republican.

This was a big month for important adult drama. I also saw *Scandal,* which is about England's Profumo affair, when the government crumbled because all these big politicos had sex with what the English call tarts and my mother calls Single Women Without Skills. This movie is very classy and distinguished, which seems a little weird; it's kind of like making a *National Geographic* special about Donna Rice. If you ask me, the big problem with *Scandal* is this: I don't believe that English people actually have sex. Julie Andrews? Prince Charles? John Hurt? Somehow I don't think we're talking waterbeds and late-night cable, or even a really warm handshake. After all, didn't the Pilgrims come to America because they heard there was petting?

Hollywood is the exact opposite of London; I mean, Jackie and Joan Collins had to emigrate so they could show cleavage. In *Scandal*, when the characters are supposed to be having an orgy, I just didn't buy it—I knew they were really all about to read sonnets aloud and make plum pudding. I went to England once, for forty-eight hours on a package tour, and I liked it; London was like a big Ralph Lauren outlet, a place where everyone wears two sweaters at once. Europe as a whole reminded me of the EPCOT Center; each country was like a boutique, with cute gifts and food that tasted perfectly fine once you heated it up or put powdered sugar on it. EPCOT is a little smaller than Europe, which is convenient, and it has less grime and decay. EPCOT is like Europe before it went to pieces and turned into ruins; if Walt Disney had been a Roman emperor, there'd be a monorail in the Colosseum and lots of expensive Zeus dolls.

The other film I saw this month is called *Lost Angels,* and it's about how rich kids don't get enough love and need psychiatrists. This is a problem that I've never really understood. Okay, so these kids don't get enough love, but they have lots of great clothes and sports cars—what's the trouble? "I love you" isn't the only way that parents can say they care: "Here are the keys" is nice, and so are "Buy all three colors" and "Okay, if it means that much, you can have two VCRs so you can make dupes."

In *Lost Angels,* Adam Horovitz plays a tormented teen who gets put in a clinic for troubled youths. I expected him to bunk with Timothy Hutton from *Ordinary People* and all the kids from *Less Than Zero.* Donald Sutherland is the hip, understanding therapist, a role that is usually played by Judd Hirsch or Marsha Mason, unless it's a movie of the week, and then the therapist is Lindsay Wagner. Adam cries and says that all he wants is "to belong somewhere." And I thought to myself, If only Adam's shrink had seen *Field of Dreams,* then he would have had the answer: Adam should play baseball. Or maybe he should play baseball in 1919—it's all so confusing. I guess it's movies like these that make people wait for *Batman* and *Indiana Jones and the Last Crusade.* Because it'll never be Indiana Alden Jones, if you ask me.

HOT FUN

S o it's summer again, and I'm out here in Amagansett with two kids and a lot of wet towels and soggy hamburger buns. I hired a Harvard junior named Lucy Twig Bartle to help me out. She refuses to be called an *au pair* or a mother's helper—she says that she wants to be my assistant. Lucy wears little khaki shorts and a man's white shirt unbuttoned just enough to make my husband, Josh, clear his throat and spill his iced tea all over the *Sunday Times* crossword puzzle. Lucy spends a lot of time pulling her hair back with a rubber band and then tugging little wisps around her face; she says that she needs her evenings free to work on some nonlinear fiction. I asked if that meant short stories, and she gave me a look that told me that I really, truly hadn't gone to Harvard. So I said, Lucy, let's pack up the kids and go see *Road House* in East Hampton.

In *Road House*, Patrick Swayze plays a man with a Ph.D. in philosophy from NYU who works as a bouncer in a bar. As I told my five-year-old daughter, Jennifer, You see what happens if you don't get an MBA? Patrick is very cute, and he takes off his shirt a lot and beats people up, but only when he has no other choice; you can just picture him discussing Harvey Wallbangers and Nietzsche with the bartender played by Tom Cruise in last summer's *Cocktail*. What's next—Judd Nelson in *Busboy*, or maybe Rob Lowe in *Coatcheck*? And speaking of Rob, I have seen the videotape in which he allegedly appears and has sex, and Rob, I have to say that I was allegedly impressed. As my uncle Manny always says, Who knew?

Lucy and I discussed Patrick, and she says he's pure *Tiger Beat*, and I have to agree. If Patrick played Hamlet, he'd do bench presses during "To be or not to be," or maybe he'd comb his hair. But that's why I like him, even though Lucy says that *Road House* is crypto-kitsch and pop fascism—this may explain why Lucy refuses to change the baby's Pampers or even make Kool-Aid.

Lucy has started making me very nervous, especially when she told me that my life is a postmodern cartoon and that for her, marriage represents only a vapid cocooning against international despair. Lucy's boyfriend, a Princeton senior, is spending the summer with his old girlfriend at her family's place on Nantucket; Lucy says that she feels dead inside, but that she can express her pain in nonnarrative fragments and by soaking her hair with lemon juice and sitting in the sun all afternoon reading the *Paris Review*. I read one of Lucy's fragments. It was just one sentence, which said, "My skin feels like abandoned celluloid until Brian calls." I said, Lucy, let's go see *Dead Poets Society* to cheer you up.

Dead Poets Society is about this New England boys academy in 1959. The whole movie looks like a Ralph Lauren ad; as soon as I saw someone with a sweater tied around his waist, I knew the school wouldn't be the kind that closed down for Rosh Hashanah or Martin Luther King Day. Robin Williams plays this inspiring teacher who makes jokes and stands on his desk and tells the boys to carpe diem, which means seize the day in Latin. All the boys start getting excited and reading poetry, and one boy decides to audition for a local theater production even though his father wants him to be a doctor. Then all the mean adults make the boys stop reading poetry and conform, and it's very tragic. Basically, this is the sort of film for anybody who's read *The Catcher in the Rye* one too many times. The whole movie is about teenagers, and none of them has acne, and they always have clean hair; all of the boys sort of look like Audrey Hepburn in a blazer. The boys also sit through an entire performance of *A Midsummer Night's Dream* without fidgeting or making armpit noises; they get all misty-eyed, as if they were watching the Lakers at the Garden.

Dead Poets Society says that if rich Wasp boys would only read Walt Whitman, then they wouldn't become investment bankers. Let me tell you, I had an inspirational teacher, but she didn't teach Poetry 101. Mrs. Carmucci taught Home Economics, and her motto was caveat emptor—let the buyer beware. She taught us to

Scotchgard slipcovers, to always mail the warranty card to the manufacturer right away, and to put dress shields in with Velcro, so they can be replaced. I wanted to share this memory with Lucy after *Dead Poets Society,* but she was weeping. She said that her boyfriend, Brian, had gone to Exeter and that's why he was a sadist; she also said that in real life, Robin Williams had left his wife and then married his son's nanny. This started me thinking: whatever happened to the old kind of nanny, with the nylon uniform and a hair net?

On the way home, Lucy told me that all she wanted out of life was Brian and a publishing contract for a collection of minimalist pieces. I told her that Brian sounded pretty minimalist in the brain department, but she didn't even giggle. She said that she had been sleeping with her literature theory professor at Harvard because he had connections at Knopf, but that so far he hadn't come across. The next afternoon Lucy and I left the kids with my mother, who asked me why I couldn't be as nice and thin as Lucy. Lucy told my mother that bad relationships keep her weight down, and my mother said, Good for you. Then Lucy and I went off to see *Vampire's Kiss,* which I thought might interest her because Nicolas Cage plays a Manhattan literary agent who thinks he's a vampire.

Lucy thought the movie was boring, but she said she liked that; she says that any truly contemporary artwork must be empty in order to reflect the passivity of global existence. Then she spent an hour trying to call Brian in Nantucket, but the line was always busy; she said she was thinking of composing a neo-opera, four hours of a busy signal and a woman sobbing in French.

Lucy quit today; she'd only been with us for two weeks, but Josh paid her for the whole summer and bought her an airline ticket to Nantucket. Before she left, Lucy told me that Josh was adorable and that I was an interesting contrast. Maybe that's why I accidentally left a squid in her Noxzema jar and told her to carpe Brian. I'm so grateful for these summers at the shore; some days I just pray for medical waste to wash up, so we can all go back to the city. Carpe *Star Trek V* is my thought for the day, if you ask me.

Over the past few months, I've seen *Indiana Jones and the Last Crusade, Star Trek V: The Final Frontier, Ghostbusters II*, and *Batman*. I took my adorable five-year-old daughter, Jennifer, with me to these movies, and yesterday she asked me, Mommy, were those all one movie? I had to admit that Jennifer had a point; all these movies seem to be about paunchy middle-aged men in silly outfits blowing things up. It's like watching my uncle Manny and the guys from his Poker Night fighting evil between hands and trips to the john.

Each of these movies has special effects, although my favorite—and the least expensive—is the toupees in *Star Trek V*. I wonder if they pass them out on the first day of shooting, first come, first served, and William Shatner always oversleeps. I have never seen anyone, at any age, with hair like William Shatner's, except maybe Burt Reynolds when he's playing a race-car driver; Captain Kirk's hairpieces look like corduroy berets, or as if they might have ear-flaps. Haven't transplant techniques advanced by the 23rd century? And is it just me, or has Yvonne DeCarlo been playing Mr. Spock? I'm really starting to worry about the crew of the starship *Enterprise*; they're beginning to merge with the cast of *Cocoon*. Every time they head off to save the universe, I'm scared that someone's going to break a hip.

During *Ghostbusters II*, I mostly thought about how much each of the stars was making; I know that people like Bill Murray and Sigourney Weaver defer chunks of their salaries and get pieces of the gross. Maybe there should be a new Oscar category for Best Deal, as well as Best Supporting Deal for Someone Who's Not a Big

Name but Is Necessary for a Sequel. Everyone in *Ghostbusters II* looks a little haggard, like the bride and groom at a wedding with a major prenuptial agreement. Harrison Ford is dreamy in *Indiana Jones,* but even he has those summer-sequel bags under his eyes; he looks like a grouchy little boy who's asking his mom, Do I *have* to make another $5 million?

Indiana Jones is a little draggy; maybe it's because of director Steven Spielberg's recent divorce from Amy Irving. Steven probably had trouble concentrating, with all those phone calls to the lawyers. I've heard that Amy may be getting as much as $100 million as a settlement after three and a half years of marriage. All during *Indiana Jones,* I kept thinking, Is there anybody I *wouldn't* marry for that kind of money? Amy, you are now my favorite actress; I'd like to see Meryl walk away with those kinds of numbers. For $100 million, Amy isn't just an ex-wife, she's a blockbuster; I want a lunch box with her attorney's picture on it.

As for *Batman,* Jennifer and I agreed that the merchandising is much more fun than the movie. Jennifer has two different Batman T-shirts, a visor, and a set of rub-on tattoos; all during the movie she kept gluing these little Bat-stickers onto my arms and legs. Jennifer said she was jealous of Michael Keaton because he could afford the Bat-suit and all the Bat collectibles; she thinks he might even have Batman's Malibu Dreamhouse. I spent most of *Batman* studying Kim Basinger's many hairstyles, which, I assume, are a tribute to the career of Suzanne Somers, who pioneered creative ponytail placement and drenched-sheepdog perms. Watching Kim playing Vicky Vale, a Pulitzer prize–winning photojournalist, it was easy to remember that Kim was once a James Bond girl, and that she did a spread in *Playboy.* Kim knows that fine acting is not about motivation but about luster and bounce.

Jennifer begged me to take her to *The Karate Kid Part III,* but I explained that if I did, the government could legally place her with foster parents. I sent Jennifer and my husband, Josh, off to see *Honey, I Shrunk the Kids,* and I went to see Spike Lee's *Do the Right Thing.* I decided that if I saw one more special effect, it might upset my menstrual cycle, the way too much exercise does; I was ready for a movie with no green slime, gamma rays, lasers, phasers, or even spiritual special effects, like the ones in *Indiana Jones*, when God punishes Nazis with matte shots.

Do the Right Thing was wonderful and very upsetting. It's all about this block in New York's Bedford-Stuyvesant area; most of the people who live there are black, but the pizzeria is run by Danny Aiello and his two sons, who are white. The movie is very funny, but by the end there's violence—let me put it this way, no one gets beamed up, and you don't have to worry about Dan Aykroyd dropping by in a jumpsuit. I've read in the papers that some people are worried that *Do the Right Thing* will inspire real-life rioting. This is very dumb: after watching *Star Trek V*, will people go out and kill Klingons? In America, movies mostly make people want to buy things, not break them: in his movie, Spike Lee wears baggy surfer jams over bicycle shorts, and I must admit I'm tempted, because the outfit looks comfortable and slimming. Spike has his sister starring in the movie, and his dad composed the soundtrack; Spike may be controversial, but he's such a mensch.

Do the Right Thing is all about racism, and afterward I thought about how prejudice affects people's jobs and housing, and how it even affects the summer blockbusters. In *Ghostbusters*, Ernie Hudson plays the black ghostbuster; in *Star Trek*, there's Lieutenant Uhura; and in *Batman*, there's Billy Dee Williams as Gotham City's district attorney. None of these actors gets to do much, and they never get as many outfits or closeups as the white stars do. As far as I can tell, black actors need either better scripts or better agents; if you ask me, people of all creeds and colors deserve to wear bad toupees and shrink their children.

And that's just what I told Jennifer, who said, Mommy, my name isn't Jennifer anymore, it's Batgirl. And I said, Fine, as long as you gross $100 million on your opening weekend. It's never easy being a Batmom, if you ask me.

LOVE AND CARNAGE

▬ ▬ ▬ ▬

This month, for our wedding anniversary, my husband, Josh, and I went to see *Lethal Weapon 2*, and we had a marvelous time. We thought about using our Frequent Flyer miles for an upgrade to Paris, or trying to get a reservation at a restaurant that's so chic it doesn't have a name, but we decided to have fun instead. *Lethal Weapon 2* is terrific, because it has an extremely high murder/pleasure ratio. This means that a lot of people in the movie get killed, but they're so evil that everyone in the audience can cheer and not feel guilty. Nowadays the best movie murder victims are rich European guys in high-fashion black outfits, sometimes with ponytails. Other years, physically deformed biker thugs, like the ones in *RoboCop*, are big, and Latin American drug kingpins and their private armies are always good. The Euro-style victims in *Lethal Weapon 2* are white South Africans, so watching them get shot between the eyes is really fun; *Lethal Weapon 2* is like a Dirty Harry movie for liberals.

My only complaint about *Lethal Weapon 2* involves what I call the Tush Factor. In the first *Lethal Weapon*, Mel Gibson gave us a full naked tush when he got out of bed, and, if you ask me, that tush was a national aphrodisiac, like a power blackout; nine months after that tush was exposed, I'll bet the birth rate tripled. In *Lethal Weapon 2*, however, there is zero tush; we get chest and a little hip, but Mel, you let us down. Even my mother, the beloved Sondra Krell-Gelman, called me and said, Libby, where is it? What's with Mel? Does he have a rash?

I was curious, so I asked Josh what he would rather see—a beautiful, naked actress or a car chase going the wrong way on a superhighway at rush hour. Josh chose the car chase, because it was our anniversary; that's why I love him. The only weird thing is that while we were making love right after we saw *Lethal Weapon 2*, Josh began making car crash noises; after a while, I started doing it, too. We were like a police car and a getaway van being driven toward each other by stuntpeople. Later, I asked my therapist, Dr. Arlene Cole-Natbaum, if this was healthy. When I looked up, Dr. Cole-Natbaum was cocking her forefinger at my forehead, as if she had a gun; she had just seen *Lethal Weapon 2* that afternoon. She fired, and I rolled off the couch; then we both sat on the floor and ate canned frosting out of the can with spoons and agreed that I was making real progress.

The next day I took my cousin Andrew, the fabulously talented art director, to see *Lock-Up*, because Andrew is a big Sylvester Stallone fan. In *Lock-Up*, Sly is put in prison because he beat up some punks who were beating up an old man. The warden is out to get Sly, so he throws him into the Hole. Sly wears only tapered boxer shorts in the Hole, but after a week he comes out with even tanner skin than when he went in, without a beard, and with his hair perfectly styled. As Andrew said, that warden threw Sly into a Bruce Weber layout; it was the only Hole with UV bulbs. I like Sly because he's a real movie star; he's always the same, whether he's on *The Arsenio Hall Show* or being pummeled by twelve armed guards. Sly worries about his fans and his image. Andrew says he's like a big, hunky Shirley Temple. Andrew says that only Sly would make a movie about a maximum security prison where there's no gay sex, and where the inmates have their own auto-body shop; it's the kind of prison that high-school boys daydream about during study hall. Andrew says that Sly has reached the point where he's not really an actor but a host, welcoming the audience to his films. Maybe someday Sly will have an anthology TV series, the way Loretta Young used to; *Sly Stallone Playhouse* could be on every week, with a different guest star getting beaten senseless.

Lock-Up has a low murder/pleasure ratio, because very few people are killed; *Lock-Up* is a Thud Movie, which means it's fun because of the sound effects for the punches. Sly also has probably the highest star-abuse figures; these figures depend on how many bullets, electrodes, or poison-tipped arrows a star endures without dying. Let me put it this way: you can kill a star's best friend with a karate chop, but it takes at least eight fully armed helicopters to make Mel or Sly even crouch behind a car. Real stars are often shot in the arm so they can pull the bullet out themselves and keep going. The easiest people to kill are stars' girlfriends; in old movies, a star would rescue the girl, but nowadays he finds her body and gets mad. Josh says that this is a common male fantasy: you have sex, and then the girl either dies or turns into a Nintendo cassette and a bag of chips.

After seeing *Lock-Up*, Josh, Andrew, and I all went to see *Kickboxer*, which is like a Chuck Norris movie, only lower-budget; it's the sort of movie where the actors wear their own clothing, and where the ancient ruins look like chopped liver in the shape of a swan. *Kickboxer* stars Jean Claude Van Damme, who is a martial-arts expert. Jean Claude has a strange accent, like Cloris Leachman's in *Young Frankenstein*; Andrew says he's called the Muscles From Brussels. In *Kickboxer*, Jean Claude goes to Thailand to help his brother compete in a kick-boxing championship. If you ask me, kick boxing looks like what kids at recess call fighting like a girl: kicking and scratching and slapping. Tong Po, the champion Thai kick boxer, cripples Jean Claude's brother, rapes Jean Claude's girlfriend, and stabs Jean Claude's dog. This all happens so that we will be happy when Jean Claude kick boxes Tong Po into a pulp. Jean Claude trains for the big fight with an older Asian man who lives alone up in the hills; this is basically the same person who trained Luke Skywalker, the Karate Kid, and Remo Williams. Now, of course, Pat Morita from *The Karate Kid* is doing toothpaste commercials as the Colgate Wisdom Tooth; I guess if Confucius were around today, he'd be helping Dolph Lundgren or Mary Lou Retton.

Jean Claude practices underwater, kick boxes a palm tree, and has his legs stretched by pulleys into a complete split; Andrew says that after that Jean Claude can either kick box or dance *Giselle*. Finally Jean Claude fights Tong Po; they both wear leather diapers and wrap their hands with rope, and then the rope is smeared with glue and dipped in ground glass. Tong Po has a three-foot-long braid, but Jean Claude never grabs it. Even Jean Claude's dog shows up for the last fight, wearing a bandage. Jean Claude isn't as glamorous as Sly or as beefy as Arnold Schwarzenegger; as Andrew put it, he's the Mary Tyler Moore of bodybuilding. After the movie, Josh tried to kick box a parking meter and broke a metatarsal in his foot; he had to wear one bedroom slipper for a week.

After seeing all these action movies, I was exhausted, and I sort of wanted to watch any episode of *Masterpiece Theatre*. Instead, Josh and I went to see *The Abyss* as our final anniversary treat. *The Abyss* is about a separated couple who rekindle their love while stopping nuclear-war devastation and greeting alien life-forms. As I told Josh, since we have two careers, two kids, and only one and a half bathrooms, our situation is very similar. *The Abyss* takes place almost completely underwater; Mary Elizabeth Mastrantonio plays a woman who designs offshore oil rigs, and everyone calls her a "cast-iron bitch." I identified with Mary Elizabeth; as an assistant buyer in juniors' activewear, I am often called upon to be decisive and forceful. I know that some people call me names, but the way I see it, somebody has to take charge and order twelve or more Ralph Lauren Indian-blanket car coats along with plenty of Donna Karan cashmere bodysuits, even if it takes an hour to get out of one if you have to go to the bathroom.

In *The Abyss,* Mary Elizabeth joins forces with her soon-to-be-ex-husband, Ed Harris; at one point, she drowns and Ed brings her back to life by calling her a bitch again. Josh said that if I ever even get a cold, he's going to try the same technique. *The Abyss* is very absorbing, and it makes you think about how hard it is to be an actor in action movies; I mean, Meryl Streep almost never has to breathe liquid oxygen while dismantling a warhead. Plus she never gets strapped to the bumper of a truck, like Mel in *Lethal Weapon 2,* or gets coconuts dropped on her stomach to help her reflexes, like Jean Claude in *Kickboxer.* I'd like to see Meryl pulverize Tong Po using only her feet, or swab the prison floor like Sly. Actually, when Sly swabs the floor, he keeps going over the same little corner, so it's obvious that he's never used a mop before. And that's how you can tell a real movie star, if you ask me.

MANO A MANO

■ ■ ■

Sometimes when my husband, Josh, is shaving, he looks in the mirror and squints and does an Elvis thing with his lips and tries to look tough. Now, Josh is a thirty-eight-year-old orthodontist who could stand to lose a few pounds, and our bathroom has pink tile and pale blue guest towels with monograms; I love him to pieces, but the only people Josh will ever scare are thirteen-year-olds who forget to wear their retainers. This is the same problem Michael Douglas has in the detective thriller *Black Rain:* Michael rides a motorcycle while smoking a cigarette and wearing a black leather jacket and jeans; he's supposed to be a rebel cop, but all I could think was, What's my aunt Doris doing on a Harley?

Michael is adorable, and he was just right in *Fatal Attraction* and *Wall Street;* if you ask me, he should never play anyone who makes less than $200,000 a year. When Michael curses and stomps around in *Black Rain,* he reminds me of Josh trying on blazers at Barneys on a Saturday; Josh and Michael think they're Dirty Harry, but they're more like Bar Mitzvah Boys From Hell. Most of *Black Rain* takes place in Japan, which looks very MTV; there are lots of electric fans, smoke, and girls trying to look comfortable in *bustiers.* The movie is confusing, but I think what happens is that Michael completely eliminates the Japanese Mafia and teaches the Japanese police to forget their ancient codes of honor and respect by saying things like Sometimes ya gotta take a side, and Watch your tail, cowboy. Michael is getting a bit plump, so he wears dark colors and is photographed mostly from the middle of his chin upward; maybe Jack Nicholson was his stunt double. Considering how many Panasonic, Sony, and Mitsubishi products I own, I also thought it was a

75

little weird that the Japanese needed American help with anything.

Sea of Love is a detective movie with another middle-aged star—Al Pacino. How come actors never want to play rebel orthodontists—guys in ripped nylon smocks who refuse to floss? Al is a treat, and *Sea of Love* is very well written and directed; it's like an Emmy Award–winning episode of *Hunter* or *T. J. Hooker*. Ellen Barkin plays a murder suspect who also becomes Al's girlfriend; she keeps ripping off her clothes and jumping on Al. Al is still very cute, but he's a little pudgy, and he never even takes off his shoes; it's kind of like watching my dad drive Daryl Hannah all wild and twitchy. Ellen has an incredible body, and she wears skintight Azzedine Alaïa–type outfits; she must be the first actress to *insist* on nudity in all her films. Ellen and Al meet through the personal ads; my dear friend Stacy Schiff once tried this route. Stacy says that the personals demonstrate the difference between male and female vanity. Even beautiful, deeply thin women describe themselves as "attractive," while 350-pound men with muttonchop sideburns and missing teeth will call themselves "handsome" because they wear perforated leather racing gloves and Jovan's Musk for Men when they drive their mothers' Datsuns. Stacy had a very bad experience with one of these men; he took her to a motel and wanted her to powder and diaper him while making fun of his SAT scores. Stacy went along with it, but she says she's tired of dates that sound like Geraldo Rivera specials; she says she's beginning to feel nostalgic for men who are just self-absorbed and who claim she's getting clingy if she lives in the same city.

To cheer Stacy up, we went to see Tom Selleck in *An Innocent Man.* Tom plays some sort of airline mechanic who gets framed on drug charges by crooked policemen and sent to prison. Tom is so gorgeous that when he arrives at the prison you expect all the convicts to mob him with autograph books, and Leeza Gibbons of *Entertainment Tonight* to pop out of a cell and ask, Tom, do you think you can cross over from light comedy to serious dramatic roles? Tom's problems are the opposite of Michael's and Al's; Tom wants to *stop* playing a TV detective and to be less yummy. Tom, thank God it doesn't work; even with maximum-security stubble and cell-block lighting, you're still a hunk.

While Tom is in prison, a black gang threatens to make him their punk; Tom prevents this by stabbing the gang's leader to death. If you ask me, this is a pretty extreme response to a dating situation. Stacy and I agreed that we would also like Tom to be our punk. Tom gets prison-behavior tips from F. Murray Abraham, who enunciates dirty words perfectly, as if he were the president of the prison's Little Theater Society. F. Murray is the American Ben Kingsley; they both decided that winning an Oscar was the same as getting knighted or becoming Geraldine Page.

No matter how much time he spends in the Hole, Tom stays tan and trim, like Sly Stallone in *Lock-Up* or Robert Redford in *Brubaker*; I'm beginning to think that the Hole must actually be a Winnebago with a wet bar and a masseur. Actors love to go to prison, as long as their characters don't actually have to be guilty of anything; going to prison is even better than having a Harley and wearing a black leather jacket and a biker earring. Josh says prison is a macho paradise—you shower only once a week, you wear the same clothes every day, there's a basketball court, and you get to talk about women without ever having to remember their cats' names.

To get away from all this boy stuff, I went to see Woody Allen's *Crimes and Misdemeanors*. This movie is partly about moral responsibility and good versus evil; Woody is like Superman in grad school, writing his thesis instead of saving Metropolis. The movie asks questions like If there's a God, why does He allow suffering? How come the wicked prosper? Why do bad things happen to good people? Woody, here are some real questions for you, things you never go into: Why does everything that tastes good have greasy fat, refined sugar, and enough cholesterol to fill a school bus? Why does God allow Jackie Mason to have a TV series? Why do bad dates happen to Stacy Schiff, even after she started using Retin-A? Answer some of these, Woody, and then you can tackle war and disease.

As a favor to Woody, I did spend a moment thinking about whether or not there is a God. I decided there is, because just this morning I got a perfect haircut, my slipcovers finally arrived and they fit like a dream, and I read in the paper that constant snacking actually lowers your risk of heart disease. If you ask me, God has good days and bad days, just like anyone; sometimes He gives us those new hangers that triple your closet space, and sometimes it's Hurricane Hugo. Woody, here's my point: The trick is to catch Him in an up mood.

Crimes and Misdemeanors is also about Woody's character, a poor-but-noble documentary filmmaker. Woody is after Mia Farrow, who works for public television, and Mia falls for Alan Alda, who's a sleazy, big-time Hollywood TV producer. If you ask me, Woody thinks that the biggest injustice in the universe involves women who won't go to bed with him. This part of the movie is much more fun than the serious part, because it's really bitchy; Woody wants to be Ingmar Bergman, but in his heart he's Rona Barrett. In real life, Woody is an acclaimed millionaire filmmaker, and he recently had a child with Mia; he's won all the marbles, so, as my aunt Sylvia would say, perk up, Mr. Gloomy. I guess Woody would rather play a lonely little ragamuffin; he gives himself these long close-ups with tears in his eyes, as if he were turning into Susan Hayward giving up her married man in *Back Street*. That Mia must have her hands full; she must need to keep telling Woody that even though he's rich and famous, he doesn't have to be happy.

Stacy and I talked about what it would be like to be married to Woody; we decided it would be like being married to Michael or Al or Tom. Every day you would tell them they were cute and young and more talented than Dustin, or at least taller. It's just like with Josh—after I tell him how sexy his new mustache is, and how he's probably one of the top five orthodontists on the Upper East Side who's under 40, he kisses me and tells me I'm great. Maybe I should buy him a leather motorcycle jacket; he could wear it with his little mirror and a toothbrush sticking out of the pocket. Movie stars and orthodontists—it's all stud city, if you ask me.

MAKIN' MOVIES

■ ■ ■

I don't know whether to hate Michelle Pfeiffer or just to start a new religion or a chain of fitness centers built around her. In *The Fabulous Baker Boys,* Michelle is unbelievably gorgeous and sexy and funny, all at the same time; she's like a triath- lete. Basically, Michelle is what God had in mind for human- ity until the original blueprints got all creased and linty; instead of shooting her, my dear friend Stacy Schiff and I went to see the movie three times. Michelle plays a hooker turned lounge singer who joins up with Jeff and Beau Bridges, who play matching pianos at Ramada Inn–type hotels. Michelle and Jeff have an affair, and I still haven't recovered; I hate to say it, but this movie may have had something to do with the San Francisco earthquake. At one point, Michelle sings "Makin' Whoopee!" in a red velvet dress while lying on top of Jeff's grand piano; if you ask me, this moment is all the proof you need that movies are much better than life.

Stacy has been single for so long that she was thinking about writing to men on death row but was afraid of being rejected; *The Fabulous Baker Boys* changed her life. The movie is so dreamy that right after the third time we saw it, Stacy went back to her office and proposed to the first man she saw, who happened to be a bicy- cle messenger, a nineteen-year-old named Miguel. Stacy took Miguel into her office, climbed onto her desk, and sang "Embrace- able You" to him; she was wearing a navy blue Ann Taylor suit, a Ship 'n Shore blouse with a pussycat bow, and her pink Reeboks, but she says that the overall effect was still very Michelle, even when she accidentally rolled onto the electric pencil sharpener. Miguel got very excited and offered Stacy his canvas delivery bag, his Walkman, his waist pouch, and his gold necklace that said PARTY MAN as proof of his love. By the time Stacy and Miguel were through, three hours later, they had destroyed Stacy's Exercycle, her fax machine, and all her spreadsheets for the past eight fiscal trimesters, but they were engaged. The people in the window of the office building across the street even held up a sign that read WAY TO GO, MCBURNEY INTERMARKETING, INC.!

Miguel moved in with Stacy that night, and they went to see *Baker Boys* together; after "Makin' Whoopee!" they were asked to leave the theater because they were disturbing the other moviegoers. As she was being thrown out by an usher, Stacy raised her fist and started a "Michelle! Michelle!" chant. Then Stacy and Miguel took the train to meet Stacy's parents out in Great Neck, Long Island; the Schiffs served cutlets and kasha, along with some Pepperidge Farm crescent rolls from the microwave and Mrs. Schiff's signature Duncan Hines bundt cake, which she always decorates with German chocolate icing and peanut M&Ms spelling Stacy's name. The Schiffs asked Miguel what his prospects were, beyond pedaling a ten-speed bicycle without brakes through midtown traffic. Miguel did not answer, as he was enjoying a second helping of kugel and also did not speak English. Stacy had not noticed that Miguel only knew Spanish; she asked herself what Michelle would do, and she and Miguel ended the evening by waking up Rabbi Waldman and getting married at 3 A.M. in the rabbi's finished basement, after the rabbi had folded up the Ping-Pong table and put away his son's water skis.

The next day, instead of a wedding shower, I took Stacy and Miguel to see *Look Who's Talking*. This movie is about Kirstie Alley, who plays a single mom. John Travolta plays a cabdriver who helps her, and he's so charming that Stacy and I agreed that if, God forbid, something should happen to Jeff Bridges, John would be an ideal choice to comfort Michelle. John has been in some dud movies lately, but he's still the best; he's a great actor without being a pain or playing a tormented Vietnam veteran. Miguel enjoyed the movie too; I speak high school Spanish, and I think Miguel said that his old girlfriend was a single mom like Kirstie and that little Miguel, Jr., was a Party Man, too. As a wedding gift, I gave Stacy and

Miguel a CD of the *Baker Boys* soundtrack and a Kryptonite lock for Miguel's bike. That afternoon, Stacy and Miguel got matching tattoos that said MAKIN' WHOOPEE 4 EVER; Stacy said it didn't hurt all that much, at least not when compared to using those new machines that rip out your leg hairs with "soothing coils." Afterward, Stacy and Miguel registered at Tiffany's, Bloomie's, and Miguel's favorite video arcade in Times Square.

By the time Miguel and Stacy had been together for two weeks, they'd seen *Baker Boys* eight more times; Miguel taught Stacy to sing "Makin' Whoopee!" in Spanish, and Stacy decided that while Michelle is perfect, she should gain ten pounds. They also went to see *Immediate Family,* which is about an infertile yuppie couple who want to adopt a baby. Upper-middle-class infertility has become very chic lately; it's like the new Lyme disease. Glenn Close and James Woods are the couple; if you ask me, maybe it's just as well that they couldn't conceive, because Glenn and James would probably produce a radiant, very Waspy psychopath—Charles Manson with his own horse. Can you imagine what it would be like to have Glenn and James as your parents? Glenn would bake something and kiss you gently on your forehead, and then James would help you shoot up. Stacy and Miguel left the movie before it ended, because they didn't want to miss the next showing of *Baker Boys*.

I hate to tell you this, and I don't blame Michelle, but Stacy and Miguel eventually separated. Three weeks after their wedding, *Baker Boys* left all the theaters in town. Stacy began to nudge Miguel about buying his own Sabrett hot dog wagon; Miguel learned just enough English to say "I hate Lean Cuisine" and "Stop asking me, you look fine." Suddenly, they seemed to have nothing in common; Miguel could not even understand why Stacy liked to ride a bicycle that didn't go anywhere. They sought counseling with my therapist, Dr. Arlene Cole-Natbaum, who told them to hold off on anything legal until *Baker Boys* came out on home video. Despite Dr. Cole-Natbaum's advice, Stacy and Miguel had their marriage annulled; the judge accepted *The Fabulous Baker Boys* and Michelle's recent *Newsweek* cover as grounds for the decree. In fact, the judge said that Michelle was now being named in more than a third of all divorce actions, right behind mental cruelty and John Travolta.

Stacy and Miguel shared a last kiss on the courthouse steps; Miguel gave Stacy a tire repair kit and his little racing cap with the Italian logo for her to wear backward, and Stacy gave Miguel a bottle of Calvin Klein's Eternity for Men and the matching soap-on-a-rope.

To try and cheer Stacy up, I took her to see *The Bear,* which is this European nature movie about the adventures a bear cub and an older bear have while hunters chase them through the wilderness. Stacy was in one of those moods, and she kept cheering for the hunters, even when the baby bear was playing with a butterfly. I thought the bears were cute, but I worried about their careers; I thought, Okay, maybe they'll get a buddy movie with Jim Belushi, but that would be it. And how could they ever go back to their caves once they'd had their own trailers? Stacy said she didn't really want to watch a movie about two dancing rugs, so we left; I still worry about those bears, though, and I hope they have enough sense to stay off *Win, Lose or Draw.*

Stacy's been feeling a little better lately. Dr. Cole-Natbaum says movie-induced romances can leave very deep scars; Dr. Cole-Natbaum herself is still recovering from Mel Gibson's hot-tub scene with Michelle in *Tequila Sunrise,* and she also suffers from a recurring rash in the shape of Harrison Ford changing his shirt in *Working Girl.* I personally have never really come back fully from that moment in *The Big Easy* involving Dennis Quaid's hand and Ellen Barkin's skirt; Dr. Cole-Natbaum has recommended disconnecting the freeze-frame button on my VCR. Sometimes Stacy looks down from her office and sees Miguel riding by—she rubs her tattoo and softly hums "Makin' Whoopee!" Stacy's mom blames her own first marriage on Bogart and Bacall in *To Have and Have Not;* even Michelle was divorced not too long ago—I wonder what movie she saw. Hollywood should be more careful, if you ask me.

LETTERS TO LIBBY

E very so often, I like to take time to answer my mail from such delightful and wisdom-filled people as Tom Parrish of Nantucket, Massachusetts, who writes, "Nobody writing about movies today has as much insight as Libby. . . . She's funny, she's a miracle, she's always dead-on target, and I love her." How I wish that Tom could share a friendly mug of International Coffees Naturally Decaffeinated Suisse Mocha with Charles T. Tatum, Jr., of Minot, North Dakota, who refers to my column as "Erma Bombeck's Evil Clone Goes to the Movies." Charles, listen to Tom; he even has beautiful handwriting.

I have received a great many letters from devoted readers who were troubled by my views on *Field of Dreams;* as Bonnie White of San Antonio puts it, "There are some people out in America who love movies about dreams, old-fashioned romance, and old-fashioned love. Those of us who do hate you!" Kristi Nelson of Lyndell, Pennsylvania, writes, on lovely pale yellow stationery sprinkled with tiny pink hearts, that "I don't think anyone died and left you the right to rank on great movies and their actors. . . . You're obviously a very shallow person to sit in your office and write a bunch of information that no one cares about." Kristi even claims that "we don't care if you're married to an extremely successful orthodontist; he's not that important—I've never heard of him!" Peter Frye of Fort Wayne asks, in all-capital block letters on loose-leaf notebook paper, "What's the problem, Libby? Are you agitated because *Field of Dreams* is a male-centered movie dealing with a man's relationship with his father? Is this somehow threatening to our ever-omniscient feminist population?"

Shawn J. Rubel of Jersey City tells me that *"Field of Dreams* is a movie about love, family, and goodness." Shawn goes on to share thoughts about my name, which he says "sounds like pumpkin-pie filling," and about my husband, Josh: "You know what they say about dentists and orthodontists—they lack imagination, creativity, passion, and personality. One can only imagine what their wives are like." Louis J. Pepe of Boalsburg, Pennsylvania, inquires whether my parents named me "after a brand of canned fruit." Marion Pilowski of Adelaide, Australia, on airmail stationery featuring a Scottie dog chasing a cat up a telephone pole in the moonlight, refers to me as "a complete superficial prat." John B. Magevney of Jacksonville, Florida, claims I am a "naive, narrow-minded, materialistic, what-am-I-going-to-wear-tonight? type of person" and says that "if you watched the movie with an open mind, you would understand that it is not just a movie about baseball but about life and dreams." Perhaps Tammi R. Coulter of Edmonds, Washington, sums things up when she says that after reading my review of this movie "three words came to mind: BITCH, BITCH, BITCH!"

Well, if you ask me, there certainly is something about hopes and dreams and old-fashioned romance that brings out the campus-clock-tower sniper in people; while we're at it, I wish someone would tell me exactly what a "prat" is. And don't people think that orthodontists have feelings, too? For your information, Shawn Rubel, my husband has a charming personality and is extremely creative; Josh was among the very first orthodontists to use rainbow-colored rubber bands on the braces of his younger patients. Josh considers every snaggletoothed, overcrowded mouth he works on to be a blank canvas, awaiting the dental artist's tin and pliers. Josh has even created braces that include tiny animal shapes, based on the world-famous circus mobiles of Alexander Calder; for a slightly higher fee, Josh will work a teenager's initials into his or her dental appliance, and he recently installed a remarkable likeness of Johnny Depp, the teen-detective star of TV's *21 Jump Street,* along the overbite of little Julie Wallowich. (Julie, I am sad to say, has just asked if Josh could change the face to look more like Johnny's rival, Richard Grieco, the detective star of TV's *Booker,* but Josh put his foot down.) Josh always says that he doesn't just make teeth straight, he helps them soar. In Josh's own words, "I don't just treat the teen, I sculpt the smile."

As for my own name sounding like a supermarket item, let me say this, Kristi and Tammi: at least it's not spelled Libbi. As for *Field of Dreams,* I still think it's a movie about baseball and the wholesome white people of the Midwest; it's the kind of movie the Reagans would watch on the plane to Japan. I have just read Nancy's autobiography, *My Turn,* and maybe the guys who made *Field of Dreams* could option it; it could be the heartwarming story of an American wife and mom who just wanted to fight drug abuse, disown her children, fire cabinet members, and stay trim. In *Field of Dreams,* a black character talks about how great the game of baseball was in 1919, but no one mentions that back then the game was segregated; it's interesting that of all the letters supporting the film, only one talked about the movie's racism. Jennifer Mills of Aneta, North Dakota, writes that "if baseball was segregated in 1919, that doesn't mean black people didn't enjoy it." Yes, Jennifer, and even if they had to drink from a separate fountain, they still liked water.

But enough of filmic controversy; let's talk about things that matter, like finding decent live-in help. As my readers know, last summer I hired a Harvard junior as an *au pair* at the beach, and frankly, she was a nightmare in Weejuns and her boyfriend's Levi's jacket. Greg Fisher of Cathedral City, California, volunteers his own services for next summer; Greg says he's "not crazy about children, but who is?" Greg is a doll, although he does hesitate, adding, "then again, maybe I should get a life." Harvey Doherty of Barrie, Ontario, comes up with a terrific solution; Harvey notes that in the James Spader Filmography in the September 1989 issue of *Premiere,* James was quoted as saying, "It's very enriching to experience a wide variety of situations and individuals," and that when he's not acting, he likes to work at "straight jobs." Harvey suggests I "give Mr. Spader a call"; Harvey, I like your thinking, but I just can't see James rinsing out swimsuits and making rainy-day finger puppets out of seashells and pipe cleaners.

I have gotten many other interesting tidbits in my mailbox; Don Pugsley of Los Angeles wrote to alert me to his performance as

Sergeant Bronson, Paul Newman's assistant, in *Fat Man and Little Boy*, which is about the men at Los Alamos who built the first atomic bomb. I know that Don is just terrific in the movie, but I haven't been able to see it because I read somewhere that it is a provocative and brave treatment of an important global topic, and I still haven't finished reading my *Cosmopolitan* book excerpt on how Christina Onassis bought love and once smothered a puppy by sitting on it. Basically, I don't think there are a lot of people who just want to hug nuclear weapons; it's a pretty safe topic. I hear that the next big Hollywood-style issue will be the destruction of the rain forests. If you ask me, we can expect a lot of canoe chases up the Amazon, and maybe Jane Fonda as the bumbling American journalist who falls in love with the charismatic Brazilian activist.

My readers often look to me for auteur guidance. Diane McKay of Brantford, Ontario, who signs herself "a faithful fan," asks, "By the way, what is your favorite movie?" Diane, this is a tough one. There are so many elements that go into making a classic motion picture: the writing, the direction, the acting, the nudity, the quality of the trailers shown with the film, whether your seat was broken, whether you had to sit next to strangers with umbrellas, how much Bruce Willis was paid—there are just so many facets to consider. As for my current all-time favorite, I'm wavering. Part of me says, Yes, of course it's *The Trouble With Angels*, featuring Hayley Mills as a parochial-school cutup; but then that little auteur voice says, No, Libby, go with that memorable movie-of-the-week from a few years back, *Portrait of an Escort*, which starred Susan Anspach as a suburban mom forced to accompany men to restaurants in order to pay for her teenage daughter's braces. Some viewers may discover cinematic eternity in *Citizen Kane*; for me, that moment of filmdom nirvana occurred when Susan, confronted by her daughter, shrieked, "Yes! It's true! I'm a *professional dater!*"

My favorite mailbag offer came from Jason Baruch, a senior at Yale. Jason writes, "Help me, Libby. I think I'm in love. I've developed an addiction to your column not at all unlike my addiction to Doritos, only this new addiction is less fattening and my mother will let me indulge on the living room couch." Jason gets right to the point: "Let's not beat around the bush, Libby. Run away with me." Jason says that he also models, and that "my analyst tells me I'm very mature for my age." He urges me to "dump Josh—I bet you have perfect teeth anyway. And he'll get over it. Orthodontists always do. Help! I wake up at night shouting LIBBYLIBBYLIBBY." Jason says that he has already legally changed his name to Jason Baruch-Beznicki-Gelman-Waxner, adding my name to his own and that of his current girlfriend. Jason pleads that if I won't run away with him, "at least send me a photograph of you bathing seminude in a vat of Newman's Own salad dressing."

I must admit, for a moment I was tempted. Jason, you're a nice boy, even with the modeling; I'm sure your mother is very proud of you, especially if you've started giving a thought to the law boards. But Jason—it could never work. The age difference doesn't bother me, because as a woman, I am only just reaching my mid-thirties sexual peak, so I would be doing you a major favor. And Josh might not notice if I disappeared for, say, a weekend, as long as the fridge was full, the television was warmed up, and the *TV Guide* was in the pocket of the recliner. My kids wouldn't notice as long as I left cash, Teddy Grahams, and plenty of new outfits for my five-year-old daughter Jennifer's favorite toy, My Little Pony, a plastic horse that has a mane you can tease and back-comb and more accessories than Zsa Zsa wore in court. My friends wouldn't notice I was gone as long as the answering machine was on so they could discuss their personal problems. But Jason, I just don't like this other-girlfriend issue, this Beznicki person. It's like I told Josh when we got engaged—Josh, if you want me, you have to give up all other women, 100 percent of your income, and any notions of personal independence, because that's what it means to love Libby. Jason, I don't know if you're really ready to join Libby's Love Corps; write again when you're out of grad school and can forward a tax return. As for the seminude photo: well, excuse me, Jason, but you're the big model, and I didn't even get a Polaroid.

As always, I thank all of my devoted readers for writing, even those whom the sensitive Erica Zwick of Seattle refers to as my "tight-ass critics." And I would like to offer a special thanks to Stacy Schiff of Manhattan, who, though unrelated, shares her glorious name with my dear friend, who is currently at a spa near Santa Fe, where her cellulite is being treated by burro rides and sacred Navaho clay wraps. Both Stacys are clearly wonderful and increasingly svelte women; but then, all of my devoted readers are wonderful, even when they're abusive, wrongheaded, and obviously writing from behind double-bolted doors at private institutions. I love you all, because that's a film critic's number-one job, if you ask me.

THE LIBBYS

O nce again it is time for me to announce my annual Libby Awards, which acknowledge achievements in cinematic excellence, good taste, and merchandising tie-ins with fast-food chains, such as those special cardboard totes that McDonald's offers featuring characters from various Disney films. One of these promotional totes caused my adorable five-year-old daughter, Jennifer, to ask me, Mommy, when we eat Filets-o-Fish, are we eating parts of the Little Mermaid? Then Jennifer asked me why I was wearing a fur and if my fully let-out natural ranch mink coat with perfectly matched skins wasn't just an animal cemetery. I told Jennifer that these were both very mature and interesting questions, and that if she wanted answers she might consider asking her new friends at military school.

Here now, the Libbys.

The Ali MacGraw Hot Rollers and Facial Sauna goes this year to Demi Moore for her work in the film *We're No Angels*. In this movie, Demi plays a poverty-stricken mother during the Depression who prostitutes herself in the dead of winter on the Canadian border, all to help her deaf-mute toddler. Demi first appears in the film taking a topless sponge bath in front of an open window, and throughout she wears mostly sleeveless housedresses with plunging necklines. She always looks fresh and gorgeous, and you expect the other people in the movie to call her Demi and ask about her baby with Bruce Willis; Demi knows that being poor really means turtlenecks and clogged pores, but why bum out the audience? She has clearly studied frontier pouting and shameless hair tossing with Ali and

Christie Brinkley, and she may in fact be the first actress to use movies as a steppingstone to modeling.

The Jackie Mason Humanitarian Libby goes to screenwriter Joe Eszterhas, who recently bragged in the press about making more than $1 million per screenplay; he seems to do this mostly by exploiting global tragedies. Joe always takes a big issue and turns it into a suspenseful vehicle for a movie star; in *Betrayed*, we are supposed to worry about Debra Winger as an undercover FBI agent fighting the Klan, and in *Music Box*, Jessica Lange plays a feisty lawyer who discovers that her dad is a war criminal. All of this is known as the Joan Crawford School of Human Atrocity; if Joan were still around, she'd want to play a beautiful American reporter who has an affair with one of Noriega's attorneys. When Joe hears about some new terrorist torture, his first thought must be: Sigourney!

The Cahiers de Leona Prix d'or goes to Michael J. Fox and the people who made two *Back to the Future* sequels almost simultaneously (*Part III* will be released later this year). Michael does have a baby, so he needs some extra money for Huggies and savings bonds; I'm sure the three films' director, Robert Zemeckis, is also tired of driving that used Rambler and counting out food stamps at the Stop & Shop. Enough about that Alaskan oil spill and those whiny earthquake victims; what about a Live Aid–style, "We Are the Profit Participants" superstar benefit for the boys of Hollywood?

The Mickey and Minnie Strasberg Medallion is awarded to the live-action movie that comes closest to animation; this year's winner is Steven Spielberg's *Always*. The skies are so blue in this movie and the acting so adorable that soon employees will appear at the gates of Disney World wearing enormous rubber heads of Richard Dreyfuss and Holly Hunter. Richard and Holly play wisecracking pilots who risk their lives to fight forest fires—Hey, Steven, how about my parents, Sy and Sondra, as daredevil race-car drivers in *Seniors at Indy*?

The How About Another Turner & Hooch Libby goes to Miloš Forman for directing the year's least-awaited remake, *Valmont*, which was a much more expensive version of last year's *Dangerous Liaisons*. If you ask me, Miloš must spend a lot of time in the auteur locker room, working on a bad case of budget envy. Miloš made a duller movie, but at least his was bigger.

The Love Is My Drug Libby and a big wet Libby smooch go to Matt Dillon for his work in *Drugstore Cowboy*. Even playing an impotent junkie thief, Matt is an important dreamboat, and this is a wonderful movie, both because it gives us Matt's terrific performance and because it shows that when not-very-bright people use drugs, they become hilarious. I once fantasized about traveling cross-country and robbing drugstores, but if I were to really do it, I wouldn't steal Quaaludes or morphine, like Matt and his friends do—I'd just grab diet pills, displays of Tic-Tacs, sucking candies, plastic rain bonnets, and postcards; I see myself as a notions' counter criminal. And, of course, as an orthodontist's wife. I have no trouble getting prescriptions; everyone I know has been sampling all the new antidepressants, although personally I still find that a bag of Halloween-size Baby Ruths is far superior to Elavil or Tofranil. Sometimes I wonder: What did the Pilgrims take for mild-but-chronic depression? Did the Indians introduce them to corn, pumpkins, and Prozac, or did everyone just quilt and make candles until they cheered up?

The Only If It's Appropriate for the Role Libby, awarded for the most appealing gratuitous nudity, goes to Sylvester Stallone and Kurt Russell for walking naked (which we see from the rear) out of the prison shower room in the action movie *Tango & Cash*. Sly and Kurt look great, like the twin-sister or wistful-French-schoolgirl centerfolds in *Playboy*. Remember when action stars were rugged, dull guys like John Wayne and Clint Eastwood, instead of rosy pink starlets like Sly, Kurt, Dolph, and Arnold? John Wayne worried about staying on a horse and being quick on the draw, while Sly and his pal worry about tan lines, styling gel, and tank tops. I hear that Sly's next film will be *Jumpsuit: The Jack LaLanne Story*.

The Here Come the '90s Libby goes to Tom Cruise, whose next movie, *Days of Thunder,* is about stock-car racing. Tom told *Us* magazine that the movie will not be *"Top Gun* on wheels." No, Tom insists, "it's about America and America's sons, really. Cars symbolize to me creative greatness. The drivers are artists. It's not just about going out there and putting your foot on the pedal." And

Tom, that's why someday there's going to be a Datsun on display at the Louvre. Tom, you're a true cutie and a Hyundai among actors, but you have to stop talking to reporters and putting your foot someplace besides that pedal.

This year's movies were sweet, but I noticed that in *Vanity Fair's* '80s Hall of Fame issue there were not many stars but lots of moguls, such as Barry Diller, who runs Twentieth Century Fox, and David Geffen, who produces movies and records. Nowadays, the financing of a movie is usually more exciting than the picture itself. Why don't they just film Barry in negotiation, or the Japanese buying Columbia Pictures, and throw in a love theme or a chase to the executive washroom? When a junior vice president in Hollywood is fired, he or she always gets $4 million in stock options and an independent production deal just to leave—now, that's entertainment, if you ask me.

FIELD DAY

his column celebrates national Sally Field Day, which I have declared in honor of all the major American actresses who have recently played spunky blue-collar women and actually opened refrigerators onscreen and pretended to iron. I've noticed that actresses get this urge once they hit forty; all of a sudden, they feel a sisterhood with lower-class women, even if they don't really know any personally. Maybe it's hormonal, because as actresses get older, they all head right for K mart, the bus stop, and kitchens with hundreds of visible cleaning products.

In *Stanley & Iris,* Jane Fonda wears a rubber snood and works in a factory that produces baked goods. I've always dreamed of working at the Hostess cupcake plant, although Jane never puts the frosting hose in her mouth, like I would. When Jane goes lower-class, she does it like nobody's business: in this movie, she has a scraggly bleached perm with a welfare barrette; a dead husband; an unwed, pregnant teenage daughter; a physically abusive, beer-swilling brother-in-law; colitis; and Robert De Niro as an illiterate boyfriend. Jane doesn't play a character, exactly; she's sort of like Joan of Arc in a poly blend. She teaches Bob to read, and right away he goes from digging ditches to a fancy executive position; she also lectures her daughter that a baby is not just "a jolt of semen."

I got the feeling that once she finished this movie, Jane thought, Okey-doke, I polished off Vietnam in *Coming Home,* feminism in *9 to 5,* and the nuclear threat in *The China Syndrome,* and now I've taken care of all the working-class women with colitis; I think I'll head for that ozone layer next—if I don't do it, it won't get done. In real life, Jane is divorcing her politician husband, looks like she had a breast lift, and was dating a younger Italian guy, and her daughter, Vanessa, was arrested; Jane, it's all so much more interesting than watching you teach Bob how to read "The girl has a fish in her hand"—why didn't you teach him to read the *Enquirer*? On second thought, maybe you should have taught him to read scripts.

Jessica Lange also plays a blue-collar widow in *Men Don't Leave*; after her construction-worker husband dies, Jessica has to sell her house and move to Baltimore with her two sons. She ends up with a job baking gourmet muffins for a caterer; catering is the hot new job for women in the movies and on TV. Kate and Allie started a catering business, and Jessica and Michelle Pfeiffer have both run restaurants in movies. Art-gallery work used to be big, like the jobs Jill Clayburgh and Kim Basinger had in *An Unmarried Woman* and *9½ Weeks*, but now it's all oat bran and eclairs. These are the sorts of jobs that the wives of movie executives might do part-time for a month or two, to fulfill themselves; somehow I don't see scones paying for Jessica's two-bedroom apartment.

Jessica grieves for her late husband, bakes, and has a breakdown for a few days, until a friend takes her for a ride in a hot-air balloon, like in a Kodak ad, and then everything's all better. The friend is a nurse, so why didn't she just slip Jessica a few Valiums? Jessica also gets a warm and supportive new boyfriend, a musician who can somehow afford a waterfront loft; this is the sort of boyfriend caterers get. He loves Jessica's kids, just like Robert De Niro loves Jane's kids in *Stanley & Iris*; we also get to watch Jessica wash dishes and fold laundry—it's like Sears pornography. Jessica's boyfriend cheers her up by taking her to do the polka at a Polish dance hall; whatever happened to back rubs and jewelry?

The minute an actor hears the words "blue collar," he thinks "pot belly" and "thermos"; when an actress goes working-class, it's "baggy cotton cardigan." Jane and Jessica both wear this cardigan; Jane even has two—a pink one for when she's in a good mood, and a gray one for her more depressed days. If you ask me, poor people don't need therapy or better housing, just more pastels. I'm very worried about all these Sally Field cardigans; I can just see Sissy Spacek going through her closet right now, wondering, Where did I put that thing? Actresses used to play madcap heiresses, or murderers, or Scarlett O'Hara; now it's all lawyers and widows, just like on TV. I'm an assistant buyer in juniors' activewear—Jane, where are you?

After overdosing on movie stars with unmatched glassware, I decided to go see *Camille Claudel*. While this movie is in French, with subtitles, it also stars Gérard Depardieu, who is so sexy that I thought the movie might seem American. It's a true story about Camille, who was an artist and an assistant to Rodin, the famous sculptor who did *The Thinker*, which is the sculpture they use in the wristwatch and laxative commercials. Camille has an affair with Rodin and then gets jealous of him, goes insane, and gets locked up for the rest of her life. Camille is not exactly a feminist role model; she's like a *Cosmo* article called "I Dated a Genius."

Isabelle Adjani plays Camille, and she also developed and helped produce the movie. Isabelle reminds me of Nicole Schlect, this girl I knew in third grade. Nicole was the prettiest girl in the class, and whenever the drama club did a play, Nicole got the lead, and she always made them change the play to *Cinderella*. Nicole would put a little smudge of dirt on her cheek for the first part of the play, and she'd say, Now I'm poor, and everyone hates me because I'm pretty. Then she'd put on the aluminum-foil crown and say, Now I'm a princess, and everyone loves me, and I will be kind to all. Isabelle Adjani is very pretty, and she never really has a facial expression that might get in the way. Even though she's playing a sculptress, she always has a manicure and smooth hands; when she goes mad, she tousles her hair like Ann-Margret used to on her motorcycle in her Vegas act. Isabelle is just like Nicole, only Nicole's now on her fourth marriage, and she's working on a book about how hard it is to be pretty; she's calling it *Fatal Beauty: Women and Perfection.*

Isabelle also went mad in another movie, *The Story of Adele H.,* which I did not see because Gérard wasn't in it. Isabelle likes to go mad in historical clothes. It's sort of the French way to get a Best Actress nomination, as opposed to the American route, which involves having a real-life personal tragedy, or being old or Meryl. Whatever happened to actresses playing Madame Curie or Mata Hari or even a modern heroine like Basia Johnson, the maid who lived the American dream and married a dying zillionaire? Even Gérard doesn't get to have fun in *Camille Claudel*; he never even takes off his coat, let alone anything else.

When women star in movies lately, their onscreen boyfriends always turn into wimps—cuddly musicians or guys who can't read but love to cook. Personally, I've always thought that blue-collar guys were just men who were too sexy to get their master's. I'm glad I'm married to an orthodontist, but I'm also glad that there's a firehouse down the block where the firemen wear little navy T-shirts and sit outside. As for blue-collar women, well, I asked my cleaning lady, Mrs. Castillo, if she was planning to see any of the movies in the Sally Field Festival. She said she wasn't, but if Jane Fonda wanted to drop by the South Bronx and clean her apartment, she'd be happy to go see *Stanley & Iris* and get out of her way. Mrs. Castillo and I agreed that we really miss Cher, and then she told me all about Rosanne Barr's wedding to this man who just got out of a drug-rehab program. According to the *Star*, Rosanne and her new husband ate two of the wedding cake's three tiers all by themselves; I bet Roseanne was married in a stunning silk organza cardigan, if you ask me.

DREAM ON

Every year or so, the cinema provides a Dream Date for all the women of America. This man can be a good actor, but talent isn't necessary; mostly, he must seem like someone who, if he met me or any of my friends, would sweep us off our feet; take us out for an intimate dinner; look terrific but not too perfect; reveal that he's both sexy and sensitive but not a wimp; make us feel sexy, thin, and appreciated; and generally behave like the exact opposite of the guys we're married to or currently seeing ("seeing" means the man is too phobic even to use the words "dating" or "going out with"). Cary Grant, as my colleague Pauline Kael has pointed out, is the ultimate Dream Date; and while I love Sly Stallone, Arnold Schwarzenegger, and even Danny DeVito, they will never be Dream Dates, except maybe for each other.

Dennis Quaid is so sexy that he almost goes beyond Dream Date-dom and into the Dangerous Zone; this is the category for guys who might say, Let's have sex in a car going off a cliff, and you'd say, Let me just leave a note for the sitter. Bruce Willis, like Richard Gere, is his own Dream Date, and William Hurt, who had DD potential, now seems more like the weird, forty-year-old graduate student your aunt Rivka would fix you up with. William has also been sued for palimony, so he might want to talk about old girlfriends, which pretty much kills the Dream Date situation. Kevin Costner was last year's ultimate DD, of the lean-and-lanky, Levi's-slung-low-on-the-hips variety; Kevin is from the same school as James Taylor, Sam Shepard, and Matthew Modine—the surfer-with-a-Ph.D., or cowboy-novelist. These guys seem almost shy, but they're still steamy, as if they'd take you for a ride in their pickup, and their dog would wear a dusty bandanna.

Kevin was datable in *No Way Out* and *Bull Durham*, but in his new movie, *Revenge*, he makes practically the biggest mistake a DD can make: he develops a major crush on himself. This crush usually occurs after a guy's just become a huge star and gets to pick his own projects; at this point, he usually chooses to play a fighter pilot or a race-car driver—either way, we're not talking Hamlet. Al Pacino played an alienated race-car driver in *Bobby Deerfield*, and Tom Cruise has played a fighter pilot and a bartender; I just saw the trailer for Tom's next movie, *Days of Thunder*, where he plays a race-car driver. The trailer said the movie was "based on a story idea by Tom Cruise"; he's shown wearing sunglasses while driving a motorcycle to the racetrack. If Tom isn't careful, he may become a Dream Dork—a man capable of dating only machines that are much bigger than he is.

In *Revenge*, which Kevin executive produced, he plays a retired fighter pilot who goes to visit his friend Anthony Quinn, who's a zillionaire Mexican mogul. Kevin falls in love with Anthony's beautiful young wife, and they run off together. The wife climbs on Kevin while he's driving his jeep, and they have sex; I asked my husband, Josh, if we should try this, and he said it would be too distracting, like trying to steer and fold a road map at the same time. Kevin and the wife also have sex in a lake, in a filthy log cabin, and on the guests' coats during a cocktail party; I'm sorry, but all I thought about were frogs, cockroaches, and dry-cleaning bills. Finally, Anthony catches the couple at the cabin. He beats up Kevin and has his wife slashed, drugged, and sent to a whorehouse; for Ivana's sake, I just hope Donald Trump doesn't want a Mexican divorce.

Kevin is nursed by an ancient desert woman, who heals him with native bracelets and gauze; when he revives, he stands up and presents his naked backside to the camera, with the gauze tucked all around, as if the Costner tush had been purchased at a very fancy boutique. Kevin finds the wife, who has been transferred to a convent; she dies in his arms, and he's very sad. As far as I could tell, the moral of this movie was: Well, at least she got to have sex with

Kevin in a recreational vehicle. Kevin wears sunglasses and has stubble; he's like a gunslinger on Rodeo Drive. Kevin is no longer a Dream Date, he's a Dream Dude. He's ready to market Costner Cologne and After-shave, with the Rugged Smell of Malibu.

This year's true DD is Alec Baldwin, whom I just saw in *The Hunt for Red October*. Alec costars with Sean Connery, who is so sexy and such a great actor that he's way beyond datability—it would be like going out with Zeus. *Red October* is an espionage thriller about nuclear submarines; it was very exciting, although I wondered if people are really allowed to smoke on subs, where you can't exactly open a window. The submarines are full of dials and switches and computer screens, and all the actors looked very busy; I didn't understand a thing they were doing, but I trusted them. Alec plays a submarine specialist, and he doesn't have much to do, but he's handsome and sly and has squinty eyes—I could just picture him in a luxurious hotel room, driving me wild and then, when I thought I would die, ordering room service, sharing childhood traumas, and starting all over again.

Alec still hasn't been in a movie where he gets to seduce all the women of America, but there has been much discussion, at least on my phone, of his black bikini briefs in *Married to the Mob* and the fact that in *Working Girl*, Melanie Griffith left him for Harrison Ford, which is the definitive no-lose situation. Harrison is an ultimate DD, especially because in real life he married a writer instead of an actress—extra DD points are awarded for marrying brunets, older women, or Joanne Woodward.

Dream Dates are restricted to the cinematic arena, while Dream Husbands exist only on TV, because on TV, everyone has kids and no sex life—couples always lie in bed in pajamas discussing Kirk Cameron's problems holding an after-school job. As a rule, any actor you can even picture wearing pajamas will never have a major movie career; Dream Husbands are men who look their best carrying a briefcase, an infant, and a bouquet of daisies. They are the sort of guys who bring you breakfast in bed—with a bud vase—on Mother's Day, even before you've had children; Dream Husbands can also be found in commercials, where they become aroused by their wives' Spring Breeze deodorant and then use their American

Express cards to bankroll spontaneous vacations to the Caribbean. Ken Olin, of *thirtysomething*, is a modern DH, because he cries and talks about his wife's diaphragm; Mark Harmon is a DH trying to become a DD, but he has day-care center written all over him.

The last film I saw this month was *Bad Influence*; it's a thriller, and Rob Lowe plays a smiling psychopath who wears linen sport jackets and corrupts James Spader, who's a yuppie financial analyst. I don't know why, but even when he plays a psycho killer, Rob Lowe reminds me of Nancy Drew. He's fun to watch, and you never believe a word he says; he's the new Natalie Wood. I happened to see and record the videotape of Rob actually having sex when it was shown on a local cable channel; in *Bad Influence*, the sex is all sweaty and glamorous, and everyone's tan, but in Rob's tape it was sort of boring, with no electronic music or lighting effects or Kim Basinger–style moans, the kind most people save for something with frosting. In *Bad Influence*, James Spader is very moist and nervous; he's not someone you really want to share anxiety with. Rob and James aren't Dream Date material; Rob is too silly, James is a twitchy bunny, and neither one seems to be an adult yet. One test of a DD is whether you'd be embarrassed to be seen in public with the guy; dating Rob Lowe would be like going out with all the New Kids on the Block. He's the only movie star who could appear in a notorious hard-core video and still seem like a Brady or a happy-go-lucky pool toy.

So my money is on Alec as the first bona fide DD of the '90s. Andy Garcia is also in the running, although he slugged his wife in a restaurant in *Internal Affairs*, which is not Dreamy behavior. Jeff Bridges is a classic DD, and Denzel Washington is coming on strong; so far, I don't think Denzel has appeared in any movie that requires aviator glasses, a bomber jacket, and a helmet. God bless Dream Dates; these are the men who get many of us through lonely nights, pints of Butter Almond, the month of February, and even entire marriages; maybe the best thing about DDs is that you'll never actually meet one and have to find out that all he really wants to talk about is his new haircut and what it's like to date models. Having a Dream Date is like making love without anyone seeing your thighs, if you ask me.

DANCE CRAZED
▬ ▬ ▬ ▬

Movies have been getting so much better lately, now that they've become more like car commercials on TV—the ones where they use an old hit song, like "Just One Look" or "What Becomes of the Brokenhearted," to sell a four-door economy sedan. In the new Disney movie *Pretty Woman*, the best moment is when the opening vamp of the Roy Orbison title song plays during a shopping montage. Even if the movie were showing a school bus being hit by a train, the audience would still be happy, because the song is so great.

Pretty Woman is about a prostitute in Los Angeles who gets hired to spend a week with a millionaire businessman for reasons I never really understood; Richard Gere, who plays the tycoon, should just have turned to Julia Roberts, who's the hooker, and said, Stay with me, because we're in a movie. Julia Roberts is gorgeous and wears very clean, very expensive lingerie, even when she's flagging down cars on Hollywood Boulevard. The movie opens with a big close-up of Julia's lace bikini underpants, so right away you know the story will probably not involve the student unrest in Tiananmen Square. After Julia meets Richard, he sends her out to buy new clothes on Rodeo Drive, but the salespeople snub her because she's so tacky. What do they do when Jackie Collins starts to browse, or when Jane Fonda comes in for her Academy Awards gown? From what I know about Los Angeles, most of the call girls eventually marry network presidents; in real life, the sales help at any Beverly Hills boutique would probably ask Julia to sign the bridal registry.

I guess Richard Gere has matured—in *American Gigolo, he* played the Beverly Hills hooker. Now he has silvery hair and acts mostly by squinting; Richard's become much more talented just by losing his contact lenses. He eventually proposes to Julia, who has insisted that he marry her rather than keep her in a luxury condo. Julia is a very prim sort of prostitute; she's like Donna Reed with a specialty in oral sex. *Pretty Woman* is basically a recruiting poster for prostitution as an alternative to grad school or even dating; I'm thinking of telling my adorable six-year-old daughter, Jennifer, to rethink her plans for Harvard Law and just head straight for a push-up bra and a big shoulder bag. I hope that Disney will remake a lot of its old movies in this new soft-core-porn format: the Three Little Pigs could be a ménage à trois, and Mary Poppins could fly into the rooms of teenage boys with premature-ejaculation problems. Pinocchio could be the first hand-carved marital aid, and as for Bambi's mom—well, let me put it this way: maybe Richard Gere could save her from that hunter.

This month I also saw *Cry-Baby*, which is a teen musical directed by John Waters. This film is delightful, although I must confess that I missed Divine, the huge transvestite who used to star in nearly every John Waters movie and who reminded me so much of my grandmother Tessie, who shared Divine's fondness for sleeveless housecoats, hairnets, and the dessert cart. Both Divine and Tessie are no longer with us, but I'm sure they're tossing mah-jongg tiles up in heaven and telling all the other women to eat something or they'll turn into skin and bones. Divine, because of his name alone, is probably very chummy with God. In *Cry-Baby*, there is a female character named Hatchet-Face, and Patty Hearst plays a school crossing guard; they are both very gifted, but neither one can fill Divine's shoes. (Together, however, they might squeeze into one of his strapless evening gowns.) Patty is very funny; it's good to know that going to prison for urban terrorism can lead to a glamorous film career.

I hope that for his future works, John Waters will hire Jean Harris or maybe Squeaky Fromme; his movies could become an important rehabilitative tool. Johnny Depp, the teen idol, stars in *Cry-Baby* as a juvenile delinquent; he lip-syncs to a lot of Elvis-style songs, and the film is every bit as good as *Viva Las Vegas* or *Blue Hawaii*, although Johnny hardly ever calls anyone "Ma'am" or

"Sir," the way Elvis used to—I'm sure Elvis even called his drug dealer "Sir." If Elvis were alive today, I'll bet he would be in a John Waters movie, especially if he had continued to avoid those Slim-Fast milk shakes; Elvis's life seems to sum up all of the great John Waters auteur themes, including diet pills, French kissing, couches that look like Thunderbird convertibles, and the cultural impact of white-trash hairdos. Some people say that John has gone too main-stream, and maybe this is true, but still, when the teen heroine of *Cry-Baby* drinks an entire jar of her own tears, people around me in the theater started gagging, which is a true John Waters ovation. John, if you ask me, *Cry-Baby* is right up there with *Grease 2*.

The songs in *Cry-Baby* are very catchy, but I wanted a more so-cially significant musical experience, so I went to see *The Forbidden Dance*, which is about the Brazilian dance sensation called the lam-bada. Some reports claim that the lambada doesn't really exist, that it's all hype, but this cinematic docu-event convinced me other-wise. It's all about a tribal princess who lives near the Amazon with her people, who all wear grass skirts on their heads. Some evil de-velopers arrive in Jeeps and threaten to bulldoze the rain forest; the tribal princess decides that the only way to save her homeland is to bring the lambada to Los Angeles. She flies to California with the tribe's witch doctor and finds work as a maid for a rich family in Beverly Hills. The parents of this family snub her because she's Brazilian; they treat her as if she were Julia Roberts trying to buy a Bill Blass sundress. But the teenage son of the family falls in love with the princess, and she teaches him to lambada in every conceiv-able position—she even has him use condoms to avoid any lam-bada-transmitted diseases.

The son and the princess enter a big dance contest, even though both of them move like they've had hip replacements. Then the princess is kidnapped by gangsters, who force her to lambada for them, but she breaks free and wins the contest. The event is broad-cast on live network TV, like most lambada festivals, and the prin-cess uses the opportunity to tell the world of the ecological danger to her beloved jungle. In other words, she has it all: a rich guy, a lambada championship, and a global platform for her views. Even an L.A. prostitute would envy her.

There is another lambada movie, called *Lambada,* about a man who teaches high school by day and lambadas by night, but I suspect that it lacks the multilevel political conscience of *The Forbidden Dance.* After all, as the tribal princess tells us in a historical note, the Brazilian government banned the lambada 50 years ago "because it was too sexy." The princess's agenda is two-pronged: Save the Rain Forests, and Legalize Lambada Now!

Personally, I am pro-choice on this issue: people should be allowed to lambada according to their own moral values and upbringing, although perhaps teenagers under fifteen should seek their parents' permission—no one should jump into the lambada before they are psychologically ready. As far as I could tell, doing the lambada involves grinding your crotch against your partner's to music that sounds like Soviet disco. I asked my husband, Josh, to lambada with me in our living room; first we moved the couch and the wing chairs, and I did a quick run with the Dustbuster when I saw what had been lurking underneath. I wondered if I should remove the Scotchgarded chintz slipcovers that give our place the English Country House Look, along with the framed hunting prints and brass accents that make me feel like Lady Libby. I decided to leave everything, so Josh and I could lambada in honor of Fergie and Prince Andrew's new baby; I did, however, switch the little porcelain bowls of potpourri from Westminster Garden Medley to the more tropical Safari Spice. Josh asked if he could lambada in his sweatpants and terry cloth shaving coat; I told him he could, even though I had taken the trouble to pull together a special lambada outfit for myself, consisting of a hot pink leotard, a plastic lei from my sister-in-law's wedding reception—don't ask—and an old corduroy wrap skirt that I had shortened and shredded. Both Josh and I also wore colorful lambada headbands, which I had stitched from chintz swatches and Velcro.

For music I played an old Herb Alpert and the Tijuana Brass album, but at 16 rpm, so it would feel more sultry and sensual. I stood very close to Josh and ground my crotch into his. I started swaying; Josh said that if I kept it up, I would give him a hernia. I wet my lips like the tribal princess did, and I murmured the movie's slogan—"If it were any hotter, it wouldn't be dancing"—into Josh's ear. Josh wouldn't stop giggling, and that was when I had my inspiration—suddenly I invented my own sizzling tribal dance, which I call the Libida. To do the Libida, you first grab the most overweight areas of your partner's body; I went right for Josh's love handles—he yelped and grabbed the cellulite on the backs of my thighs; suddenly we were grinding away, and our lips met.

Soon Josh was pinching the skin underneath my upper arms; I started tugging on his jowls. By the time he reached my stretch marks, I was ready to save the rain forests and the whales and to fill in all the potholes on Lexington Avenue; I was on fire with tribal lust and environmental awareness. I bit one of Josh's chins, and he whimpered, Come on, baby, scrub that oil spill off my sea otter. What can I say, except that we did the Libida until it was time to watch Deborah Norville on the *Today* show the next morning; in fact, Deborah Norville may just be the antidote to the Libida.

As Josh and I were getting dressed for work, I had a marketing vision: suddenly I saw the Libida spreading like wildfire, or even like the hustle or break dancing, all across America. I could see Libida Dancewear nooks in major department stores, Libida Nites for Interested Singles at churches and synagogues, and early-morning Learn to Libida classes for frisky seniors at Florida malls. I saw aerobic videocassettes for Lo-Impact Libida-cize, and maybe even an unauthorized paperback tell-all called *Libida! The Dirty Dance That Replaced Dieting*. Then I realized, no—the Libida belongs to everyone and should not be commercialized, or at least the licensing should be restricted to a signature fragrance, L'Air du Libida, and I ♥ Libida mugs and key chains, with all the profits going to a foundation to fight liquid protein.

The Forbidden Dance is proof that movies can make a difference—in both the political arena and the bedroom. I hope that there will be many more lambada films, and that the trend doesn't peter out the way roller disco did after *Roller Boogie* and *Skatetown, U.S.A.* Maybe Meryl Streep could work up a Brazilian accent and bring her very special elegance to the lambada; maybe Richard Gere could recapture his humanity along the Amazon. Richard is very involved with halting the Chinese occupation of Tibet and helping the Dalai Lama; Richard, why not whirl him out on the dance floor for a Dalai Lambada? I also hope that the Libida can be a cultural bridge between the U.S. and our South American neighbors, and even Eastern Europe; my dream is to Libida in the rubble of the Berlin Wall. We are living in exciting times, and I'd like to put a little Libby into global liberation; the Libida can save the planet, and your marriage, if you ask me.

X-HAUSTED

There was a controversy at Wellesley College recently when Barbara Bush was invited to speak at the annual commencement ceremony; many students felt that Barbara, as First Lady, was just a fancy Republican housewife and not a woman of accomplishment. These students may have a point; if you ask me, Barbara is like something out of the Talbot's catalog—she's one of those women in a madras wrap skirt and a sun visor, pouring martinis out of a thermos on the seventh hole or chain-smoking at a Yale-Harvard tailgate with a plaid blanket over her knees. For the Wellesley commencement, and as a role model for today's young women, I would have suggested that the college contact Carré Otis, the star of the controversial film *Wild Orchid*.

Carré is a model turned actress, and she has lips the size of a sectional sofa; her hair is always in frizzy tendrils around her face, and I think she has studied speech with Brooke Shields and Cheryl Tiegs. Her voice is high and tinkly, like a mouse on helium; in *Wild Orchid*, Carré plays a brilliant corporate attorney. Her character supposedly speaks at least five languages, and as my aunt Sylvia would say, she can't say no in any of them. Carré gets sent, along with her boss, Jacqueline Bisset, to negotiate the purchase of a hotel in Rio. Now, if I were on trial for murder one, somehow I don't think I'd want to be represented by Carré and Jackie, and not just because neither one of them wears underwear. Jackie is actually very funny; she acts like an executive by getting agitated and calling everyone "honey" on her cordless phone. It's like watching Faye Dunaway playing the secretary general of the U.N.

Carré and Jackie go to Brazil, where they both become the love

107

slaves of Mickey Rourke, who's some sort of international financier and sex god. Mickey does not seem to have bathed since his film career began; his hair is greasy, and his cheeks look like he's storing something up for the winter. In the credits of his movies, I always expect him to be listed as playing someone called Willie the Geek. He speaks softly, rides a motorcycle, and wears sport jackets and tuxedos without shirts or, I imagine, dress shields; all of this causes Jackie to quiver and Carré's voice to get even squeakier. Mickey gives Carré a sensual education by forcing her to sit next to another couple who are having sex in a limo; this strikes me as being almost as sensual as sharing the backseat with a small child eating an ice cream cone. Then Mickey has Carré pretend to be a prostitute and sell herself to a strange man, while Mickey watches through the window—I hope Carré doesn't want to make partner. Then Jackie and Carré both dress up in men's suits for carnival season and go dancing in the streets; Jackie also wears a mustache, but then, she is the head of the firm.

Jackie finally picks up a handsome young beach hustler and has him strip while Carré watches; Jackie also sampled a nude boy in *Rich and Famous,* so I guess this is her screen trademark, like Bette Davis's cigarette or Rosanna Arquette's overbite. Mickey shows up and kicks the hustler out; Carré tells Mickey to "just reach out and touch me." Earlier, Mickey told Carré that "sometimes you have to lose yourself in order to find yourself," a philosophy that also applies to house keys. Finally, Mickey grabs Carré and they have steamy sex, or at least I've heard that they do in the uncut European version. In the R-rated American version, all you see is Carré sitting on Mickey's lap while they both make erotic faces, but this seems appropriate, since everyone knows that no one would ever really have sex with a lawyer. I don't understand why *Wild Orchid* would get an X rating, unless X stands for an incoherent plot and the use of atmospheric dwarves in restaurant scenes. By the end, Carré has closed the big hotel deal, so she is clearly Wellesley material, as both a legal mastermind and an insatiable topless plaything.

Kim Basinger was Mickey Rourke's love slave in *9½ Weeks,* in which he made her eat strawberries, dance half-naked, and be late for work. Mickey's movies are very successful in Europe, but probably as comedies; all the French and Italian people can giggle and say, Oh, look, ze Americans still think you have sex wiz ze ice cubes. Frankly, my idea of hot sex involves a lavish hotel suite, beautifully laundered sheets, room service, and lots of fashion magazines to read afterward; great sex should combine all the best parts of staying home from school when you're sick.

This month I also saw director Pedro Almodóvar's *Tie Me Up! Tie Me Down!*, which received an X rating. In this movie, a man gets released from a mental hospital and immediately kidnaps an ex–porn actress, beats her up, and ties her to a bed. Before long, she falls in love with him. I have been out of the dating scene for a while, but my dear friend Stacy Schiff says that a man is still required to at least rent *Honey, I Shrunk the Kids* and provide microwave popcorn before tying someone to a bed. In interviews I have read, Almodóvar claims that his movie is really a metaphor for marriage and committing to a relationship. This is the same sort of reasoning that Lina Wertmüller used for her movie *Swept Away*, where Lina claimed that when the man slugged the woman, it was really a metaphor for the evils of capitalism.

Here is my question: how come, in all these metaphors, the woman never gets to smack the man? I would love to see Carré Otis tie up Mickey Rourke and at least give him a shower with Dial soap; it could all be a metaphor for personal hygiene. Because I have an open mind, I decided to try a sensual adventure of my own. I waited until my husband, Josh, fell asleep in front of the TV, and then I quietly used two of his Father's Day neckties and a pair of my control-top panty hose to tie him to the recliner. When he woke up, he couldn't move, and right away he started yelling that I was cutting off his circulation and that his feet were asleep. I sat on his lap and asked, Don't you feel like a metaphor for marriage and commitment? He said, No, for that we would need boiling water, napalm, and a red-hot poker. Then I said I wouldn't untie him until he said he loved me; he said he'd scream until the super came up to investigate, and he'd tell the super that he loved *him*. Then I told Josh that he was my love slave, and that I was going to rip off his imitation-Lacoste shirt and sell him to a strange woman; Josh told me that I *was* a strange woman and that I didn't have to untie him, just get off his lap and turn the channel to *The Simpsons*.

Suddenly I began to feel like Mickey Rourke, so I went into the kitchen and got a glass of ice cubes from the automatic ice maker built into the door of our fridge; while I was there, I grabbed a Weight Watchers Chocolate Mousse Bar from the freezer. I went back into the living room and rubbed an ice cube on Josh's bare stomach; he started whimpering and said that this was just how the other kids used to torture him at Camp Tiwonda for Authentic Crafts and Teen and Preteen Weight Loss. Then I slowly and erotically sucked on the Mousse Bar, which really made Josh moan, because he claims that NutraSweet is an aphrodisiac. Then I told him that Stacy and I were going to dress up in two of his white nylon orthodontist's smocks and go out to Roseland. Finally, I told him that instead of physically abusing him, I was going to make him watch *Life Goes On*, the sensitive TV show about a family with a child who has Down's syndrome; even before the first commercial, Josh was begging me to get the pliers.

When I untied him, we both agreed that kinky sex probably works only in Europe; Josh said that in America, going on forced errands is sexier than bondage. We both decided that if we were Mickey Rourke, we would wait until Carré Otis had gotten undressed and into bed late on Sunday night, and then we would make her pull on a raincoat and run down to the store for milk, Carnation Instant Breakfast, and a bag of Chip-A-Roo's. I told Josh that there was one last X-rated film out this month, called *The Cook, the Thief, His Wife & Her Lover*. I had read that it opens with someone being smeared with excrement and peed on; Josh said it didn't exactly sound like Indiana Jones being chased by a big boulder. I'd also heard that pasty English actors are thrown naked onto rotting meat covered with maggots, and that the whole movie was a metaphor for civilization. Josh said he thought there should be more movies that were metaphors for flush toilets and nice fresh sirloins. I decided I didn't have to see this movie because the title was too long; as a rule, I don't see movies with more than one comma.

There has been a lot of fuss lately about censorship in America and the supposedly obscene works being funded by the National

Endowment for the Arts, so I looked at the book of Robert Mapplethorpe's photographs, the ones that have been causing such a tizzy. If you ask me, Jesse Helms and those other senators are actually upset about the national endowments on the nude guys in those pictures; the senators don't want their wives comparison shopping. Even the pictures of S&M sex were sort of sweet, like UNICEF greeting cards from hell; at least there were no pictures of Carré Otis serving a subpoena. I don't mind if my tax dollars support dirty pictures; what if Mapplethorpe had photographed one of those half-billion-dollar Stealth bombers? Personally, I think X ratings and all this to-do about smut only leads to a lot of disappointment once you see what everyone's talking about. Mickey Rourke is just a metaphor for Mickey Mouse, if you ask me.

HAPPY BIRTHDAY
TO ME
▄▄ ▄▄ ▄▄

My name is Jennifer Waxner, and I am seven years old, because I just had my birthday party. My mommy, Libby Gelman-Waxner, says that she is too tired to move a muscle and I should write her column into the cassette recorder and then my daddy will type it up, if he knows what's good for him. My mommy is lying down in her bedroom right now with a damp washcloth over her eyes, and she says that giving a children's birthday party is the tenth level of Hell but I shouldn't say Hell. I loved my party, and Mrs. Escadero, the cleaning lady, says that all the stains will come out of the wall-to-wall, even where Jonah Kleinert threw up candy corn and those cookies my grandma brought from the French bakery that looked like somebody already threw them up.

Because my mommy is an important film critic (even though she is not on TV), she said that I could have a movie party, so I invited all my friends, plus Jonah Kleinert, to see *Total Recall* and *Another 48 Hrs.*, even though Jonah chases me with boogers on his fingers, but my grandma says that Kleinert Kustom Kitchens makes a fortune and I could do worse when the time comes. I also invited my best friend, Amanda Barkman, whose daddy is in jail for insider trading and whose second mommy used to be a flight attendant on a big plane, so my grandma says I should feel sorry for Amanda, because now she might as well be Tricia Nixon. My other guests were all from my first-grade class, so they are all gifted and reading at a sixth-grade level, except Max Pletkoff, who is dyslexic, which Grandma says means "probably adopted" in Latin. I also invited my mommy's therapist, Dr. Arlene Cole-Natbaum, because my mommy wanted to make sure everything was low-stress, except Dr. Cole-Natbaum spent most of the party in the bathroom crying about how men are threatened by women with doctorates and asking if Jonah's father was really available.

First we all went to see *Total Recall*, which is about Arnold Schwarzenegger, who is a man my daddy says he used to look like back in college when he played lacrosse. My grandma says that Arnold is really like one of the Teenage Mutant Ninja Turtles and that someone is inside working him. In the movie, it is the future, and Arnold has no memory or something, and he goes to Mars and kills everybody, which was the part I liked. My mommy asked if I knew that the people in the movie are actors and didn't really die, and I said, Mommy, I'm not a total butthead, and then Grandma said, Libby, your child has a mouth like a garbage disposal, but Dr. Cole-Natbaum told her not to repress my creativity, so I asked Dr. Cole-Natbaum why her husband left her for a twenty-three-year-old holistic healer, and she asked Jonah if he was free on Saturday night, and Jonah said he was but that his bedtime was 8 P.M., and Dr. Cole-Natbaum said he clearly has problems with intimacy.

Amanda and I started to have a fight about whether the little bits left in the bottom of the popcorn bucket are really kitty litter and whether it was better to have your head chopped off with a big knife or blown off by a laser gun, and Amanda said the laser was better because your clothes would stay clean, and then I asked my mommy why the mutant Martian lady had three breasts, and Dr. Cole-Natbaum said it was because men are pigs. Then the movie was over, because Arnold gave all the people on Mars air to breathe, so it was a happy story, and my grandma said that Arnold's being a movie star proves that America is a great country, and Dr. Cole-Natbaum said it's only because he has large breasts.

After that, we all went into the theater across the hall at the cineplex to see *Another 48 Hrs.*, and my grandma told the usher that we were just children and we had lost our stubs. Amanda said, But isn't that illegal? and my grandma said, Call your father in the cell block and ask him, dear. *Another 48 Hrs.* is about a black man named Eddie Murphy who wears nice clothes and a white man named Nick Nolte who drives a used car, and together they kill everyone in California, and my mommy said that this was good, because the black person and the white person are friends and throw guns to each other. Eddie Murphy calls all the women in the movie bitches, and my mommy said that bitches means supporting actresses, so Amanda and I decided to tell our teacher that we want to be bitches in the school play about Columbus, and my grandma said, Oy gevalt, Libby, when did we become the Manson family? Jonah Kleinert said he heard on TV that Eddie Murphy got $9 million to be in this movie, and my grandma said we should get profit participation just for sitting through it. After the movie was over, Dr. Cole-Natbaum asked all of the children what the movie had taught us, and I said it was never to run out of ammunition in a whorehouse, and Amanda said, No, the movie taught us that sometimes even if you shoot, punch, and stab somebody, they can still pop up and hit you, and Jonah said, No, the movie taught us that Eddie is worth it, because he delivers an opening weekend, and my mommy said, Who wants cake and ice cream? and Amanda and I said, Are you crazy, we'll be on the StairMaster for the next five years.

After the movies, everybody went back to our apartment for more of the party, and Mommy asked us if we wanted to play Duck Duck Goose or Farmer in the Dell, and I said, No, I want to play Summer Action Blockbuster, and that I was the star and the party was really the sequel to my last birthday. I said that I was a rebel detective and Shange-Arimba Lachman was my partner because she is black—even if her parents are Columbia professors—and Amanda started crying because she wasn't my partner, so I said she could be my agent-manager and get 20 percent of all my earnings, and she said okay, if she could have other clients and produce my albums. Then I said that Jonah was a South American drug kingpin who hated recycling and that all the other kids were his mindless killing machines and that Dr. Cole-Natbaum was his sexy drug-addict girlfriend, and she said that Prozac was for chronic depression and had changed her life. I said that Grandma was the police chief who didn't like it when Shange-Arimba and I broke the rules and killed people, and that my mommy was a lifelike android who had developed emotions, and that was when she said, It's time to open presents, so Shange-Arimba and I killed everyone really fast.

My favorite present was from Caitlin Tisch, because it was a gift certificate from Bergdorf's, and my grandma said it was very thoughtful, and my second favorite was either my baby doll that makes sucking noises and then burps, just like Jonah Kleinert does in the back of the classroom, or my Pretty Li'l Pony that gets toe-nail polish when you put water on its feet, or my Jumbo Bucket of Super Sludge, which I put on a cookie and told Jonah it was tofu. Dr. Cole-Natbaum gave me a copy of her unpublished novel about her relationship with her mother, and I said thank you, because Grandma pinched me and said, What do we say to the nice lady who can write prescriptions? My mommy and daddy gave me a whole bunch of cool stuff, so I asked them if they were getting divorced, and my mommy said, What a question, and my daddy said no, that would be for *his* birthday. My baby brother, Mitchell Sean, gave me a lot of books, but I know they're really from my mommy and daddy, but I kissed Mitchell Sean anyway and then shot him because he was a double agent working for Jonah.

The birthday cake was really good, because it was from an expensive place and had rum in it, and the clown guy said that we should all come see him on Broadway whenever one of the other Cats gets sick. And then Amanda said that at her birthday they had a magician, and Caitlin said that at hers they had a wine tasting, and Shange-Arimba said that at hers Alice Walker read from her works and made balloon animals, and Jonah said at his next birthday there's going to be a shooting range with live bunnies, so I started crying because my party was so dinky, and my grandma said, Stop, there are children in Europe who would give their right arms for Barbie paper plates, and Amanda said, Not in Paris. Then everybody started crying, and my mommy was about to call 911 when Grandma said, I have a dollar here for every smile, and Jonah talked her up to $1.50, and Caitlin said she could take the smile as a deduction.

Then Dr. Cole-Natbaum told me that birthdays were meaningless and that I always had to nurture the child inside of me and that lots of women are still fertile after forty, and Grandma said, Shoot her, and I did, and my mommy said, Jonah, the Interplak tooth polisher is not a toy and the cat doesn't need whiter teeth, and Don't touch those videocassettes, they belong to Jennifer's father for his poker nights, and Can't all the children who are left wait downstairs with the doorman? My mommy will be back next month, and she says that when I have children, I'll understand why we can't go to see *Die Hard 2* later tonight, which I think is pretty barfy of her, if you ask me.

—Jennifer Waxner

THE ENTERTAINMENT FACTOR

I'm not really concerned about Americans' tanning too much or eating too much saturated fat; I'm worried that, as a nation, we may be getting too much entertainment. Between Arnold Schwarzenegger's heading the President's Council on Physical Fitness and Sports, Bugs Bunny's fiftieth birthday, and Tom Cruise's turning up in his underwear on every magazine cover, I'm getting nervous. Every time the doorbell rings, I think it's Michael J. Fox with a Diet Pepsi; it's as if all the celebrities in the world got together and said, Now that Sammy Davis, Jr., is dead, there's a show-business love vacuum, and somebody's got to fill it. Even such fancy, reclusive types as Warren Beatty are trying to make commercial blockbusters; ever since Warren did those back-to-back *Donahue* shows, I've been thinking about getting a court order to stop him from harassing me.

Maybe there should be a rating system for all this entertainment, based on the sun-block model; if a movie has an Entertainment Factor of 34, it means that the star will be appearing on all three network morning shows simultaneously, claiming to be a very private and/or boring person. *Days of Thunder* has an EF of 40. It's Tom Cruise's movie about how exciting and philosophical it is to be a stock-car racer. As he does in all his movies, Tom plays a cocky but gifted rebel who needs an older male star to teach him how to be even cuter. Tom's onscreen baby-sitters have included Paul Newman, Dustin Hoffman, and Bryan Brown; in *Days of Thunder*, Robert Duvall does the burping, and you can practically hear him saying, Yes, Mr. and Mrs. Cruise, have a good time, I'll look after him and make sure he has a growth experience. Actually, Robert Duvall, who builds the cars Tom drives, seems to be turning into Walter Brennan; he wears a baseball cap, has ear hairs, and always seems as if he's about to call someone "young feller." When all of these older actors look at Tom, don't they think, Hmm, he's half my age, half my height and he's making $10 million? Why don't all those actors get together and say, Okay, in the next movie, after the near-fatal accident that's supposed to make Tom shape up, couldn't he die?

After watching *Days of Thunder*, I decided that driving a race car is basically like playing Pac-Man, only you can get killed. At one point, Tom says he loves racing because he wants to "control something that's out of control"; this theory may also explain Tom's home permanent. All of the cars have sponsors, so there are huge ads for things like Havoline motor oil and Tide painted on the hoods; I read an article about how the racetracks are trying to attract more women, so soon a car will probably say MODESS ... BECAUSE.

During the movie's only sex scene, Tom explains the thrill of racing by balancing two packets of Sweet 'n Low on his girlfriend's naked thigh while they're in bed; the packets represent cars, and the girlfriend's crotch is the finish line. I guess Tom chose Sweet 'n Low because if he used real sugar, the cars would end up on her hips. The girlfriend is there mostly to act prissy and beg Tom not to race; this sort of role used to be played by Natalie Wood in a tight cashmere sweater, but because of the women's movement, the girlfriend in *Days of Thunder* is a neurosurgeon. This relationship is obviously an homage to *Road House*, where Patrick Swayze, a nightclub bouncer, falls in love with Kelly Lynch, the doctor who bandages him. This is all a major step forward for feminism; now even women with Ph.D.'s can stand on the sidelines and shut their eyes. Nicole Kidman plays Tom's girlfriend, and like most surgeons, she has lots of frizzy hair in her eyes and wears tight white pantsuits to the track.

After seeing *Days of Thunder*, I experienced entertainment burns over two thirds of my body; I was so entertained that I couldn't think or form sentences for almost 72 hours. And after watching Jay

Leno on *The Tonight Show* telling Tom how much *Rain Man* had moved him, I developed actual celebrity hives on my back and upper arms.

Dick Tracy is also far too entertaining; the whole movie is art directed in glossy primary colors, so it's like being buried under a pile of Fiesta ware and crayons. The film is very tasteful, and there's not a lot of violence; it's an action-adventure movie for people disturbed by the mindless bloodletting of *Driving Miss Daisy*. While I was watching, I tried to imagine Madonna, who plays Breathless Mahoney, in bed with Warren, but I'd read too much about their relationship, so I kept picturing their publicists having wild sex. Warren is very sweet as Dick Tracy; he's like a nice man running a nursery school, offering everybody Ritz crackers and paper cups filled with apple juice. All Warren and his movie want to do is entertain you; *Dick Tracy* makes the Muppets look like serial killers. I give *Dick Tracy* an Entertainment Factor of 15, because it could cause only brief blackouts or a new feeling for brown; it's a St. Joseph's Chewable Movie for Children.

This month I also saw *Bird on a Wire*. In this movie, Mel Gibson and Goldie Hawn are so entertaining that they may have to be gunned down by federal agents so they can never entertain again. Mel is a reformed drug smuggler on the run, and Goldie is a high-powered attorney, and they get to show off their behinds; someday soon they may both be squatting in the cement at Grauman's Chinese. I also saw *Gremlins 2: The New Batch*, which was very funny, but it had so many rubbery, shrieking little gremlins that I felt like I was trapped in the "It's a Small World" ride at Disneyland after all the little singing dolls from other lands had dropped acid. Disneyland is the Manhattan Project for entertainment; it's where entertainment first attained enough critical mass to destroy the planet.

By the end of the month, I was so overentertained that I was unable to see either Bill Cosby in *Ghost Dad* or Alan Alda's new movie, *Betsy's Wedding*. Bill and Alan are competing to become the newest in-flight auteur—someone whose career exists entirely on Delta nonstops to Albuquerque. Both Bill and Alan used to be talented and appealing until, after starring in long-running sitcoms, they became pathologically entertaining, so entertaining that now they can be viewed only by audiences wearing lead-lined rubber jumpsuits and thick Lucite goggles. Overentertainers do things like win People's Choice Awards or any awards created solely for the purpose of having a TV special; they also develop a need to overentertain in all media. Bill Cosby has had books ghostwritten that offer his thoughts on fatherhood and love and marriage; personally, I would only take Bill Cosby's advice on tax-free investing. Scientists are currently developing a vaccine for overentertainment, by combining snippets of Bill's last movie, *Leonard Part 6,* with the moments from the Barbara Walters special in which Roseanne Barr wept; if you ask me, the trailer for *Back to the Future Part III* could be the key ingredient.

The last movie I saw this month was *Arachnophobia,* which was all about killer spiders infesting a small town. The ads call this movie a "thrill-omedy," because it's half sort of funny and half sort of disgusting—in other words, pure overentertainment. Maybe when you start seeing thrill-omedies, it's time to start gardening or performing any activity during which the possibility of watching Robin Williams grabbing his crotch is severely limited. Right now I'd like to go down and check my mailbox, but I'm worried that an *US* magazine special issue on the 300 Most Desperate Hunks might be waiting. I'd turn on the TV, but what if *Entertainment Tonight*'s Mary Hart is interviewing Julia Roberts on how the press distorts her feelings about her relationship with her career? The phone is ringing—what if it's David Lynch telling me that the first *Twin Peaks* episodes are now available on video? Is overentertainment the homelessness of the '90s? Do we dare leave future generations a world in which the opening applause for Arsenio Hall takes up almost as much of the show as his hugging the bandleader does? If Warren does any more press, will Shirley MacLaine start to look like the shy one? Overentertainment: let's get it on the ballot, if you ask me.

AFTERLIFE,
AFTER LUNCH

■ ■ ■ ■

Last week, I bought my adorable seven-year-old daughter, Jennifer, her first pet, which was a gerbil, because she wanted a mouse, but I explained that we'd have trouble with the co-op board. And just yesterday, Jennifer came home from school and Jordan the gerbil was dead. Jennifer had named him after her favorite New Kid on the Block, so I tried to explain that the death was not an omen. I put Baggies on my hands and placed Jordan in an old Estée Lauder Youth Dew box, and Jennifer and I dropped the box down the incinerator shaft. All of a sudden, Jennifer was asking me about the larger topics, like death and heaven, so I did what any caring parent would do to make the random ways of the universe more comprehensible: I took Jennifer to see Patrick Swayze and Demi Moore in *Ghost*.

In this film, Demi and Patrick live in a gorgeous TriBeCa loft that is filled with things like jukeboxes and life-size statues of angels; it's like a window dresser's supply room. Demi makes artistic ceramics on her potter's wheel; she has a bowl haircut that makes her look like an effeminate member of the Three Stooges. Patrick works as an investment banker, and frankly, while I would happily let him handle my body, my finances are another matter entirely. Patrick wears very fitted business suits and stands near the computers in his office; he reminded me of the lead dancer in a summerstock production of *How to Succeed in Business Without Really Trying*. Patrick's hair has been frosted in what is clearly an homage to my aunt Florence, who was recently voted Ms. Sassy Senior by the population of Legacy Village in Boca Raton, Florida. Patrick is adorable, but whenever he has to have a thought, he scrunches up his forehead, as if his brain hurts.

Early in the movie, Patrick gets shot and dies, but he immediately becomes a ghost whom only a medium, played by Whoopi Goldberg, can contact. Even when he's sitting on their custom woodwork, Demi can't see Patrick, so she cries all the time. Every tear is so perfect, she always looks like a ceramic Pierrot ashtray from an airport gift shop. Eventually, Patrick and Whoopi track down Patrick's murderer, and God lets Patrick and Demi have one last dance. Then Patrick is allowed to climb a big glowing white ladder to meet a lot of glowing white creatures who look like wads of Kleenex. Patrick's murderer gets killed, and little screaming black special effects grab him and drag him down to hell.

After the movie was over, Jennifer had a lot of questions, and so did I. First of all, if there's a merciful God, why did He give Demi those bangs and let Patrick go to heaven, especially after his last two films, *Road House* and *Next of Kin*? And how will Patrick's death affect the *Dirty Dancing* sequel? Will Demi's pottery pay for the maintenance on the loft, or will she kill herself because this movie makes dying look simply like a fabulous form of lighting? What if the little screaming black things took Jordan the gerbil to hell, where he'll never get to meet Patrick?

Once we got home, I sat Jennifer down and explained things to her. I told her that heaven is a place where everything fits without alterations, where everything stays spotless because the angels take pride in what they do and don't drink, and where Retin-A is available without a prescription. I didn't want to frighten Jennifer, so I told her that hell is basically like the smoking section of a restaurant—a place where everyone's clothes smell bad and the utensils and glassware have water spots. I said that most people and all animals except pit bulls go to heaven, and that the Richard Nixon Library & Birthplace in Yorba Linda, California, is spoken of as the entrance to the underworld in the Dead Sea Scrolls. Jennifer asked if dying is painful, and being a loving and modern mom, I told her the truth: that it hurts, but nowhere near as much as childbirth does. Then Jennifer asked which was worse, dying or not getting into a decent college, and I said, God willing, you'll never have to know.

Then Jennifer asked if there is a boys' heaven and a girls' heaven, and I had to be honest—I told her there is only a girls'.

I felt that Jennifer and I had bonded, so I took her to Columbus Avenue for some frozen yogurt, and then we went to see *Navy SEALs*. This movie is about a special group of military men who, as far as I can tell, are sent to Arab nations to rescue hostages and massacre bystanders while making frat-house jokes—the SEALs are like surfers with grenade launchers. Charlie Sheen plays a wild rebel SEAL who charms a half-Lebanese woman journalist by making anti-Muslim wisecracks. The journalist eventually sleeps with one of the other SEALs and then tells him where some terrorists are hiding—it's as if Barbara Walters had sex with one of Qaddafi's bodyguards and revealed Cher's private number. Jennifer said the movie was racist and fascist and sexist, so I bought her two new Barbie outfits and Barbie's exercise studio. This was all part of Jennifer's moral education; I believe in reinforcing fine values through desirable, high-quality merchandise. I told Jennifer that Republicans are just people who don't know where to shop, and that's why they end up with Scottie dogs and little strawberries all over everything.

Jennifer also wanted to know who was better, Christians or Jews, so I told her that all people should be friends, even if it means putting up with alcoholics singing Christmas carols and beating their wives. I told her that all people are basically the same, even if some of them can ice-skate and others can get Ph.D.'s and cure diseases that afflict all mankind. I said that Christians and Jews had all started out as one tribe, until one group decided it wanted to drive small foreign cars and have cheap affairs and the other group decided to plant trees in the desert and fight social injustice in the Deep South. I mentioned that God loves all religions equally, even if there are certain homes He visits more often because there's always enough potato salad and the carpeting has been professionally cleaned. Jennifer asked if God loves brunets more than blonds, and I said that He loves them both equally, but that, of course, He's no fool.

Then Jennifer asked me some even tougher questions, such as Why is there war? and Why are there handguns? and Is linen really supposed to be worn wrinkled? I told her that all these things are tests from above; God gives us war and guns to see if we can make peace and He gives us white linen slacks to keep us humble. Other divine tests include *America's Funniest Home Videos*, opera, unions, eating doughnuts covered with powdered sugar, trying to stop eating those chocolate-covered mini-doughnuts after you've had twelve, wondering which personal products are okay to leave out in the bathroom, leprosy, and men who turn up the collars of their polo shirts. These tests make life interesting. As I told Jennifer, What would life be like without other people to talk about after they've finally gotten off the elevator?

Jennifer asked what God looks like, so I told her He looks just like Harrison Ford in *Presumed Innocent*, the screen adaptation of Scott Turow's best-seller, only with a better haircut. In this film Harrison is a lawyer with a Julius Caesar look; he cheats on his wife and child with a glamorous, sexually insatiable woman prosecuting attorney; the woman is murdered and Harrison is arrested and put on trial. I used this film as a moral lesson for Jennifer: it showed her that even a law degree and a marriage license can sometimes spell trouble. The nympho prosecutor is played by Greta Scacchi, who cross-examines witnesses while wearing designer suits, a deep tan, and enough turquoise eye shadow to recoat a Navaho bracelet; if you ask me, Greta could only prosecute defendants on *Wheel of Fortune*. Jennifer asked if lawyers are bad people, and I said, Of course not, lawyers are brave and necessary, because someone has to defend plastic surgeons.

After all this mature discussion about life and death, I went out and bought Jennifer another gerbil. I gave it to her that night and explained that it was Jordan's twin brother and that it was better because it was newer; I believe that morality begins at home. I tucked Jennifer in, and I told her that Gelman-Waxner women believe in truth, equality, and paying off Visa with MasterCard. Death can never harm us, because God loves a woman with hips. Then Jennifer asked why bad things happen to good people, and I said, At least some of the bad things have sprinkles on top, and I've heard that Dr. Salk is working on cellulite next. Moral choices are always difficult, but, as I told Jennifer, they're nothing compared to finding flattering bridesmaids' dresses or a bathing suit that doesn't ride up; heaven is just sleeping in thick wool socks and a football jersey, if you ask me.

LIBBY "NOIR"

— — — —

As a cultivated student of the filmic medium, I have often heard the expression *"film noir"*; after seeing several current examples of this genre, I now realize that the exact translation of *film noir* is "sexy and really, really boring." *Films noirs* explore the dark underbelly of America, which certainly beats Colonial Williamsburg as a weekend getaway, and they always feature the same characters: a hot, dangerous male drifter; a hot, dangerous, bored small-town slut; and at least one disgusting fat man who gets brutally killed, right after which the drifter and the slut have really great sex, usually near a ceiling fan and venetian blinds. Everybody in *film noir* sweats a lot, and deodorant and Irish Spring are never mentioned, so maybe *film noir* also means "unpleasant to stand behind at the cash machine."

The first *film noir* I saw this month was *Wild at Heart*, which was directed by David Lynch, who also co-created the TV show *Twin Peaks*. I saw *Wild at Heart* at a brand-new multiplex in SoHo, where there is a café that serves French pastries and at least ten different bottled waters, and where at least one of the theaters is always showing a blasphemous foreign film that portrays Jesus as either a cabdriver or a teenage girl. Everyone in the audience had asymmetrical haircuts, glasses with thick black frames, and clunky rubber-soled shoes. They looked like French opium addicts, but if you ask me, they were all probably assistants at public-relations firms uptown. All of these people loved *Wild at Heart*, and they all felt that David Lynch is a quirky visionary who deals in subconscious dream imagery, and after a while, I wished I was home watching a

Golden Girls rerun. I have never been able to sit through a whole episode of *Twin Peaks*; it's a postmodern soap opera, which means that every time someone onscreen eats a piece of apple pie, you can hear a thousand grad students start typing their doctoral dissertations on "*Twin Peaks:* David Lynch and the Semiotics of Cobbler."

In *Wild at Heart,* Nicolas Cage is the studly drifter in a snakeskin jacket, and Laura Dern is the small-town sexpot; they hop into a flashy convertible and hightail it through the South, hoping to escape Laura's nasty mother and to discover surrealistic vignettes of American grotesquerie. Nicolas and Laura have lots of sex, and the screen turns different colors, just like it did for Mitzi Gaynor in *South Pacific.* The sex is really conventional, though; only Laura is naked, and the sheets are always awkwardly tucked around anything really interesting. Eventually, supporting actors die in car accidents, or get set on fire, or have their heads blown off with shotguns, and all the people in the theater thought it was visually arresting and a stunning treatment of classic American bloodshed, which is not what they'd say about the same sort of thing in a Rambo movie, where at least it's fun and there aren't any allusions to *The Wizard of Oz.*

After Dark, My Sweet was my next *film noir,* although I suspect it might actually be some sort of NASA stress test; they could show it continually to astronauts to see how long humans can exist in space without entertainment. This movie was not just boring, it was like a two-week sleep-over visit from my aunt Frieda, my uncle Morty, who has to keep his right leg elevated so the blood clots won't reach his brain, and their son, Heshy, who has started an international computer call-board for other 42-year-olds who still live at home and are interested in cyborg comics and the Talmud. *After Dark, My Sweet* is like the fulfillment of some ancient curse; it's as if God had said, By 1990, if people are still going to the movies and not getting enough fresh air, I will send down a punishment.

Jason Patric is the hunky drifter in this movie. He's an ex-boxer with beard stubble and a crumpled brown paper bag that he carries everywhere; after a while, I started to look for the matching shoes.

Jason is gorgeous beyond belief, but this is *film noir*, so he's innocent yet troubled and violent, which means a lot of squinting, as if he's trying to duplicate Patrick Swayze's EKG. How do people become drifters, anyway? Do they take an aptitude test that says, You excel at stumbling along the highway, not changing your underwear, and getting hooked up with small-time criminals? Jason joins forces with Bruce Dern, who looks like Big Bird on methadone, and Rachel Ward, who plays the local slutty alcoholic widow; between the three of them, it's like the Olympics of terrible acting, but believe me, Rachel breezes off with the gold. I don't think Rachel could believably scream for water if her hair was on fire; it's like she was put on the planet to make Ali MacGraw feel better.

Rachel, Jason, and Bruce plot to kidnap a rich little boy, and they do it and then sort of forget about the kid; it's like watching a suspenseful crime movie in which everyone has Alzheimer's. I must confess that I didn't stay to see the end of *After Dark, My Sweet*, because I felt like I was dying, and I didn't want my children to remember me as a segment on *A Current Affair* entitled "Death Without Butter: Movies That Kill."

My last *film noir* was *The Hot Spot*, and like the other *noirs*, it takes place somewhere really arid, in a sort of bleached-out town completely populated by animal skulls and art directors. In this movie, Don Johnson plays the drifter, and he lives in a cheap motel room with a flashing neon sign right outside the window; sexy drifters always request that room. Don is broke, but his '40s-style wardrobe is always impeccably dry-cleaned; he gets a job as a used-car salesman and messes around with Virginia Madsen, who plays the steamy slut married to Don's boss, and also with Jennifer Connelly, who plays a beautiful, innocent girl working as an accountant. Eventually, Don robs a bank, Virginia gives her husband a heart attack by tying him to the bed and wearing lingerie, and Jennifer snatches the Olympic honors from Rachel Ward without even trying. I read that Jennifer is currently enrolled at Yale, in the tradition of Jennifer Beals and of Brooke Shields, who went to Princeton. Jennifer, you're a knockout, but get that degree.

Virginia is naked a lot in this movie; at one point, she and Don are tussling in the moonlight out at a sawmill, and she jumps into a huge hill of wood chips. Then she climbs the hill while the camera shoots her from underneath and behind; she grabs Don, and they fall into the sawdust and make churning, passionate love. Doing it in sawdust does not strike me as particularly erotic; it would be like having sex in the salad bar at Sizzler—everything would stick to you and itch. Don keeps unveiling his naked behind, as if it were an engagement ring from Fortunoff's; after about the fourth rear display, I began to wonder if Don even *had* a penis. Then I remembered that Pamela Des Barres, a famous groupie, wrote in her autobiography about how well endowed Don is—Don, she didn't write about how pink and hefty your tush is, if you catch my drift. If Virginia is going to risk a sawdust infection, or even Dutch elm disease, the least you can do is swivel.

Since I couldn't figure out why people like *film noir,* I tried to put myself, Libby, in a *film noir* situation. I pictured myself lounging between my Wamsutta percales while my husband, Josh, was out correcting overbites; I imagined that I was listless and in heat. If a drifter came to my door, I decided that the first thing I would do would be to send him out to wait on line for tickets to *Miss Saigon.* Then I would make him finish college or get some sort of vocational training, since I couldn't very well introduce him to people by saying, This is so-and-so, you'll love him, he's a drifter. Then, if he still tried to entice me into killing my husband or pulling a bank job, I would say, Excuse me, do you have any idea what it's like for a woman in prison? Listening to Jean Harris whine all day about her royalties? Discussing a possible appeal with Joel Steinberg at the prison mixer? Then, if by some mad chance the drifter did convince me to kill my husband, I'd just say, Let's wait a few years; Josh is an overweight Jewish man from a family with a history of prostate trouble—time is on our side. If the drifter wanted to have sweaty, wild sex with me while we waited, I would tell him just what I tell my adorable seven-year-old daughter, Jennifer, whenever she wants the latest thing from L.A. Gear: if you still want it a year from now, then we'll see.

Maybe I'm just not a *noir* type of person; I think that lust and destiny and doom sound like home-shopping-club colognes. *Film noir* is like Jerry Lewis: it's something French people only pretend to like in order to upset Americans. Maybe to get back at them, we should all pretend to like Isabelle Huppert movies and that new glass pyramid in front of the Louvre. That'll fix 'em, if you ask me.

I have been wondering why there are so many gangster movies around right now; my dear friend, the still tragically single Stacy Schiff, says that Hollywood just likes to save money on actresses. These movies usually have only one woman character, and they're always directed by nice, nerdy boys. The first gangster film I saw this month was *GoodFellas,* which was directed by Martin Scorsese, who was an asthmatic child and then went to New York University's film school. If gangsters were the ones directing the movies, would they be about a bunch of film students with pocket protectors having shoot-outs at a revival house over whether John Ford is better than Howard Hawks? Would Robert De Niro start playing really intense cinematographers?

GoodFellas is based on the book *Wiseguy,* which is a true story about a mobster, but the title was already being used by that TV show that once starred Ken Wahl, who is dreamy beyond belief, even if he's getting a little chunky for blue jeans. Ray Liotta plays the main gangster in *GoodFellas,* and his Mob friends are played by De Niro and Joe Pesci, and all they do is drive flashy cars, steal payrolls, and shoot clumsy waiters, which certainly beats leaving only a 5 percent tip. Lorraine Bracco plays a Jewish girl who marries Ray; on the soundtrack, Lorraine says that she was turned on when he let her hold his gun. To research this, Stacy and I went to a local sporting-goods store and asked to see something attractive in a small pistol. The clerk let us hold several models, and I must confess, Lorraine has a point. All of a sudden, I felt like I would have no problem getting my children to sit up straight. I pictured myself pointing my piece at a Zabar's salesclerk and saying, I know you're only up to number 32, and I'm number 86, but I have people coming over for Sunday brunch, and I need that lox *now*.

Stacy said that with her rod, she could probably find a nice cardiologist to marry her within 45 minutes; if the subject of prenuptial agreements came up, she would just take off the safety catch, aim the barrel somewhere below her fiancé's waist, and say, But darling, I love you so much, please don't spoil it. Stacy and I agreed that women would make much better gangsters, because instead of dealing in heroin and prostitution, we would just force Isaac Mizrahi to stop designing those cat suits that make women look like they forgot their skirts and can never go to the bathroom. We would also demand protection money from any woman with visible abdominal muscles, and from anyone who has ever said, I wish I could *gain* weight. We would take out contracts on Marla Maples, Judge Souter (if he doesn't behave), and maybe on Barbara Bush's dog Millie, because the concept of a First Pet with a book on the best-seller list is almost as annoying as Kitty Dukakis's tell-all; maybe in a few years, Millie can write another book about her problems with Milkbone dependency and rubber-hydrant abuse.

Stacy and I decided that our Mob would be organized around Stretch 'N' Tone aerobics classes instead of crime families. Instead of doing leg lifts, the women could discuss muscling in on any manufacturer that uses the word "Lite" on its packaging when the product is still loaded with sodium and tastes like a sponge. The woman in each class with the flabbiest inner thighs would get to be the don, or even the donna; she would be respected and feared, and any woman who crossed her would be forced to put on ankle weights and do a hundred low-impact lunges to reggae music. In *GoodFellas*, a lifetime mobster becomes a "made man" in some sort of mysterious ceremony; in the women's Mob, a member would join the inner circle after letting everyone criticize her personality for ten minutes. Eventually there would be violent feuds between rival Abs, Thighs, and Buns classes, and women would be found hanging from meat hooks in floral garment bags and at the bottom of the

East River, their feet encased in cement and those pumps that are supposed to feel like sneakers. Rival donnas would be shot in cold blood, execution-style, their corpses slumped over salads, their Filofaxes still open, their lip liner ruined.

Stacy and I started feeling very powerful, as if we were about to appear before a Senate subcommittee and claim we knew nothing about the unexplained disappearances of Lynn Redgrave, Jenny Craig, and that woman on TV who claims you can get rid of your cellulite by taking seaweed pills and stimulating the backs of your thighs with a hairbrush. We went to see *Miller's Crossing*, which is a gangster movie directed and cowritten by Joel Coen and produced and cowritten by his brother, Ethan; I think the Coens also went to film school, because in their photographs, they look like chess champions, the kind who wear ski pajamas and build forts with their mashed potatoes. Neither Stacy nor I could really follow *Miller's Crossing*; it seemed to be about gangsters in the '30s rubbing out one another and wearing hats. There was also a lot of art direction in this movie; whenever an actor sat next to an antique lamp, I thought he was about to start an affair.

There's a lot of gangster slang as well; the characters have nicknames like "Mink" and "The Dane," and they say things like What's the rumpus? and You treated me high-hat. Stacy and I decided that our Mob would need lingo, too; when Stacy and I see each other on the treadmill, we now say, Where's the blubber? and Don't treat me high-carbs. My Mob nickname is "Control Top," and I call Stacy "No Dressing"; my husband, Josh, is "Love Handles," and my mother is "The Nudge."

Stacy and I almost went to see *State of Grace*, which is about Irish gangsters in Hell's Kitchen, but we decided that our Mob would never operate in bad neighborhoods; our motto would be "Crime and Croissants," and we would always need a getaway cab. We almost decided to go see the new Steven Seagal movie, *Marked for Death*, but Steven insists that his name is pronounced suh-*gahl* instead of the Jewish way, so Stacy and I decided that a boycott was in order. Steven is married to Kelly LeBrock, the model who was in those Pantene ads in which she said, Don't hate me because I'm beautiful; Stacy and I decided that our Mob might have to force Kelly to drink some Vidal Sassoon Finishing Rinse. Steven also has a very long ponytail, which makes him look like a really mean prep-school girl with a field-hockey stick behind her back; I think Steven and Kelly may ultimately need marriage counseling from Brigitte Nielsen.

I called my therapist, Dr. Arlene Cole-Natbaum, and asked her if America's fascination with criminals indicates a deviant national psyche, and she said no, she's much more worried about America's fascination with watching little children lose their pants on those home-video shows. She said most convicted felons are just people who were not taken to museums or Broadway musicals as children; she said most of the murderers on death row have never owned a copy of *Peter and the Wolf.* She also said that watching gangster movies provides a healthy outlet for men who would otherwise be tempted to do Marlon Brando impressions by stuffing their cheeks with hamburger rolls at barbecues.

Finally, Stacy and I went to see *Postcards From the Edge,* which is a delightful film that stars Meryl Streep and Shirley MacLaine and was adapted from Carrie Fisher's novel about being a drug-addicted actress in Hollywood. Stacy and I decided to make Meryl, Shirley, and Carrie all honorary members of our ladies' Mob. This movie is sort of about not using dope and about mothers and daughters, but mostly it's about movie stars having fun not playing gangsters. It was directed by Mike Nichols, who is married to Diane Sawyer; Stacy and I decided that Mike and Diane are so famous and so perfect that they probably make love by exchanging autographs. Diane interviewed Baryshnikov on *PrimeTime Live* recently while sipping champagne in a Venetian gondola; she's not exactly Dan Rather in Beirut.

Sometimes Meryl can get a little Diane-ish, but in *Postcards,* she's adorable. She wears a Levi's jacket and even sings a country-and-western song, so it's like watching Queen Elizabeth get tipsy on wine coolers at a royal picnic. Meryl even gets to have love scenes with my spiritual fiancé, Dennis Quaid. This inspired me; if

Meryl, a 41-year-old mother of three, can smooch with Dennis with his shirt open, then there's hope for us all. Dennis is engaged to Meg Ryan in real life, so I may have to schedule a Malibu rubout. Dennis, you're my moll, so show some respect, if you ask me.

A BOY NAMED SIOUX

■ ■ ■ ■

I have often wondered what would have happened if, instead of having my own room with a canopy bed and a Snoopy phone in Great Neck, I had been kidnapped as a child by Indians and raised as a Sioux. Now, thanks to Kevin Costner's *Dances With Wolves*, I have my answer. In this three-hour cinematic epic, Mary McDonnell plays a white woman who was brought up in a tepee after her pioneer family was slaughtered and scalped. As a squaw, Mary behaves just the way I would: she wears stunning suede outfits trimmed with shells and Ralph Lauren–style Santa Fe fringe; she does her hair in a flattering shag look instead of too-severe tribal braids; and after her first husband dies, she holds out until a white movie star shows up. Mary is called Stands With a Fist because she once hit an Indian girl who gave her a hard time. In my high school yearbook, the Great Neck *Senior Serenade,* I was voted Best Accessories and Most Likely to Marry Within Her Faith, so the comparison is obvious.

In this movie, Kevin plays a Civil War hero and pacifist who moves out to the prairie alone and becomes an honorary Sioux, even without having read any Time-Life books on how the Indians were good guys. Kevin is also the director, and he told *Us* magazine that "this is a bonding film for all. You could put it anywhere in history—the Berlin Wall, Kuwait." At the film's Los Angeles premiere, Melissa Gilbert said that Kevin and his movie "gave me so much inspiration as an actress. We are not just meat puppets! We can do so much." Demi Moore said that she "came out to support Kevin tonight. I just finished producing my husband Bruce's new film. It is all a risk for me, carrying out a vision." Believe me, you don't want to know what Rosanna Arquette had to say. Someday I hope that a Sioux movie director-star will make a film about how he moved to Bel Air and befriended everyone at Kevin's premiere; it could be called *Dances With Low SAT Scores*.

Kevin brings a real Laurel Canyon sensibility to the plains; he directs like a man with a single earring, if you know what I mean. He teaches the Indians to say "Hi," smokes whatever is in their pipes, and lets his hair get long and bleached and blown-dry; when one of the braves gives him a ceremonial necklace, I expected Kevin to say "Cool." He grins and stumbles and faints a lot, so the tribe is bound to find him adorable; he's like Dick Van Dyke in the tall grass. All of the Indians are sweet and gentle and generous, except when they are attacked by a neighboring tribe and are forced to massacre them with hatchets, arrows, and Kevin's rifles. Kevin learns to speak Lakota, a Sioux language, and he sketches and writes in his journal about how the Indians are the only decent people he's ever met. Now, I'm sure that many Indians are just terrific, but Kevin gets a little Shirley MacLaine about everything; this movie is sort of like watching a Ken doll get to know the Care Bears. All of the white men except Kevin are evil soldiers; they shoot Kevin's horse and pet wolf and use the pages of his journal as toilet paper. This makes the audience cheer when Kevin and the Indians strangle the white guys with chains and drown them.

Kevin basically avoids the really tough questions about Sioux life. At one point, the Sioux holy man asks Kevin if he and Stands With a Fist are going to try for a baby right away—did the Sioux make rawhide diaphragms? And while we're at it, what did the Indians use for toilet paper, anyway, not to mention roll-on and cologne? Whenever I see a western, all I really think is, I'm glad it's a movie, because I bet that until the turn of the century, when Johnson & Johnson arrived, the world was pretty gamy.

Sometimes I wonder what my life would be like if I just picked up and moved to the Middle East and became the sex slave of Saddam Hussein; that is just what happens to Debra Winger in *The Sheltering Sky*. This movie is based on a famous novel by Paul Bowles, but the book is one of those flat trade paperbacks instead of the nice, chunky supermarket type, so I don't trust it. Debra and John Malkovich play a bored, rich couple named Kit and Port, which sounds like a rap group; they go to the Sahara looking for an answer to their spiritual ennui. Eventually, they both expose their pubic hair and wear many neatly pressed outfits, even when they're sleeping on dirt floors in foreign-legion outposts. John is a very odd actor; he's like a transvestite who is too lazy to pull on her gown, so he just pouts and slinks around in his underwear. Eventually John dies of typhoid, and Debra behaves like any well-adjusted widow; after a decent interval, she decides to get out of her shell and meet someone new. Of course, in Debra's case, the interval is about fifteen minutes, after which she runs into the desert, hitches a ride with a caravan, and joins the harem of a Tuareg chieftain in a turban. I'm curious about life in a harem, although the movie is not very clear about it—is everything scheduled, like, If it's Tuesday, you must be Fatima? Eventually Debra leaves the harem and wanders around aimlessly, and the movie ends; when the lights went up, everyone in the theater turned to the person next to them and asked, What time is it?

The Sheltering Sky is about existential issues, like Why Are We Here? And What Is the Meaning of Life? and If There's a God, Why Does He Let Movies About Ennui Go On for More Than Two Hours? As my own mother, the beloved Sondra Krell-Gelman, would say, You've got ennui? I'll give you ennui—leave me alone, get a job. And yet, once in a while, I too feel a spiritual emptiness, and I too take a journey, usually to the aisle at Gristede's marked COOKIES, CRAX, AND SNAX. Mallomars, I have found, hold most of your larger answers: the plain vanilla wafer part represents arid suffering; on top of that is fluffy white marshmallow, which represents mankind's attempt at creating an artificial happiness to cover pain; it's all sheltered by a coating of pure chocolate, which of course represents love. Some claim that the coating also represents God, but I think of Him as more of a Drake's Yodel, the only perfect food. It's all there, right in the cookie, although despair is never far off because, of course, sometimes Gristede's is closed, and then you have to go into the desert and join a harem, or at least check out whether area rugs are really cheaper in Algeria once you factor in shipping and customs.

Edward Scissorhands is another fable about the human spirit. Edward is a boy who was created by a kindly old man in a castle who gave him shears for hands and died before replacing them with fingers or a less dangerous utensil. An Avon Lady finds Edward and takes him to live in suburbia, where all the housewives are nice to him; Edward falls in love with a blond cheerleader but can't touch her without slicing. Eventually the town turns on Edward and chases him back up to the castle because he's too sweet and innocent to live among creepy human beings who do terrible things like wear stretch pants and want to have sex instead of just hug.

Some people say that this film is an allegory about Jesus or the role of the artist in society. Jesus, if you ask me, actually had something on his mind besides hedge clipping, and I don't remember anyone chasing Picasso, or Warhol, or even Tim Burton, who conceived and directed this movie, back up to his castle. Tim also directed *Beetlejuice* and *Batman;* I've noticed that after a director earns his first $50 million, he usually makes a movie about how tough it is to be a sensitive soul. In real life, people are nasty to black people and gay people and people in wheelchairs, but Tim is only worried about the guys with big eyes and scissors popping out of their elbows. It's really an issue for our times. No one ever suggests that Edward get a pair of really big gloves; no one even X-rays him to see what the kindly old man used as ingredients, aside from Cabbage Patch dolls and videocassettes of *Rain Man.*

All Edward really needs is to meet Kevin Costner, who would befriend him and help him kill all the bad people. Eventually Kevin would glue a manicure kit to his own hands out of empathy and call himself Dances With Band-Aids. And then maybe Edward could date Debra Winger, and she'd ask him for spiritual answers—if she's willing to have sex with John Malkovich on Algerian gravel, then she's up for anything. Let's bring back Pinocchio; at least he sang and danced and didn't represent anything. Life is hard enough without movie directors thinking about life all the time; they could hurt themselves, if you ask me.

LETTERS TO LIBBY

— — —

At least once each year in my column, I like to share the mail I receive from my many devoted fans worldwide; I am always touched that so many readers take the time to drop me a note in between their electroshock sessions and parole-board hearings. This year there was much controversy surrounding my comments on Mickey Rourke's work in the Brazilian sexfest *Wild Orchid;* Jillian F. Schneider of Mount Prospect, Illinois, was offended by my claim that Mickey hasn't showered since his career began: "I feel sorry for Libby that she is so blind to his charisma. I go to all his movies, whether the plot sounds interesting or not." Others were less upset; Lavinia Fitzpatrick of Azusa, California, feels that "Mickey Rourke should go down in history books as the most unclean person in the United States. I agree with Libby—someone needs to get the man some SOAP!"

Rebecca Dubroski of Hazleton, Pennsylvania, was angered by my remarks on film and TV *noir;* she says, "I am glad that, unlike Libby, I can be bored enough to watch every episode of *Twin Peaks* at least four or five times. I only wish I could get my hands on a copy of the foreign version, so I could be bored even more." Patty Hinkson of Las Vegas, Nevada, was rattled by both my and *Premiere's* treatment of *Ghost.* She writes, "Obviously, none of the staff have ever known the love of a soul mate. I'm disappointed in all of you, BUT my belief in the moviegoing public has been restored. We saw it! We shared it! We saw couples in the audience holding each other—imagine that! We saw strangers feeling together, and we drowned ourselves in tears of love. And when we left the theater, we were all holding hands with the person we had come in with."

Patty, I'm glad that you liked *Ghost*, but—take my word on this—try to avoid those midtown theaters with the strangers feeling together.

Sometimes it can seem that, as John Umpherville of Toronto perceptively notes, "being a film critic must be a thankless job." Eric Levy of Trumbull, Connecticut, took a moment to say, "I have put up with your column long enough. You have the nerve to call yourself a journalist, and yet you find something rude and offensive to say about everything." Jennifer Banbury of New York City declares, "Reading Ms. Gelman-Waxner's column has become akin to listening to commentary from a popular junior high school girl who wears Guess? jeans and believes there will never be a movie as good as *Grease 2*. I realize that *Premiere* is no *Cahiers du cinéma* (nor would I want it to be), but surely Ms. Gelman-Waxner could benefit from reading François Truffaut's compilation of his own film reviews, *The Films in My Life*. It seems to me that Ms. Gelman-Waxner could be using her talents more appropriately on the staff of *Tiger Beat*." And all that from a Jennifer.

Tammy Denotter of Oskaloosa, Iowa, objects to my statement that "lawyers are bold and necessary—someone has to defend plastic surgeons." "I am in law school," Tammy says, "and know that's just poor taste on Libby's part." Tammy refers to my "full-of-garbage opinions" and goes on to fearlessly state, "I am also a Republican, and I'm proud of my values." Tammy, have I got a guy for you: Rob Stover of West Vancouver, British Columbia, who writes that "a couple of weeks ago, my young Shetland sheepdog began to choke on some food. I took drastic action immediately and showed her one of Libby's 'witty' articles. My puppy promptly vomited upon seeing it." And do I get a thank-you for saving a life? Peter Bishop of Arlington, Virginia, concludes that "Libby Gelman-Waxner should be fired. I found her blatant prejudice unconscionable. Characterizing Christian men or any group of people as wife-beating alcoholics who have cheap affairs is malicious."

First of all, let me say that Christian men are swell, and if you don't believe me, just ask Jessica Hahn. And second of all, I wish that Tammy Denotter could chat with someone like the handsome, open-minded Jeff Lane of Louisville, Kentucky, who writes, "You must be the finest creature walking upright on the face of the Earth. You are also one of the nicest wives I have ever read about. That Josh is one lucky plump little tooth straightener to have a woman of your caliber." Donna Acerra, one of the brightest and, I'm sure, most popular women in Bethlehem, Pennsylvania, asks, "Is it possible to devote an entire issue to Libby's observations?" The most stunning and articulate citizen of Davenport, Iowa, Barbara Zoeckler-Nelson, says, "If I never read one other thing in *Premiere*, her column would be the one I would turn to. I literally fall on the floor—not from a standing position, but from the couch—whenever I read her reviews. After all, I'm 65 and have to be careful about low calcium deposits." Nick Hart, obviously the most respected and admired resident of Houston, adds that "since I've found Libby, the mail cannot be delivered fast enough." Perhaps Jennifer B. Cunningham, widely regarded as the most perfect human being in all of Chicago, says it best when she writes, "Before I even take off my coat, I have to read Libby. Her wit, style, and sincere admiration of Mel Gibson's physique are the cornerstone of your magazine."

Of course, like any film critic dedicated to rewarding excellence in the cinematic arts, I especially appreciate the letters with sexual overtones. Leonard W. Dick of Boston is "particularly interested in the plight of your friend Stacy Schiff. I believe I might be able to set her up with a man I think Stacy will enjoy meeting. That man is I." Leonard is "a graduating M.B.A. from Harvard Business School"; he also attended Harvard College, he's worked for Morgan Stanley on Wall Street—"and I'm Jewish." Leonard "would love to take Stacy to dinner" and predicts that "maybe something good will happen and you will march at our wedding." Leonard, much as I'd love to, I cannot pass your letter along to Stacy; as a single career woman over 30, she is very fragile, and I am afraid that your credentials alone might cause a stroke or seizure—if not in Stacy, then in her mother, who now considers Stacy's volunteer work with the homeless to be a mixer situation. I'm afraid I must also discourage Óscar Rollón of Madrid, who read the column guest-written by my adorable seven-year-old daughter, Jennifer, and "fell in love with her." At nineteen, Óscar feels "a little old for her, but I can wait, and we all know that age is not important, love is important. If you say no, I won't insist. I would have a lifetime of heartache, though. I probably would become a priest and go to South America and fight against the drug smugglers." Óscar, you're an international sweetheart, but Jennifer won't start dating until late next year, and we need you in Colombia, busting those cartels.

As for me, Libby, my dream pen pals include Steve Kobb of Houston, who sent me a photo of himself working out in a homemade Libby Gelman-Waxner T-shirt that his wife gave him. Steve, it's a shame we're both happily married, but as Elizabeth Taylor or Zsa Zsa or my aunt Florence—who just buried husband number three and is off on a Seniors Ahoy cruise to Saint Martin—might say, You never know. For the time being, I'll just keep rereading my letter from Patrick McSparin of Tyndall, Florida, who claims, "I am writing to tell you that I want you more than anything in the world." Patrick cites "your perfect eyes, perfect hair, perfect teeth . . . and that body!" I do not find these comments sexist, as Patrick also yearns for "your mind . . . your rapier wit. . . ." Patrick is an enlisted man in the Air Force and knows that he'll "just have to live with the fact that you will never be mine." Patrick, every time I see an airplane, or even an article on the Pan Am bankruptcy, I'm going to think of you. Maybe you can find comfort in the words of Alison Jones of Greenwich, Connecticut, and her friend Alicia Gordon, who have come to see that "true happiness comes from hard work, a low-fat, high-carb diet, and racy Lily of France bras with a good underwire." As Alison and Alicia sum it all up: "Life is too short not to be like Libby." I love all my loyal readers and lonely servicemen everywhere; I'm just an esteemed film critic, a provocative contemporary philosopher, and a USO canteen, if you ask me.

THE LIBBY AWARDS
— — — —

This year's Libby Awards are being televised for the first time ever—as I write this, my husband, Josh, is circling me with his brand-new video camcorder, and if he does not stop televising me very soon, I may be forced to videotape him playing with his spare tire while he watches *Nightline;* I don't think Ted Koppel ever imagines that people hide pretzels in the folds of their skin while watching a debate on Lithuania. Despite all the turmoil in the world today, cinematic excellence and good taste must be recognized and rewarded; and so here now, the Libbys. And Josh, I'm warning you: do not shoot my upper arms, if you know what's good for you.

The Classical Gas Libby goes to Glenn Close for her role in the filmed version of *Hamlet.* Glenn plays Mel Gibson's mom, and her whole performance is devoted to showing what a wild young tamale she is. She runs around the castle in low-cut gowns and soul kisses Mel every chance she gets; she's like the Queen on a Hot Tin Roof. Glenn's hair also changes length from scene to scene; sometimes she has twelve-foot-long braids, and then all of a sudden, it's a Pre-Raphaelite shag. I think Glenn based her performance on Cher's "If I Could Turn Back Time" video, the one where she's basically just wearing panty hose and bumping hips with her thirteen-year-old son, Elijah Blue, while a battleship full of sailors cheers her. Glenn shows us that not only can Shakespeare be sexy, he can even be zany. Josh, go point that thing at the kids, so we can cherish those precious moments of their childhood while you were still alive.

The War Is Hype Libby goes to Sally Field, the woman for whom all awards were invented. Sally plays Betty Mahmoody in *Not With-*

out My Daughter, a film based on a true story; Betty is an American woman who marries a nutty Iranian who takes her back to Iran and tries to get her into a chador. Eventually she is forced to kidnap her own child and head for the border. The ads for this movie showed Sally hefting her daughter around like a sack of potatoes or an oversize Academy Award; after the war in the Gulf began, there was an item in *The New York Times'* Chronicle column reporting that Sally had been forced to hire bodyguards because of death threats. My question is this: Who told the Chronicle column? I'm not suggesting that Sally's publicist called in the tidbit to capitalize on global unrest, but let me put it this way—just for playing someone named Betty Mahmoody, Sally's earned her Libby. Josh, in just 30 seconds, I'm going to get very angry and aim that thing at your ankles, so everyone can see how wearing cheap nylon socks wears off your leg hairs.

The Dead Is Better Libby goes to a trio of films—*Ghost, Flatliners,* and *Jacob's Ladder*—all of which make death seem almost as glamorous as the prostitution in *Pretty Woman.* In *Ghost,* Patrick Swayze achieves magical powers after being shot and killed; in *Flatliners,* a group of medical students kill one another with injections in order to explore death and then are revived, I assume, to get a movie deal. *Flatliners* is the kind of film in which the young doctors are played mostly by gorgeous actors who clearly had trouble with high school; Julia Roberts becomes a surgeon-of-tomorrow by wearing eyeglasses. After death, these kids discover, you confront the evil things you did in life; this does not bode well for Joel Schumacher, the film's director, who was also responsible for *St. Elmo's Fire* and *The Lost Boys. Jacob's Ladder* takes place in the mind of a dying soldier in Vietnam; the soldier hallucinates about the forces of good, which are symbolized by his Waspy wife and towheaded children, and the forces of evil, which are represented by a sexy Latin spitfire who works at the post office. Eventually the soldier dies, but he gets led up to heaven by Macaulay Culkin, the star of *Home Alone;* Macaulay's grosses make him a natural choice for the role of God. And while we're at it, I'd also like to award a Libby to all the articles in newspapers and magazines that discussed the success of *Pretty Woman* and *Ghost;* these articles usually concluded that Hollywood's action/adventure cycle is over, and that these new hits appeal to the female audience's desire for romance. I agree that *Ghost* and *Pretty Woman* embody common female fantasies; at one time or another, every woman dreams of being a hooker who marries a millionaire, or of being a woman whose husband is dead. While Josh is not dead, he probably wishes he were; right now I'm videotaping his closet, especially the stack of *Sports Illustrated* swimsuit issues that is hidden underneath the revolting pair of ancient Jockey shorts he uses to blow his nose when he can't find a handkerchief or a Kleenex.

This year's *Bedside Bonanza Libby* goes to *Awakenings*. This Libby is awarded annually to the work that takes a terrible if gimmicky illness and uses it as a metaphor for remembering to smell the roses. Just as Dustin Hoffman's autism helped Tom Cruise mature in *Rain Man*, Robert De Niro's sleeping sickness in *Awakenings* helps Robin Williams decide to come out of his shell and date nurses. Somehow I don't think chronically ill people really want to be used as wakeup calls for the rest of us, or as Oscar opportunities; it's bad enough to be sick without having to cope with endless visits from celebrities who want to imitate you in soft-focus. Robin is getting so huggable that pretty soon the only roles open to him will be Santa, the Easter Bunny, and Winnie-the-Pooh; he's turning into a telethon for himself. Actually, Robin looks a little like Josh, whom I'm now taping on his hands and knees, begging me not to record the waist size on the tag of his Levi's for all posterity to see.

Finally we come to my annual *Film Criminal* award, given to the person whose cinematic achievement should actually be punishable by a prison term or assignment of community service. This year's Film Criminal is not a single individual but a film—*Once Around*. This movie is about how warm and wonderful and crazy family life and love can be, and it basically proves that Lizzie Borden was right. Holly Hunter plays a spunky, feisty, childlike single woman whose only ambition is to get married; as my still tragically single friend Stacy Schiff noted after watching Holly's performance, At least *I* have a cat. I have this recurring dream in which I'm in a movie theater watching Holly play the daughter of Sally Field and Robin Williams in a warm, human comedy entitled

Meet the Munchkins. In it, Holly's love interest is played by her partner in *Once Around*—Richard Dreyfuss, a fellow who can twinkle and cavort and love life as well as any Gummi Bear. *Once Around* was cowritten by Malia Scotch Marmo; somehow I feel that Malia may well be an ideal mate for Phil Alden Robinson, who directed *Field of Dreams*, or maybe Bruce Joel Rubin, the corpse-loving screenwriter of both *Ghost* and *Jacob's Ladder*. I would recount the plot of *Once Around*, but we are at war and Pepto-Bismol may soon be rationed; let's just say that the movie gives human emotions a very bad name, and that at one point Richard screens home movies on Holly's pregnant stomach. Instead of renting *Once Around* after it is cleared for video release by the American Dental Association, you should ask for my own effort, *Josh Waxner: The Man and His Toenail Clippers*, which will be available very soon. While I have enjoyed my afternoon of videotaping, I enjoyed awarding the Libbys even more; next year they'll go network, if you ask me.

LAMB CHOPS

▬ ▬ ▬

There are so many reasons why I will never go to see *The Silence of the Lambs*. First of all, just from reading the reviews, I already have to sleep with a nightlight. I even had my dear friend Stacy Schiff see the movie and tell me where every bit of suspense and terror is located, and I'm still too petrified to go. Second, the movie is about the hunt for a serial killer who skins his victims and then makes himself an outfit out of their flesh, and as an assistant buyer of junior activewear, I just don't see this as the spring line, hanging on a rack beside the new neon florals, if you catch my drift. And finally, the movie has become the subject of political controversy, since gay activists claim that the killer is portrayed specifically as a gay maniac.

In order to get clear on the issue, I called my cousin Andrew, the art director who lives in the Village with his friend Robert, who is also an art director; they have been together for almost ten years, and you should see the kitchen equipment. Their apartment is so gorgeous, I'm afraid to touch anything in it; it's like a museum of perfect taste, from the track lighting focused on the African tribal masks to the collection of American folk art, including a Pennsylvania Dutch weather vane that they recently purchased at an auction for $11,000. The weather vane is mounted on a plain white pedestal set against a stark white wall, right next to a framed label from a Depression-era orange crate. While I love the weather vane, I do sometimes wonder what the Amish farmer who bought it one hundred years ago at a hardware store would think of Andrew and Robert's collection of more than three hundred souvenir salt and pepper shakers and that Mapplethorpe photo hanging in the foyer of the two fellows peeing on each other. I'm crazy about Andrew's place, but whenever I bring my adorable seven-year-old daughter, Jennifer, to visit, I have to warn her: Don't take the Barbie doll out of the display case—she's vintage and, according to Andrew, one of the few remaining sun-and-surf Barbies (with the accompanying beach thongs, visor, and raffia tote) still in private hands.

Anyway, I asked Andrew about *The Silence of the Lambs,* and he says it is annoying when serial killers are portrayed as demented transvestites or gay, since the vast majority of such criminals are straight. Andrew and I decided that perhaps serial killers need to form some sort of antidefamation league or support group to correct their image. Andrew says movies are very powerful, and that *The Silence of the Lambs* could lead to more homophobia; I said it could also lead to more bad dreams, jitters, and clogged sidewalks when both the 8:30 and the 10 o'clock shows are completely sold out.

Andrew and I decided to boycott the film, along with carob chocolate, any TV movie based on a real-life small-town love triangle/murder, and all Sinéad O'Connor interviews; Andrew says the people with taste must make their voices heard. To celebrate our new movement, we spray-painted TASTE NOW and FREE IVANA'S TOPKNOT on the sidewalks in front of Trump Tower and then went to see *Scenes from a Mall.* I thought this would be a perfect movie because it was directed by Paul Mazursky, stars Woody Allen and Bette Midler, and is set in a shopping mall; I thought, If only this film could help me lose fifteen pounds, it would be the ultimate human experience. I'm sad to report I was wrong; *Scenes from a Mall* is like a comedy with the jokes snipped out. It's not really serious, but it's not anything else, either; it's just sort of lazy. Woody and Bette play an upwardly mobile two-career L.A. couple; they're basically like me and my husband, Josh, if we had wardrobe and makeup people. Andrew says the problem with the movie is that Bette is a great actress and, as an actor, Woody can only do his one shtick.

Andrew and I considered going to see *He Said, She Said,* which is a movie about a love affair told from both the man's and the woman's point of view, with a male and a female director each in charge of the appropriate half. I decided that the basic idea of this movie was sexist, since it assumes that your gender determines how you will behave; Andrew said he wished there was a gay version called *He Said, He Said*. We both agreed to go see *L.A. Story* instead. Steve Martin wrote and stars in this film, and it's mostly delightful. Andrew decided that Steve is a true dream date, because he's romantic without congratulating himself about it; he just likes to dance around and have a great time—he's like the antidote to Woody.

The last film Andrew and I saw was *The Grifters*, which we loved. Everyone in this movie is a small-time criminal; the stars are Anjelica Huston and Annette Bening, and it's nice to see women getting a chance to play felons for a change, just like Robert De Niro and Joe Pesci. I always love those TV documentaries on female criminals, the ones called things like *Bad Girls* and *Women Who Kill*; personally, I think that when a woman kills her husband or child, the courts must always ask, Right before the incident, was she trying to make dinner? Was the murder victim asking why the family was out of milk? Had the woman involved been forced to take public transportation?

In *The Grifters*, Anjelica plays the sexy mother of John Cusack, who's also a crook; as my mom says, Monkey see, monkey do. Since Anjelica ultimately robs her son and worse, she cannot technically be considered a good role model, but I empathized with her; children are so demanding, and they never understand that sometimes Mommy can't make Kool-Aid freezer pops because she has to bleach her hair, put on a tight skirt, and head for the racetrack to skim Mafia profits. Cub Scouts and prison terms, homeroom cupcakes and stolen cars—it's always a balancing act. I salute this film for portraying the double bind of the working mom; someday I hope that serial killers will receive the same sympathetic treatment in the cinema. Progress is so slow in Hollywood, but we shall overcome, if you ask me.

SEX, DRUGS, AND EXTRA-STRENGTH EXCEDRIN

— — — —

Personally, I think it's interesting that while there haven't been any wide-screen cinematic biographies of Socrates or Proust or Mother Teresa, we now have a multimillion-dollar film on the life of Jim Morrison, the lead singer of the Doors. Jim lived to be twenty-seven, and he made a few albums that you can still buy if you're really at loose ends. Director Oliver Stone's movie *The Doors* is basically *Jim: The Life of an Alcoholic Moron.* Jim starts out in film school with a befuddled expression and corduroy pants and sideburns; after a few more scenes, he begins wearing leather pants and becomes a drunken, abusive star. For the rest of the movie, every scene is identical: Jim looks dazed, swigs from a bottle of whiskey, and mumbles or lip-synchs. If you ask me, Jim's underlying appeal is very simple: he was pretty, he lived in the '60s, and he died. With this as a guideline, I predict that some day, once nature takes its course, we can look forward to movie biographies of Priscilla Presley and Keith Partridge.

Oliver Stone, who also cowrote *The Doors,* may very well be America's favorite kind of person: the talent-impaired genius. This means each of his films, such as *Platoon* and *Born on the Fourth of July,* is an Important Statement From a Major Artist; this also means that most of his films are loud and endless and that everyone in the audience gets a migraine after the first twenty minutes. In *The Doors,* Oliver wants to create an ecstatic Dionysian frenzy, which means the camera spins around a lot and the actors look like frightened deer, because no one's told them exactly how to act Dionysian and frenzied. Meg Ryan plays Jim's heroin-addicted girlfriend, and she keeps grinning and saying things like Jim Morrison, you get back in here, or Jim Morrison, you can't fool me. I don't blame Meg, but after a while she starts to sound like Harriet Nelson calling the boys for dinner—Ricky Nelson, you get in the house this minute! Put down that syringe!

Meg is also forced to discover Jim's dead body in a Paris hotel room while she's wearing a terrible '60s wig with bangs. *The Doors* is a tribute to bad wigs; Kyle MacLachlan, as another band member, gets to wear at least three different strawberry-blond bath mats on his head. At one point, Jim takes the band into the desert for some sort of mystical drug experience, during which he sees many meaningfully wrinkled Indians in buckskins and war paint. Later, while Jim is being Dionysian onstage at a concert, these Indians reappear as fantasy figures, dancing beside him and the many bare-breasted women who run up from the crowd. The Indians serve the same function they did in *Dances With Wolves:* they make the far more highly paid white movie stars seem soulful and important and in touch with ancient truths. Do Indians enjoy being used this way, as spiritual elves or cosmic merit badges? Has Oliver ever met any Indians outside of Frontierland in Disney World?

To Oliver, the '60s were a period of wild sexuality and orgiastic freedom; he's the Hugh Hefner of directors. If you ask me, the '60s were about two things: Paul McCartney, the cute Beatle, and Goldie Hawn doing the frug in a bikini with peace symbols painted on her tummy on *Laugh-In.* I was very little during the '60s, but I remember my older sister Shelley, now twice divorced and an executive vice president in creative concepts at Worldwide Foods, having a terrible fight with my mother over whether John Lennon had shamed his family and all of Liverpool with that haircut. Shelley's first husband was Ira Hirsh, whom she met while they were both seniors at Columbia; Shelley and Ira then moved to a commune in New Hampshire for two years and had a child, Serenity Raga Hirsh. At the time, Ira was a member of the Weather Underground, and he brought Bobby Seale to my cousin Andrew's bar mitzvah and demanded that all of Andrew's Cross Pen and Pencil gift sets be returned to the people. Ira also disrupted the hora during the reception and remolded the chopped-liver swan on the buffet into a clenched fist—it was still quite tasty.

Shelley and Ira divorced after Ira wanted to swap Shelley for Cindy Klausner, the woman who ran the commune's continental-breakfast outreach program, which distributed cappuccino, a choice of brioche or elderberry muffin, and a fabric napkin to the only welfare family in town. Shelley did not want to have sex with Milton Klausner, Cindy's husband, who was also the commune's landscape architect (the commune, one of the very few to be housed in a Georgian-style garden apartment complex, was called the Moonrise Unity Whole Planet Countercollective: An Alternative Lifestyle With Underground Parking and Storage). The commune fell apart after a group acid trip, during which Shelley saw God in the form of a white wicker hamper with a matching Kleenex dispenser; Shelley says that these coordinated bathroom accessories told her that the '60s were over and that business school was Zen Buddhism plus security.

Shelley got custody of Serenity, who demanded to be renamed Allison once she started first grade at Dalton. Shelley's second husband was Carp Carlisle III, by whom she had a son, Carp IV. Carp is an old family nickname—it's short for Carpenter; you can imagine how much all of this pleased my mother, who still refers to Carp III as Satan in Deck Shoes. Carp III was an investment banker who secretly wanted to write show tunes; his dream was to compose music and lyrics for a musical comedy about the history of golf, entitled *Teed Off!* The score, when it was completed, included such numbers as "Nine Holes in My Heart," "A Country Club for Two (and Their Descendants)," and "Over You, Under Par." Shelley played that last song for the judge at the divorce hearing, which led to a settlement that my mother says almost justifies the anguish she continues to suffer over having a grandchild who sings "The Little Drummer Boy" and calls her Grandmum. Shelley's new career at Worldwide Foods is booming; she's currently test-marketing International Gums, a group of chewing gums inspired by the palates of many lands, including Hot Curry flavor from India, Sugarless Toffee from England, and Bubble Rice Bran from Japan.

Clearly, Shelley has learned from the '60s in a way that Oliver Stone has not. The point is to keep moving, as Shelley always says. I understand that Oliver's next film is about the Kennedy assassination; what's after that, Ollie—the Judy Carne story? A searching look at both Herman and the Hermits? A savage inquiry into the death of Mama Cass? Though I worship at the shrine of auteur filmmaking, sometimes enough is enough, if you ask me.

LUNCHEON AT THE
WALDORF
━━ ━━ ━━

Recently I was nominated for one of the most esteemed and prestigious prizes in all of contemporary journalism, a National Magazine Award in the category of "Essays and Criticism"; prior to being nominated, I had never heard of these particular awards, but I was still profoundly grateful and honored. The awards, according to the brochure, "honor editorial excellence and encourage editorial vitality in magazines"; editorial vitality may be more of a cholesterol issue, but it's still an impressive goal. The awards are given by the American Society of Magazine Editors (ASME), and the presentation luncheon was held in the Grand Ballroom at the Waldorf-Astoria; I attended, and I was surprised to find myself the only nominee in a floor-length, strapless ice-blue satin gown, as inspired by the Oscar-night ensembles of Kim Basinger and Geena Davis.

The Waldorf is lovely, and the tulip-heavy centerpieces were springtime-perky, but, sadly, there was no orchestra and therefore no opening number or Best Song competition; there were also no paparazzi to besiege me, so I took out my Instamatic and annoyed all the people at the *Newsweek* and *McCall's* tables. I sat among my peers at the *Premiere* table, which was certainly the most dignified and well-mannered group; I shudder to think of the antics, not to mention the outfits, at the Condé Nast tables or those of *Progressive Farmer* and *American Baby*. I felt proud to represent my magazine, although I did have to scold one of our editors for tossing bits of her Parker House roll at the *New Republic* people, and I was forced to perform the Heimlich maneuver on a staff writer who had swallowed his Life Saver during the entrée. I resisted the Tiramisù, as I was fearful of a disfiguring dairy mustache during my acceptance speech; finally the awards presentation got under way, presided over by Osborn Elliot, a dashing professor from the Columbia School of Journalism, and Ruth Whitney, a woman who embodied her position as the editor-in-chief of *Glamour*.

The categories included such things as "Fiction," "Public Interest," and "General Excellence for 400,000 to 1 Million Circulation"; like any overexcited nominee, I paid no attention to these winners and had to be nudged by my editor as a reminder to applaud. All I could focus on was the Alexander Calder–designed statuette that each winner received; these trophies were shaped like abstract Swedish elephants, and I could just picture one of them on my coffee table, nestled beside the remote control, the *TV Guide*, and a box of Nilla wafers; the statuette would also make a marvelous jewelry caddy, if I moved it to my bedroom bureau. While I have always envied the People's Choice Awards crystal obelisk and the Emmy lamp base, it became clear to me that the ASME elephant was by far the most desirable electroplated *tchotchke* of all.

My category was near the end; my favorite earlier award went to *Family Circle* for an article entitled "Toxic Nightmare on Main Street," which had uncovered contamination dangers in Jacksonville, Arkansas. When this piece won, all the women at the *Family Circle* table leapt up and shrieked, as if they'd just won a collective Miss Congeniality ribbon or the color war at camp. The other winners were more low-key, with all the boy editors giving one another manly handshakes while discreetly stroking their elephants. At last, it was time for my category, and just as I had done so many times over the past weeks, I scanned the list of my fellow nominees and wished we could all be onstage together, clutching hands in swimsuits while Osborn Elliot asked each of us a Personality question.

The first nominee was David Rieff, who wrote an essay on sensitivity for *Esquire*; David is Susan Sontag's son, so I figured he didn't really need an award, because his mom has plenty. The next nominee was Robert Sherrill, who wrote about the savings-and-loan scandal for *The Nation*; I'm sure this was an excellent piece, but as my own mother supportively said, Would you read it? Lance Morrow was nominated for three essays in *Time*, including one called "The Anatomy of Hate"—Lance, I know you're very gifted, but why not something more upbeat? The final nominee was Hans Christian von Baeyer, who'd written three columns for a magazine called *The Sciences*, including a piece called "A Ripple in Gravity's Lens"—Hans, I thought to myself, where's the winning tingle, where's that Dances With Magazines glow? I was positive that I was a shoo-in, even though *Entertainment Tonight* had neglected to handicap the odds for these awards. I tugged up my blue opera-length satin gloves, and I put on tortoiseshell eyeglass frames with window glass in them, so I'd look like a real starlet—intelligent but with cleavage. Even though there was no network coverage, I smiled in a carefree but sincere manner, as if my preaward attitude were being examined coast to coast.

When the winner was announced, I was as shocked as you will be to hear the name: Hans Christian von Baeyer. My first thought was that he had one more name than me, and that's why he won. My second thought was: Hans Christian von Baeyer? It sounds like someone who writes fairy tales about aspirin. Other thoughts tumbled through my mind as I faked applause, making a clapping motion but no noise: Libby, I told myself, be happy for Hans, he looks like a wonderful, overeducated fellow; don't be a sore loser. It's fine, I thought, so I don't get that little tin elephant that looks like it was on sale at the Pottery Barn. And why didn't they announce a first runner-up in case, God forbid, something should happen to Hans in the Waldorf lobby and he'd be unable to serve?

To get over my disappointment and to avoid dwelling on conspiracy theories, however valid, I slung the train of my gown over my arm and marched into B. Dalton to buy a copy of Ali MacGraw's autobiography, a volume that was cruelly overlooked by the Pulitzer people, even though it includes a section on Ali's stay at Betty Ford. And then I thought about the starving people all over the world, and the victims of natural catastrophes, and innocent people serving time in prisons, and I realized—I don't care about them. I lost an award, and it's going to take many family-size bags of peanut M&M's to cheer me up. But I do not bear Hans any ill will, even if he could have begun his acceptance speech by saying, "This really belongs to Libby." In my speech, I intended to acknowledge my friends, my family, all the little people at *Premiere*, and American magazine editors everywhere—but it was not to be. As Whoopi Goldberg must have said a thousand times, there's always next year. For now I will concentrate on Ali and myself—it's the gals who never win anything who can really make a difference, if you ask me.

OUTLAWS WE LOVE

— — —

This month, my dear friend Stacy Schiff and I spent a week at the Golden Gully Spa and Stretching Retreat in Arizona in order to meditate, cleanse our bodies of toxins, and avoid our real lives. All the buildings at Golden Gully are adobe with logs sticking out of them; Stacy and I shared a cottage called Mesa Mist with a mother and daughter from Beverly Hills who were recuperating from matching breast augmentations and a record producer's wife from Detroit who had been kicked out of Betty Ford for secretly taping the group sessions with Elizabeth Taylor. Each day, a schedule was posted on our door; the first morning included a Fifteen Minute Hike in Sandals or a Low Heel, a Half Hour of Splash-Nastics in the Lap Pool With Your Instructors Rick or Amy, and a Lecture on Bran Retention With Dr. Emile Melinmite, Founder and President of the Creative Colon Institute and Enema Guild of Barcelona. By the time evening rolled around, Stacy and I were more than ready for a movie, so we signed out a pair of burros and rode into town to see *Thelma & Louise* at the Golden Gully Pueblo-Plex.

Thelma & Louise is about an Arkansas housewife and her waitress friend who take off on a weekend fishing trip and eventually become outlaws, shooting would-be rapists, robbing convenience stores, and having orgasms with cute young guys; well, after a day of kelp tea and inspirational Walkman tapes like "Slap Yourself Thin," you can imagine what a revelation this film turned out to be. Stacy and I left the theater and immediately rented a T-Bird convertible and headed for the Mexican border, just like Susan Sarandon and Geena Davis do in the movie. We don't believe in guns, but we did fill several condoms with water in the ladies' room of a filling station, and we hurled them recklessly at passing vans with offensive bumper stickers or erotic airbrushing. By dawn we were somewhere near Albuquerque, and we sauntered into a 7-Eleven, determined to shoplift sun block, Big Gulps, and a bag of those potato chips with one third less salt and oil. "Heck, we're outlaws," I told Stacy, and we loaded up with canned frosting and Double Stuf Oreos; we paid for everything, because we figured that the empty calories were rebellion enough.

Soon we grew really wild; as we raced through the desert, Stacy stood up, grabbed the windshield, and yelled, "I'm over thirty and single, and I've got a great big ol' butt!" When a passing trucker made an obscene gesture at me, I didn't blow up his rig the way Susan and Geena did, but I did shout, "All men are pigs, including my husband and especially most of the Supreme Court!" Two really cute guys in a Jeep pulled alongside of us a little later, and Stacy and I considered following them to a motel, but we decided to do something really lawless instead: we checked into the Albuquerque Hilton and told room service it was our birthdays and we needed two German-chocolate layer cakes, which we proceeded to eat without utensils. Then we went to bed without taking off our makeup or putting on any Estée Lauder Advanced Night Repair Protective Recovery Complex. "We're a-goin' straight to *hell!*" Stacy howled as we called her mother and left an anonymous message telling Mrs. Schiff that her daughter had gained twelve pounds and had let the room-service waiter see her without lipstick.

The next day, I called my husband, Josh, and informed him that Stacy and I were outlaws headed for Mexico, and he said not to bring back any more serapes or colorful pottery because our living room already looks like a tag sale at Taco Bell. I told Josh we were never coming back, and to tell the kids that Mommy was a legendary bandito, but Josh said he'd just tell them Mommy was jogging too much in the hot sun without loosening her visor, and then he had a call-waiting beep and put me on hold and I hung up. Before crossing the border, Stacy and I decided to see the Madonna documentary, *Truth or Dare*, to inspire us further. "Popcorn *with buttery topping,"* Stacy told the boy at the refreshment counter, and I could see him tremble at our raw heedlessness.

Madonna has always been my hero, which is why I enjoy the intimate, exclusive interviews she's been giving to every magazine except *U.S. News & World Report.* In her movie, she sings and dances and stretches out on her mother's grave and simulates masturbation onstage; while the film is wonderful, by the end I felt Madonna had received more coverage than the war in the gulf and certainly deserves a parade in every major American city. Madonna also wanders soulfully around her hotel room in a bathrobe while someone on the soundtrack says that she's like a child lost in a storm; of course, children lost in storms rarely have camera crews in their bedrooms, but Warren Beatty is the only one in the movie who mentions this. Toward the end of the film, Madonna plays truth or dare with her entourage, who dare her to demonstrate oral sex on a bottle, which she does. After watching the movie, Stacy and I decided that, as outlaw chicks, we had to try this, so we bought two bottles of San Pellegrino and attempted to swallow them, although Stacy said that first the bottles should promise to marry us or at least tell us we were special. Stacy immediately chipped a tooth on the bottle cap, and we called Josh, since, after all, he is an orthodontist, and he told us to fly right home and he'd have Stacy's molar bonded and even throw in a cleaning.

Stacy and I looked at each other; if we headed back East, would we lose our outlaw credentials? What would Madonna do in this situation, and how would it affect her insatiable need for her father's approval? After buying embroidered peasant blouses in both Natural Jute and Sunset Peach, along with some silver bangles that were really no bargain, we figured out a scenario: we'd go back, and Josh would fix Stacy's tooth, but afterward we'd aim his air hose at his feet and make him dance. And since I read in *Rolling Stone* that in reality, Madonna hates to perform oral sex, I would tell Josh that if Sean Penn and Warren Beatty could do without, so can he. Stacy and I flew back in first class, and we told the flight attendant that our names were Killer and Slash, although we changed them over Michigan to Jan and Melissa, which were the names we always wished we'd had. The in-flight movie starred Jim Belushi, so we threw our smoked almonds at the screen; pretty soon, I imagine, Jim will actually be appearing live on transcontinental flights. Finally Stacy and I made a pact: we swore that someday we'd both be as wild and thin as Susan and Geena, who look awfully toned for southern white trash. Thelma and Louise and Madonna are my kind of women; we're all outlaws with personal trainers, if you ask me.

DYING CUTE

Most twelve-year-old girls dream of either being a ballerina, marrying their pony, or having a long talk with Christian Slater about his hair. In her new movie, *Dying Young,* Julia Roberts experiences another swoony preteen fantasy: she takes care of a really cute, rich guy who has a fatal disease. The guy, played by Campbell Scott, has leukemia, but he's so rich and so crazy about Julia that it doesn't matter; even after he has chemotherapy, the bathroom he vomits all over is really gorgeous, with postmodern glossy black tile and moody MTV lighting. Julia plays a beautiful girl with lots of Mercurochrome red hair who seems vaguely annoyed at becoming Campbell's paid companion; her basic attitude toward his illness is oh, *gross,* until he starts spending money on her.

Campbell takes Julia to a fancy French restaurant, and pretty soon they're running off to rent a fully furnished Victorian beach house on the California coast. Each part of their romantic idyll is shot like a different kind of soft-focus commercial; when the couple wakes up under antique quilts as the sun rises through lacy curtains, it's like a Taster's Choice instant-coffee ad, and when they ride white horses through the surf, it's like a Free Spirit tampon spot. Finally, they go to visit Colleen Dewhurst, who runs a picturesque mountain vineyard, so the whole movie goes Gallo Chablis. By this point, Campbell and Julia have fallen in love, even though they have nothing in common and Julia keeps pouting; it's a good thing Julia isn't supposed to be a registered nurse, because her hours and special duties might really upset the union. Basically, Campbell loves Julia because she has so many layered waif outfits, and Julia loves Campbell because he needs her and because she's way too sensitive to ever bring up the terms of his will.

The movie climaxes at a party on Christmas Eve, with snow on the ground, so Julia naturally wears a strapless white chiffon evening gown that supposedly once belonged to Colleen; the gown fits perfectly, so we can assume that at one time Colleen was a foot taller and emaciated. The film ends as Julia promises to stay with Campbell for his next round of chemo; Campbell is so grateful that he doesn't even mention all those tabloid headlines about Julia canceling her real-life wedding to Kiefer Sutherland at the last minute in order to run off with the far dreamier Jason Patric. In the TV ads for the videocassette of Julia's last movie, *Sleeping With the Enemy*, the announcer promises that with each rental you can also get a special video interview with Julia, in which she clowns around and looks wistful. Julia has been in only a handful of movies, but she's already an industry at 23; I think her memoirs and skin-care line are long overdue.

Dying Young tries to make having a fatal illness romantic; in another new film, *Regarding Henry,* Harrison Ford plays a sleazy yuppie lawyer who gets shot in the head during a holdup. He loses his memory and a few motor skills, but he becomes a much better person, kissing his wife in public and taking his daughter out of boarding school. This may very well be the first film to promote head injury; I expected the ads to say, "It'll make you want to get shot in the head!" As a rule, it is probably best to avoid making leukemia and bullets the equivalent of a dozen roses and a box of bonbons; my personal choice for an ideal preadolescent romantic fantasy occurs in the new Arnold Schwarzenegger blockbuster, *Terminator 2: Judgment Day*. In this sequel, Arnold returns as a good Terminator sent from the future to protect a little boy who will grow up to save the world. Arnold is almost indestructible, and he has to do everything the little boy tells him to; overall, Arnold the Terminator is my ideal mate, a big hunk who behaves like a devoted maid, with no time off.

Arnold fights off the bad Terminator, who is mostly a fantastic special effect and who also looks a little like a blond Hitler Youth, so Arnold will seem more American. Arnold also shoots, stabs, or blows up lots of people, but the little boy gets upset and commands him to stop killing; after this, Arnold only shoots people in the knees and tells the little boy, "They will live." The little boy's mother is played by Linda Hamilton, who constantly scolds him for getting into danger, since he has to grow up and save the world. This is just what my husband, Josh, claims his mother always told him; of course, Josh grew up to be an orthodontist, but to his mother, that beat saving the world any day. *Terminator 2* is incredibly exciting: anytime there's a glass building onscreen, you know it will explode; anytime you see a truck, it always says GASOLINE or LIQUID NITROGEN on the side; and anytime you see a helicopter, you know it's going to fly into a bridge. The movie is also very funny, because Arnold is playing a sort of cuddly action figurine; I read that the studio paid Arnold for this film partially by buying him a private jet—if Arnold really has a sense of humor, he will blow it up. *T2* is supposed to have cost almost $100 million to make; I wish it was tax dollars, because I'd rather spend the money on Arnold than on Stealth bombers.

The last cinematic work I viewed this month was *Point Break*, in which Keanu Reeves plays Johnny Utah, a star college quarterback who went to law school and then became an FBI agent. Keanu is a cute little puppy, but he still seems to belong in a mall, especially when he pronounces "definitely" and "really" like he's still in *Bill & Ted's Bogus Journey*. Keanu is after Patrick Swayze, who plays Bodhi, the king of the surfers and also a New Age philosopher and bank robber. Keanu and Patrick challenge each other in all sorts of macho rituals, including skydiving, night surfing, and fistfighting; somehow neither Patrick nor Keanu really seems like a Hemingway type. Between Patrick's peroxide shag and Keanu's Valley Boy diction, they seem more like the Landers sisters, or Marilyn Monroe and Jane Russell in *Gentlemen Prefer Blondes*. This is very much to their credit, since I don't think I'd like any performer who could convincingly portray a character called Johnny Utah. As for Patrick, he's become so glamorous that it's impossible to think of a profession you'd believe him in; Patrick needs to be physical, so maybe his next role will be a combination, like a dance instructor who's also a hit man, or a go-go boy/circuit judge.

Point Break is the sort of movie that is all buzzwords, the kind that seem to get Hollywood executives all hot and bothered: "surfers," "bank robbers," "skydiving," "wet suits." Marriage counselors in Los Angeles probably suggest that dysfunctional couples use these words as foreplay, peaking with "Cruise," "Julia," and "android." For my money, I'll stick with Keanu, Patrick, and Arnold—guys with such really obvious stunt doubles are secretly pussycats, if you ask me.

GIRLZ N THE HOOD

▄ ▄ ▄

This month, I went to see two films by hot young black directors, Spike Lee's *Jungle Fever* and 23-year-old John Singleton's *Boyz N the Hood*. I called up my friend Jameesa Shamile-Jonque and invited her to come with me; Jameesa teaches African-American Literature at Columbia, and she gets very irate when freshmen ask if the syllabus includes Bill Cosby's books. I met her when we were at college together, and she told me I was the whitest woman she'd ever met; I told her that compared to most girls from Great Neck, I was Miriam Makeba, and we both laughed and circulated a petition demanding more 3 Musketeers bars and no apples in the dorm-basement vending machines. When I asked her to go to the movies with me, Jameesa said I was just a honkie who wanted a black tour guide; I told her if she didn't go, I'd tell everyone her real name is Joyce, and we made a date.

There had been incidents at some of the theaters showing *Boyz N the Hood*, so I was a little nervous; Jameesa said if people had any brains, there'd be violence at films like *Return to the Blue Lagoon*, where audience members could shoot the projector. I agreed and said I'd considered firebombing the Kevin Costner remake of *Robin Hood* because it was so boring and because Kevin looked scraggly and smelly, like a Venice Beach drug dealer after a night in police custody.

Jameesa and I went to see *Jungle Fever* first. It's about a black architect who has a love affair with his white secretary; his wife throws him out, and all hell breaks loose. The architect also has a brother who's a crack addict, and the secretary's ex-boyfriend starts seeing a black woman and gets beaten up. At times, everyone in the movie just sits around and discusses a topic, like Mayor Dinkins or finding a decent husband. After a while, the movie seems to be about a million different things, but I liked that; Spike's movies make most other films look anorexic. I told Jameesa that most white movies nowadays are about bank-robbing surfers or bumbling detectives who hook up with wisecracking orphans; Jameesa said maybe all the white movies have been made already, and that when you start doing films like *Bingo!*, where the star is a dog who can drive, maybe it's time to give the whole Caucasian thing a rest.

Jameesa says black actors have mostly moved up from playing Hattie McDaniel to playing Eve Arden and that it's nice to see a movie where they don't play sidekicks to Mel Gibson or Billy Crystal. I asked Jameesa about her new hairstyle, which has cornrows and coils; I wondered if the little seashells knotted to the ends of the braids hurt when they bounce on her forehead. She asked me if it hurts when I have my roots touched up, and I said, Stop it, Joyce, and we debated whether it was politically correct to leave our empty popcorn container under the seat. I asked Jameesa if she would ever marry a white guy, and she said it would be a tough decision. She asked me if I would ever get divorced from my husband, Josh, and marry a black guy, and I said it's pretty hard to top an orthodontist, and she said, What about a black ear-nose-and-throat man? and I said, Don't tease.

Boyz N the Hood is about growing up in a black neighborhood in L.A., where there are gangs and assault rifles and police helicopters. The movie is very gripping, because it showed me things I'd never seen before; Jameesa said the black people sounded normal for once. The movie follows three characters as they get older, and it reminded me of a Humphrey Bogart–James Cagney type of movie, where one guy is clean-cut and decent and is only interested in the nice girl next door, while one of his friends is a hunk and another one is a ne'er-do-well headed for crime. Everything is very well balanced, and sometimes the characters make speeches about Life; Jameesa said she noticed this, too, but we agreed that the script was so fresh that it didn't really matter. I asked Jameesa if she meant "fresh" as in the Fresh Prince, the rapper, and she asked if I meant "fresh" as in Don't be fresh to your aunt Estelle; finally, we decided we both meant "fresh" like in pasta with an expiration date. *Boyz N the Hood* stars a rapper named Ice Cube, who's very talented; I asked Jameesa if I could change my name to Twist of Lime, and she said no, I should be called Tab With Lemon, and I asked if her nose ring ever sets off the alarm at airport security.

Jameesa and I decided that Spike Lee is a more glamorous director than John Singleton. Spike's movies always have drop-dead clothes and gorgeous furniture and jazzy camera angles, as if he just loves making movies; Spike is great because he's like an activist Vincente Minnelli. The female characters in both Spike's and John's movies are a little sketchy, and the camera tends to ogle them; Jameesa said a black woman director is not a bad idea, and I said someday I'd direct a film about religious intermarriage called *Goyz N the Hood*, and Jameesa said, Libby, have you been snorting Slim-Fast again?

Both the films we saw were very well made but also depressing; when I mentioned this, Jameesa said, Welcome to the world, and I said, Aren't we right near Bergdorf's? Jameesa said I shouldn't ignore the bad stuff in life, and I agreed, but I asked her if I could maybe watch the news in a Romeo Gigli blouse. Jameesa said when I shop, I have soul; I said someday I hope everyone in the world can go to sample sales, regardless of race, creed, or gender preference. I said I was brought up to believe in a rainbow coalition, because my mother told me, If a sweater is a classic, you should get it in every color.

Just to even things up, the last movie Jameesa and I saw was *Mobsters*, which is about four white teen idols who play famous gangsters as kids; it's like *Young Attila the Hun* or *Murder, Inc.: The Junior Achievement Years*. Christian Slater plays "Lucky" Luciano, and Richard Grieco plays "Bugsy" Siegel; the movie is so terrible that you expect the actors' agents to appear with them onscreen, reassuring them about why the whole thing is surefire. Costas Mandylor, who plays Frank Costello, is the cutest New Thug on the Block, but he doesn't get to do much. Lara Flynn Boyle plays Christian's girlfriend and manages to have sex and get shot without disturbing the most obvious red wig in motion picture history; Lara looks like Louise Brooks crossed with Pippi Longstocking. After we left, Jameesa said, You see what happens when you let white guys make movies?

Finally, I asked Jameesa if she thought black people and white people will ever be friends, and she said they'd better be. That made sense, so as a gesture of equality, I told Jameesa to buy the Kamali lace skirt *and* the chunky Saint Laurent gold earrings with the fake rubies; we agreed that bankruptcy is the true universal language. If the races would only encourage each other to reach their Visa limits, then we could really have harmony on the planet, if you ask me.

MAKING NICE

▬ ▬ ▬

hanks to a bunch of recent movies, the '90s are finally starting to get an identity; if the '80s were about greed, the '90s
are about need. If I were writing for *New York* magazine, I'd
do a cover story called "The New Niceness," and I'd man-
ufacture T-shirts that said HUG ME, I'M HOMELESS and POOR
IS BETTER. In *Regarding Henry*, Harrison Ford quits being a
lawyer because all lawyers are yuppie scum. In *The Doctor*,
William Hurt is a surgeon who learns that having a sense of humor
means a person is chilly and self-involved. In *Doc Hollywood*, Michael J. Fox finds out that treating indigestion in a small town is
much more rewarding than being a plastic surgeon in Beverly Hills.
Somehow, I can't see the people who wrote and directed these
movies giving up their BMWs and heading off to volunteer at free
clinics in Appalachia or doing pro bono work for the ACLU.

The latest movie in this trend is *The Fisher King*; almost all you
need to know about it is that Robin Williams plays a homeless person who imagines himself to be a knight on a mythical quest. This is
a film for people who thought that *Field of Dreams* and *Dances With
Wolves* were too sarcastic. After seeing it, I decided that there are
certain things that Robin Williams must never be allowed to do onscreen, by federal statute if necessary:

1. Smile through tears.
2. Hug another man, who will then act embarrassed.
3. Clutch a child's toy.
4. Talk dirty so it sounds cute.
5. Rip off his clothes as a rite of freedom.
6. Twinkle, cavort, or exult.

In *The Fisher King*, Jeff Bridges plays a radio personality who makes snide remarks about yuppies, and his show triggers a psychopath to walk into a trendy restaurant and machine-gun the clientele. Jeff feels terribly guilty about the incident and leaves his job and becomes a drunk. In a weird way, the movie seems to be opposed to free speech—the screenwriter apparently thinks that people should only say nice things, especially on the air. *The Fisher King* is about someone like the radio maniac Howard Stern finding his soul—does anyone really want to hear Howard speaking out compassionately for the disenfranchised? Would that really help relieve the stress of people listening to the cab radio while stuck in midtown traffic?

Jeff hits bottom, living with a lower-class woman and finally meeting up with Robin in the gutter. Robin wears adorably designed tatters and lives in an enormous abandoned basement decorated with candles and brick-à-brac; it's an ideal meeting place for reunions of the *Beauty and the Beast* fan club. The homeless people in this movie are all winsome and sweet, like a Children's Crusade; none of them ever spit at people or demand money. It's important to help the homeless, but maybe we shouldn't turn them into Cabbage Patch Kids; I can just see a *Fisher King* boutique at Bloomingdale's, full of fingerless gloves and patched overcoats. In New York recently, a group of homeless people were living in front of the Coliseum; the city offered them their choice of shelters and gave them the option of staying together elsewhere as a tribe. Most of them got huffy and moved into Central Park; I personally think they were just waiting to see a menu and a wine list.

In *The Fisher King*, Robin and Jeff take off all their clothes at midnight in Central Park, and they lie on the ground and gaze up at the stars. The movie takes this to be an act of magical liberation, but the actors keep twisting into incredibly contorted positions to avoid frontal nudity, so some of the magic wears a little thin. Robin used to be a college professor, but his wife was shot by the very psychopath who went berserk over Jeff's radio show. Now Robin has retreated into a dreamworld, having developed the sort of lyrical mental illness that people get only in the movies—it's like Disney schizophrenia. *The Fisher King* is one of those movies that insist that insane people are really wiser and nicer than money-grubbing regular people and that only the homeless are truly sensitive and honest; in *The Fisher King*, all the street people are elves.

Everyone in the '90s keeps saying they're so sorry about the way they acted in the '80s; every insider trader who went to prison has a mea culpa book deal. It reminds me of how, after Watergate, G. Gordon Liddy became a TV actor and Nixon wrote his memoirs and got a library; in America, no one is ever really sorry, they just try to merchandise their apologies. When Hollywood starts promoting poverty and the joy of running around Central Park naked, it can get pretty offensive, especially to women. In *The Fisher King*, only the male characters are allowed to think about the Meaning of Life; the women just think about men. I don't mind so much when Hollywood promises me that someday I'll get to marry Cary Grant; I do mind when Hollywood tells me that if I'm really lucky, he'll be homeless.

I have this horrible feeling that we're in for a lot more movies about selfish yuppies finding their souls. I asked my husband, Josh, if we should give up our careers and our co-op and go live in a small town or a doorway on Avenue A. Josh asked if East Hampton counts as a small town, and I decided it might be nice to live in the revolving door at Saks, because you'd get exercise and always be the first one there for sales. We decided that while it's morally reprehensible to have a second mortgage, Cinemax and HBO, and a salad shooter, being homeless is probably not really more satisfying; homeless people, in fact, might even choose a doorman building over a shrub near the duck pond. Only moviemakers think this is a difficult decision.

All of the '90s New Niceness is making Donald Trump look awfully good; of course, in the movie version, Marla would leave him for someone living in an appliance carton. I love Hollywood because it has no soul; only Hollywood would try to market a recession. I'm investing in mismatched shoes and cologne that smells like day-old urine; I'm trading in my squash racket for a squeegee and a rag at the entrance to the Holland Tunnel. Poor isn't just better, it's hot, if you ask me.

This month was my anniversary, and my husband, Josh, bought me all the things on my list and a very ugly purple suede belt to show that he was creative, but thank God I've trained him to keep receipts. Josh always says he doesn't want anything, so I bought him two nice corduroy shirts at Paul Stuart from our children, then I threw his college sweatpants down the incinerator and bought him a fancy new pair, because Donna Karan says that for men, the black cashmere sweatpant is the new jean. Josh said maybe they're the new jean for Donna's husband, but they make him feel like he's touring in *Chorus Line*. I told him not to be ungrateful, and we went to the movies to see how we stack up next to Hollywood couples.

First we saw *Dead Again*, which is a murder mystery starring Kenneth Branagh, who also directed, and his wife, Emma Thompson. Kenneth also directed and starred in *Henry V*; he's been acclaimed as the new Olivier and Orson Welles, and while he's very gifted, he's also a little pushy, like a child at a dinner party who wants to do card tricks, play the piano, and recite a poem when you wish he'd just go upstairs and watch TV. Emma seems taller and more interesting, which makes the two of them just like every other couple in the world. Josh and I decided that Kenneth and Emma probably had really great sex after Kenneth was on *The Tonight Show*; Josh says they probably felt like we do when we get our IRS refund.

The next film we saw was *Paradise*, starring real-life husband and wife Melanie Griffith and Don Johnson. They play a blue-collar couple in South Carolina; he works on a shrimp boat, and she sits in their big house all day and sews. They don't have any kids, and she doesn't have a job, so after a while I started to wonder—Melanie, how many curtains do you need? In the movie, Melanie and Don are estranged because they lost their little daughter three years earlier, and Melanie feels guilty because she was sewing when the child choked on a piece of candy. Since the child's death, Melanie has been unable to have sex, but if you ask me, she could just knock off the sewing. A little boy comes to stay with Don and Melanie and heals their emotional wounds, like Dr. Ruth in a polo shirt; this is the kind of movie that alternates between tearful hugs and nature-study close-ups of swamp grass and whippoorwills, and after the first five minutes, you know that the climax will involve getting the little boy into physical danger—if *Paradise* were more fun, Lassie would rescue him.

Even though they're supposed to be working-class, Don and Melanie always seem as if they're on their way to Swifty Lazar's Oscar party at Spago; their all-cotton, country-casual outfits look as if they came from the local Emporio Armani, the one between the K Mart and the Piggly Wiggly. Don and Melanie are wonderful actors, but they're too pampered to play small-town folks; when Melanie washes dishes or hangs laundry, she looks like Marie Antoinette discovering Clorox, and when Don's out on the shrimp boat, you wait for the other fishermen to gush over his new blond highlights. Josh and I decided that Don and Melanie should play us in our home movies, unless we can get Patrick Swayze and Demi Moore; they all can be counted on to wear the latest $900 Melrose Avenue prescription sunglasses while playing housewives and mechanics. They all have luscious skin and great haircuts and look as if they're carried around very gently by teams of masseurs, colorists, and astrologers; they're the kind of actors who stay in touch with reality by having a chartered jet fly them to their Montana ranch so they can sit around in old clothes and play charades with Jack Nicholson.

Finally, Josh and I saw a really romantic movie and an anniversary treat—*Frankie and Johnny*, which Terrence McNally adapted from his off-Broadway play. I have seen Terrence's work at the Manhattan Theatre Club, one of the few not-for-profit locations where you can still feel comfortable in fur. His plays, such as *The Lisbon Traviata* and *Lips Together, Teeth Apart*, are classics; I don't know why people get excited about Sam Shepard and David Mamet when Terrence writes hilarious, moving plays, and you don't have to bring Advil and a magazine.

In *Frankie and Johnny*, Al Pacino plays a short-order cook and Michelle Pfeiffer is a waitress; he chases her until she finally gives in and stops being depressed, which is the perfect New York love story. Al really looks as if he works in a diner; he's a dork with a Karate Kid headband, and he doesn't have much of a sense of humor, all of which somehow makes him charming. Michelle is so unbearably gorgeous that sometimes I did expect Al to ask her if, instead of waiting tables, maybe she should consider becoming a big movie star. But she is so incredibly funny and talented that she's irresistible, and I forgave her for being a total goddess; I even liked how the costume designer put plastic barrettes in her hair to make her look plain. This movie lets you feel swoony without being embarrassed, because it's so well written; there's even a scene in which Michelle and Al kiss in front of a truck full of flowers, and Josh and I just sighed and held hands and realized that love was every bit as good as the bag of Mrs. Field's macadamia-nut brownies we'd smuggled into the theater.

Frankie and Johnny also has a spectacular supporting cast, including Nathan Lane as Michelle's best friend and Kate Nelligan as a tough waitress; they're both adorable beyond belief and funny without seeming as if they're getting ready to do guest shots on *Who's the Boss?* This movie is Hollywood at its best, because it's glamorous and touching without condescending to people who carry their own groceries and work in diners or on shrimp boats. While I don't see any blue-collar people socially, *Frankie and Johnny* convinced me that they all must be very nice, and while I'm not about to eat in a diner, I will no longer feel sorry for people who do. Josh and I decided that we were Frankie and Johnny with a silver pattern, and Josh told me that if he had to choose between me and Michelle, he'd give me a generous settlement and the apartment. I told Josh that if I had to choose between him and Al, I'd take Don Johnson, but afterward, I'd feel very cheap.

Then Josh and I walked past a Korean flower stand and kissed; we went into Gristede's and kissed in front of the Entenmann's display rack and bought a Golden French Crumb Cake, which is what I bet Liz Taylor fantasizes about even more than diamonds. I'm glad that Liz is thin again and that she got married to a construction worker; maybe she was inspired by *Frankie and Johnny*, too—though she did take her new husband to her hairstylist, who gave him a platinum bouffant that makes him look like the son of Siegfried and Roy. I think that Liz and her construction worker and Frankie and Johnny all understand that while flowers and hairdos are nice, food is love, and sharing sugar is real poetry, if you ask me.

KID STUFF

A few months ago, during those Senate hearings, everyone was asking if Clarence Thomas was qualified to be a Supreme Court justice. Of course he wasn't, and for three very good reasons, aside from Anita Hill: First of all, he was such a big whiny crybaby, acting as if the rules applied to everyone but him. Second, he wouldn't say how he felt about abortion or anything interesting; maybe the senators should have gotten tricky and asked him what he thought of the Holly Hunter TV movie on *Roe* v. *Wade*. And finally, Clarence simply wasn't qualified for a position of such high authority because he isn't a mother. It's hard being black and rough being interrogated on TV, but that's nothing compared to raising children in a world with John Hughes movies.

I took my adorable eight-year-old daughter, Jennifer, to see *Curly Sue*, the latest cinematic work that John wrote and directed, and she wouldn't speak to me for three days afterward; she even threatened to call the Child Welfare Administration and tell them I was an unfit parent. This movie is about a homeless con man and his little mop-top daughter, who bamboozle their way into the life of a chilly woman lawyer named Grey. Grey falls in love with both of them and punches her snooty boyfriend, and then everyone lives happily ever after in her fancy apartment. It's the sort of movie where the big yocks come from people getting doors slammed on their noses: does John Hughes sit around emergency rooms and howl? Jim Belushi plays the con man, and Jennifer asked me to explain Jim's career.

I told Jennifer that Jim had a very famous brother named John who died and that the government pays film companies to hire Jim as a memorial. I told her that some film companies think Jim is like Tom Hanks, only cheaper, and I used this as a parable to explain why we pay more for silk instead of Dacron in the same color. Then Jennifer asked me about the little girl who plays Curly Sue; she asked how come Curly Sue's parents in real life didn't stop her from making this movie, and I told her I thought Curly Sue ate them.

Then Jennifer asked why women lawyers in movies are always so uptight, and I said it's because John Hughes only likes mommies and that Kelly Lynch, who plays Grey, scored an important victory for women everywhere by not having to kiss Jim Belushi on the mouth. Then Jennifer asked which was worse, war or *Curly Sue,* and I told her that wars are better because at least they end.

Then I took Jennifer to see *Little Man Tate* because it also has a child star and I hoped he would be a better role model. This film is about a child genius, played by Adam Hann-Byrd, and he is totally adorable. Jodie Foster directed and also plays his waitress mom; Jodie's sleek page boy and funky-chic outfits are a little glamorous for a blue-collar gal, but it doesn't matter because, let's face it, Jodie is just the coolest. She went to Yale, she lost the weight, she won the Oscar, and now she's a terrific director; she's done everything I would do if I had the time.

Dianne Wiest plays a grown-up genius who wants to enroll Adam in her genius school; because Dianne is smart, she also has to be a little icy and unemotional, almost as if she were a woman lawyer. Eventually Jodie and Dianne collaborate on raising Adam, so he can have birthday parties and still read Camus. This movie is so sweet and fun that the plot doesn't really get to be a problem. Jennifer asked me if she was a child genius, and I said of course, just look at how successful your Barbies are. Jennifer has five—one is a supermodel, one is a single mother with imaginary quints, two are surgeons, and the fifth is the personal shopper for all the others. I decided that there should be a new doll named Jodie for women twenty-five to forty; she could come with a toy Oscar, an Armani wardrobe, a pile of tiny scripts, and a fabulous assistant she met at school. Jodie would be a megaseller, because all the women I know would bring her to step aerobics, networking saunas, and prochoice cocktail fund-raisers. Some women might prefer a more mature Candice Bergen doll, but so far, Jodie hasn't been squandering her credibility on Sprint ads. I also saw that there's actually a new doll called Happy to Be Me, with measurements that are slightly larger and more realistic than Barbie's; if you ask me, this is obviously a loser doll, and that's why she doesn't have a matching Ken with a spare tire and jowls. If we're going for toy-box verismo, why not make a doll that can be filled with Jell-O so a child can perform low-calorie liposuction with a straw.

Jennifer asked me if she should start going out on auditions as a child actress, so we discussed how much rejection there is in show business and how childhood should be a special, carefree time. Jennifer decided she'd rather be a child agent and represent all her toys and sweaters. She's been playing with her Fisher-Price cellular phone all morning, explaining to her Paddington Bear that no one is casting and that all the good scripts go to Meryl or Big Bird. Then she called Mike Ovitz and told him that her pink sweatshirt with the hearts was the next Julia Roberts and that both her ballet slippers were out of rehab and dying to work.

I was so proud of Jennifer, although, like all moms, I wondered when she'd start looking for a studio job, and I asked my husband if an eight-year-old would still be too young to direct her first feature. He said of course not, look at Steven Soderbergh, but I still don't want to push Jennifer too soon and end up with a little Cimino on my hands. As I said earlier, there's nothing as tough as being a mom and having to explain to your child why *Muppet Babies* was preempted so we could try and figure out Clarence Thomas's alleged fondness for finding pubic hairs on Coke cans. And now we're stuck with Clarence for good; it's like having John Hughes on the bench, if you ask me.

HOLLYWOOD, PHONE HOME

▬ ▬ ▬

A while back, there was a picture of Barbra Streisand and Donna Karan mugging for the camera in *People* magazine; they looked like two yentas hitting the mall in White Plains, and they were adorable. I'm sad to say that in *The Prince of Tides*, which Barbra directed, she also plays the Most Exalted Perfect Empress of the Known Universe. She's Dr. Susan Lowenstein, Manhattan's richest, most stunning, and most irresponsible shrink; she spends the whole movie analyzing Nick Nolte, though Nick's sister is her actual patient. She has an oak-paneled office with mission furniture, a penthouse with servants and Biedermeier, and a country place with enough ruffled-chintz throw pillows to keep Mario Buatta in business for a year. She's married to a handsome, world-famous concert violinist, her clothes are always wrinkle-free silk, and Nick keeps telling her how gorgeous she is; she's like the heroine of a Judith Krantz miniseries, only even better, because she's both flawless and deeply sensitive, like a therapist with psychic powers. If Barbra were my shrink, I'd know she wasn't really listening; this is a woman who just released a four-CD set that includes her awards ceremony appearances, her singing "Hatikvah" to Golda Meir on the phone, and a mechanically engineered duet with herself at thirteen. Barbra's only spontaneous moment in *Prince of Tides* comes when Nick tosses her a football and she screams, "My nails!"

There's another part of this movie, which takes place in the Deep South and is beautifully directed, and Barbra isn't in it. Jason Gould, Barbra's real-life child, plays her son in the movie, and he's a charming actor, except for the fact that he has to decide between becoming a quarterback at Exeter or a world-famous concert violinist like his dad, and when he whips out his violin in Grand Central station, his playing is dubbed by Pinchas Zuckerman. It's as if I called in Balanchine to choreograph my daughter's role as a dancing strawberry in her school play.

Barbra's been famous and reclusive for an awfully long time, but if she's lost touch with reality, then Steven Spielberg has left the planet. Steven's new movie, *Hook,* is about what would happen if Peter Pan grew up—has anyone been wondering about this? Steven told *The New York Times* that Robin Williams, who plays Peter, becomes "a wonderful man-child," so I suspected I might need my popcorn bucket for more than just popcorn, if you catch my drift. When the movie starts, Peter is a busy executive with a cellular phone, and he misses his little son's baseball game; this part of the movie is like *Regarding Peter* or any of those movies about yuppies who need to rediscover their souls. Peter returns to Neverland, but I guess Steven found his soul by directing a movie rumored to have cost $75 million.

A lot of this story hinges on that little boy hitting a home run, just the way the little boy in *Parenthood* had to catch a fly ball or be doomed forever. I bet Steven Spielberg was a nerdy kid who hated gym—why is Little League his ultimate test? When Peter gets to Neverland, it looks like an enormous Toys Я Us warehouse, full of junk that didn't sell. The Lost Boys are ethnically balanced, like a "We Are the World" UNICEF card, and they're led by a teenager named Ruffio, who has a skateboard and a punk wig—Ruffio is like a rich 45-year-old white guy's version of somebody really hip. Julia Roberts plays Tinkerbell, and she keeps telling Peter that he can't fly unless he has a Happy Thought; she started to remind me of my aunt Sylvia telling my brother David that he needed an enema. Peter's Happy Thought turns out to be his son; he also has a little daughter standing a few feet away, but I guess she's more of an After Thought.

Peter Pan is mostly about hating grownups, but *Hook* is all about the problems of pudgy adults. If Steven really loved the original story, how could he make this dopey movie? How would he feel if someone made a sequel about E.T.'s mid-life crisis starring Howie

Mandel? Steven is one of the most gifted directors who ever lived, but in interviews he keeps mooning about rediscovering the child within and how he's just a big kid. Barbra's also been chatting a lot about healing her inner child and how her mom was never proud of her. If Steven and Barbra still want to run back to the playground, where does that leave the rest of us?

I called my mother, the beloved Sondra Krell-Gelman, and I told her that I wanted to rediscover my inner child. She said that I was absolutely perfect until I turned fifteen and then I had a fresh mouth and wore too much black for almost three weeks. She said that I had sulked all through Passover and claimed that Aunt Sylvia was responsible for the bombing of Cambodia because she couldn't tell which was Sonny and which was Cher. She said that I had stomped away from the seder table and stayed in my room writing Joni Mitchell lyrics on my arm with a Bic pen, not caring that it might give me blood poisoning. I told her that all of my behavior during that period was just a response to infant mortality in the Third World and the breakup of the Beatles, and that she had never really loved Paul enough. She asked which one was Paul, and I suddenly rediscovered my childhood despair and almost hung up; then she remembered that Paul was the cute one, and she said that she never liked Aunt Sylvia either, because Sylvia had always said that Nixon was very well groomed, and then we both wept and bonded. Then she said that I should stop worrying so much about my inner child; she said that in her experience as a mother, inner children just cause morning sickness.

So what should we do with Hollywood? If you ask me, we should just hand it right over to Bette Midler, who makes me believe in grown-up happiness. Bette's movie *For the Boys* follows a pair of entertainers from World War II to the present, and it's just bliss. Barbra's and Steven's movies pretend to be about life, but they're mostly show-biz tricks; *For the Boys* is about show biz right up front, which keeps it honest. Bette sings wonderful songs that aren't chopped up into videos, and she and James Caan have a fascinating, quirky relationship; James is amazing as one of those veteran comics, like Bob Hope, who seem to exist only for TV tribute specials. Bette is my hero; her head isn't full of Malibu, and she's having too much raunchy fun as an extremely consenting adult to ever worry about the brat within. She's a big star, but she's not a fortress like Barbra or Steven. She's just pure joy, and we should get her to the Mideast peace talks right away, if you ask me.

THE LIBBY AWARDS
■ ■ ■ ■

Now that my esteemed colleague Pauline Kael has retired from regular reviewing, I have become the nation's foremost auteurist film critic. This is a major responsibility, and I must confess that there are times when I wonder if I am really up to the job. Sometimes I think that maybe, in order to fulfill my duties, I should award different numbers of little stars or little film cans to the works I review, or polish my style so that I can be more like Rex Reed, who wrote that the film *For the Boys* was "for the boys, the girls, and the whole human race." In order to feel more adequate and to get more personal breadth, I have begun taking a course one night a week in Topics in Modern Philosophy and Wine at the Alternative Life-Space, an adult-education facility I discovered through a flier in the lobby of my apartment building. It is in this spirit of continual growth and inner brain renewal that I offer this year's Libby Awards.

The Lucy and Ethical Libby goes to Oliver Stone for *JFK,* his film about the Kennedy assassination. Oliver has told the press that while much of the movie may not technically be true, it will serve as a countermyth to negate the Big Lie of the Warren Commission. I thought *JFK* was very absorbing, even though it claims that the military-industrial complex and just about everybody in America joined in a conspiracy to kill Kennedy before he could end the Vietnam War, because without a war nobody could make money selling helicopters. After seeing *JFK,* I got so paranoid that for a while I decided that *I* was involved in the conspiracy, but then I figured out the true culprit: the entertainment-industrial complex. Without Vietnam, there'd be no *Born on the Fourth of July,* no *China*

Beach, no *Miss Saigon,* and Oliver would never have won an Oscar for *Platoon.* So let's reopen those government files: where was Oliver Stone on November 22, 1963, and, more crucially, where was his agent?

The Why Bad Things Happen to Rich People Libby goes to *Grand Canyon,* which I normally would have said is all about yuppie angst, but Lawrence Kasdan, the movie's director, told *The New York Times* that "yuppie" is a "very superior, derisive, derogatory, condescending" word. Lawrence cowrote the film with his wife, Meg, and there's a picture of her in the *Times* leaning on Lawrence's shoulder; both of them look very brave and soulful, like the soldiers in the Iwo Jima statue would if they were dealing with contractors for their new kitchen. *Grand Canyon* shows how urban violence and modern despair affect a group of sensitive people in California; as Lawrence told the *Times,* the film does not claim that "a middle-class person's circumstances are as desperate as someone living in South Central L.A. . . . The premise of the movie is pain hurts, no matter what your circumstances." My teacher, Dr. Ira Sam Vanoff, associate professor of Total Thought and Cheese Selection, says we should applaud Lawrence's thesis and that "pain hurts" is closely allied to Socrates' theorem that "happiness is good" and Foucault's Third Law, which states that "Gallo's sauvignon blanc is good with Cheerios."

The Why Good Things Happen to Rich People Libby goes to the Disney remake of *Father of the Bride,* which is about a rich L.A. family that stages a zillion-dollar wedding for their button-nosed young daughter, so of course I found it very moving. Few cinematic works dare to explore the spiritual cost of negotiating with a caterer or the lasting impact of floral arrangements on character. I asked Professor Vanoff why there were almost no minorities in *Father of the Bride,* and he smiled wisely and said that it's all part of Disney Zen, a discipline that teaches us that the meaning of life can only be found in contemplating the zany activities of Caucasians and talking mice.

The Existential Affairs Libby goes to the film *Rush,* which asks the question Would you be willing to become a strung-out junkie with dirty hair if it meant you could have sex with Jason Patric? *Rush* is a very depressing, well-made movie in which Jennifer Jason Leigh plays an undercover narcotics officer faced with this very dilemma. It led me to such similar metaphysical questions as Would you have sex with Jason Patric if it meant the Berlin Wall would go back up? Would you have sex with Jason if it meant the United States would take home only bronze medals from the Winter Olympics? Would you have sex with Jason if it meant having to have dinner with him first and discussing how he hates it when the media treat him like a hunk instead of a serious actor? All of these issues can be tabled for now, since Jason is seeing Julia Roberts, which illustrates Schopenhauer's dictum that the *National Enquirer* can create reality, if you ask me.

IN BED WITH LIBBY

▬ ▬ ▬ ▬

Like everyone else in the United States, I currently have the flu or some other unnamed bug for the 48th time this year, and after three days in bed, here are my questions: When members of primitive rain-forest tribes get sick, how do they survive without soap operas, *Magnum* reruns, and *Geraldo* focusing on Men Who Claim to Have Seen Merv Griffin in a G-string? Do they just watch toucans interview chimps about sex with their sister-in-law? If we can put men in space so often that it doesn't even preempt any shows, why can't we invent a top sheet that won't bunch up? Is NyQuil really just green vodka? Is the flu a punishment from God or just a network plot to boost ratings for the *Home* show, a program that has, I think, suggested decoupaging lampshades as a cure for PMS? Does Cher's half-hour infomercial for hair-care products actually have more depth than her film roles, especially when she's shown a close-up of an unconditioned hair shaft and almost vomits? If I don't shower for another two days, will the germs multiply on my body or just get disgusted and leave?

In order to cheer myself up, I have decided to read through the accumulated mail from my fanatically devoted readers, despite the fact that none of them cared enough even to send cheap frozen tulips from the corner deli to help speed my recovery. Eddie Bradford of Boulder, Colorado, says I should abandon my column for what I'd "probably do best—write contents descriptions for the sides of cereal boxes." Ward Calhoun of New York City dreams of "Libby dehydrating in the middle of the desert in *The Sheltering Sky*, having her head shaved by Edward Scissorhands, and, best of all, being found and then left for dead in the middle of the prairie by

Lt. John Dunbar in *Dances With Wolves*." Brian Wells of El Cajon, California, tells my editors that my review of *The Doors* upset him. "She never even met Jim Morrison," Brian writes, "so she had no right to talk about him the way she did." Feminist Sue McLean of Fort Worth, Texas, sent a particularly direct note to "Dear Sirs" instructing them to "Get rid of the bitch!"

As an American, I'm very proud that Eddie, Ward, Brian, and Texas Sue have the right of free speech, even if that right is directed at a woman and working mom who is too weak to reach the electric-blanket controls or even the box of Brach's Bridge Mix, which might contain the antidote to her probably fatal sniffles. In these last minutes before my very moist death, I can take comfort in the words of Franklin Sellers of Millville, Pennsylvania, who writes that "I just want you to know you're loved despite mean criticism from obviously ignorant readers who're bitter about their own lack of insight." Of course I am too modest, even while hallucinating from cough syrup and a variety pack box of Froot Loops, to quote Oscar Rollón of Madrid, a metropolis perhaps more sophisticated than Fort Worth, who claims that "the movies are exactly the way you write they are" and "you should be a Japanese bionic-computer woman to be so perfect" and "you should have the international fame you deserve, and all the people in Europe, Africa, Asia, and Australia should adore you." The blind worship of my brilliant readers is really the best medicine, although not as surefire as Pepperidge Farm cinnamon toast dripping with butter, which my husband, Josh, is making me, since it's a medical fact that you can't gain weight when you're sick. I may pull through after all, and I can take strength from the thoughtful conclusions of Georg Turner of Collegedale, Tennessee, who assures me, "You're so much more interesting than Siskel and Ebert, even if you are egotistical, shallow, and vain."

I have just told the nanny to take the children to the gifted end of the sandbox in the park, because it's not healthy for them to see Mommy still in the same robe. While Mommy loves her little Jennifer and Mitchell, they could learn a thing or two from David Plunkett of Evanston, Illinois, who wrote an entire assignment on my work for his class in Rhetoric of Popular Criticism at North-western University. David sent me a copy of his Pulitzer-caliber paper, which I give an A+ and a Bart Simpson sticker because it describes my column as "devoted to personal exposition and glandular criticism." I am thrilled to think that I am now being deconstructed on America's campuses, right beside courses in particle physics, Tolstoy, and the semiotics of *The Jetsons*.

Being read for college credit has enabled me to sit up, fluff my pillows, and unearth the roll of toilet paper I've been using since my Kleenex ran out. (Frankly, I don't trust those new tissues with lotion in them, because they feel like I've already used them.) To bring down my fever, I read a letter from Hans Christian von Baeyer; Hans, faithful Libby-ites may recall, viciously triumphed over me in the Essays and Criticism category at last year's American Society of Magazine Editors Awards. The judges' obviously tainted decision remains uninvestigated to this day, although Oliver Stone has expressed interest in exposing the cover-up, which, I believe, reaches all the way to the offices of *Family Circle*. Still, Hans has written me such a sensational letter that I can no longer think of him as a conniving magazine-world starlet. He calls my piece on the awards "funny, perceptive, and grudgingly generous" and reveals that he was not allowed to keep the bronze elephant trophy that he snatched from my grasp. "My editor kept it," Hans shockingly reports. "I thought he might have been generous enough to let me have the little *tchotchke*. But he didn't. He gave me a certificate—like the Wizard of Oz." Hans, all I can say is, Welcome to the ruthless, anything-for-a-knickknack cesspool of American magazine editors.

Someday I know I will be well again, maybe even well enough to finish the issue of *Us* magazine in which Disney chairman Michael Eisner says that the Euro Disneyland near Paris is "a representation of American culture at its best, we think: clean, safe, creative, theatrical." I'd have added that our American culture is plenty cleaner and safer than some of that grimy French stuff in the Louvre. Even with the prayers of Michael and Goofy, I don't know if I'll be healthy enough to forgive Stacey Mankoff of Manhattan for sending me that famous chain letter with Xeroxed responses from Jane Fonda, who says, "I'll do anything out of fear," and Sally

Field, who claims, "I don't believe in this, but just in case. . . ." To Jane, Sally, and especially Stacey, I send my very own form of a chain letter: the chain flu bug. Remember, if you pass it along to just five people, in four days you will receive good luck! I'm feeling better already, just picturing Stacey huddled in a fetal position beneath a ratty down comforter covered with orange-juice stains, toast crumbs, and damp washcloths. It's all just a chain of Libby-love, if you ask me.

MENTAL PICTURES
— — — —

Welcome. I'm glad you're reading. Are you glad? I'm Dr. Arlene Cole-Natbaum, Libby's psychotherapist. On my advice, Libby is taking this month off and is resting comfortably at the Breezy-Cure Inn, a psychiatric bed-and-breakfast in East Gretchen, Connecticut. Libby suffered a brief transemotional incident after losing the betting pool at her Oscar-night party by one category; her only error lay in her poor choice of Best Animated Documentary Involving Unemployment. She ran from the party, I am told, and was found by police later that night, wandering along the West Side highway, flagging down motorists and asking them why Barbra wasn't even nominated. Libby was easily subdued, except for an episode during which she claimed to be Jodie Foster, raised her arms, and tried to part the waters of the Hudson River. I have examined Libby extensively, and I believe that the root of her seizure lies in a temporary chemical imbalance caused by glimpses of Barbra's mall-crimped Oscar-night hairdo and by the sight of Audrey Hepburn dressed as Gandhi.

Libby will return next month, her mental stability restored by a regimen of low-sodium, low-fat sedatives with just a touch of real maple flavoring, coupled with a series of mild electroshock treatments consisting of repeated exposure to the Oscar gowns of Geena Davis. I have assured Libby that I will take this opportunity to educate her readers in the enduring value of therapy, even for individuals who remain undisturbed by Warren Beatty's naming his baby Kathlyn, thus ending the reign of the Caitlins. The critical importance of the therapist in modern life can be seen, of course, in Barbra's portrayal of a psychiatrist in *The Prince of Tides*. Barbra was stunningly groomed, tender, incisive, and even willing to sleep with her patient's hunky brother in order to foster a healthy therapeutic environment. I found Barbra's work to be highly realistic, although in my own practice, I wear a bra, a slightly lower heel, and occasionally conceal a Walkman in my voluptuous curls for use during sessions when a patient wishes to reexperience his birth for a third time, including ketchup.

While Barbra, especially in her Jungian use of the crossing of the legs, is clearly a role model for therapists everywhere, I found the behavior of actress Jeanne Tripplehorn in the film *Basic Instinct* to be even more exemplary. Jeanne plays a police psychologist, a role that I understand will be spun off into a series for Angie Dickinson, to be called *Brain Doll*. Jeanne plays both the therapist and the lover of police detective Michael Douglas; like Barbra—and Richard Gere in *Final Analysis*—Jeanne understands that only when a therapist has sex with a patient or a member of the patient's immediate family can the healing truly begin. Jeanne at one point allows Michael to rip off her clothes, hurl her against walls, and bend her over furniture; soon, I pray, this mode of highly interactive session work will also be available to dentists, dermatologists, and even veterinarians dealing with your more tousled and wet-lipped sheep and ponies.

Michael's cop is a trigger-happy, ex-alcoholic ex-cokehead who finds himself falling in love with Sharon Stone, who plays a bisexual novelist/heiress who refuses to wear panties and who kills her lovers with an ice pick just as they reach orgasm. While some may find this film to be a homophobic, misogynist movie-of-the-week-with-pubic-hair, to me it's just another day at the office. How many times a week do I find myself saying to a patient, "Why do you use an ice pick? Why not conclude your lovemaking in a more positive manner, perhaps by picking up a magazine?" If Michael were my patient, I would help him to explore his inner violence, his attraction to unavailable serial killers, and his need to appear nude from the rear, even with those stick legs.

Film is an important tool in the treatment of most psychiatric disorders; I have just taken Libby off her sedatives and prescribed daily viewings of the new Woody Allen film, *Shadows and Fog*, a work now believed to have been seminal in the "sleeping sickness" of the patients in *Awakenings*. This film is a Kafkaesque fable, and the urge to create a Kafkaesque fable is, of course, the tertiary stage of Auteur's Syndrome, the most malignant and incurable of all mental conditions. In earlier centuries, individuals suffering from Auteur's Syndrome were kept locked in gloomy attics and louse-ridden asylums and were allowed to create deeply personal yet utterly derivative works only with dust bunnies and splinters. In our more enlightened era, therapy is possible: Woody has been treated with awards, biographies, and multiple starlets, sadly to little effect. Woody seems to be entering the syndrome's terminal phase, auteur dementia, a progression marked by an inability to film in color, the metaphorical use of circus performers, and the writing of such lines as the following, assigned to Jodie Foster in her role as a feisty prostitute in *Shadows and Fog*: "Men are only interested in one thing—that furry little animal between our legs."

I must close now, as I am already late for an hour with my own therapist, Dr. Sarabeth Molten-Schulfein, who was a student of R. D. Laing, Wilhelm Reich, and Jenny Craig. I have been having recurring dreams in which Armand Assante and Antonio Banderas, the seething Latin stars of *The Mambo Kings*, arrive at my office and demand Hollywood-style therapy. I asked Dr. Molten-Schulfein what these dreams meant, and she said they meant that I was very lucky. She then once again asked me to describe these dreams in rigorous detail, while we both nibbled still-frozen Sara Lee Chunky Chocolate Snack Muffins and thumbed through the latest issues of *Vogue, Self,* and *Playgirl.* Sound mental health really *is* all about basic instincts, if you ask me.

—Arlene Cole-Natbaum, M.D.

FAR AND AWRY

——

Have you ever noticed how England and America are good at different things? Like, the English are able to make richly crafted, emotionally resonant period films, and Americans are good at not going to them. This month I saw *Howards End,* the Merchant Ivory adaptation of an E. M. Forster novel, and *Far and Away,* an original story of Irish immigration that reunites Tom Cruise and Nicole Kidman, the stars of *Days of Thunder. Howards End* stars Vanessa Redgrave, Emma Thompson, Helena Bonham-Carter, and Anthony Hopkins; in the production notes for *Far and Away,* Tom Cruise says that Greenbroke, the horse he rides in the film, "was as steady as a Ferrari's engine."

For years I thought that Merchant Ivory was a mail-order business like Victoria's Secret or the Bombay Company; I thought they sold fancy chamomile-scented guest soaps or decorative plates commemorating favorite episodes of *Upstairs Downstairs.* I saw some of their earlier movies and I always expected one of the actors to turn to the camera and say, "I'm not an English aristocrat, but I play one in this film. You can own a signed reproduction of this silver tray or my Harris Tweed waistcoat for only eighteen payments signed with a quill pen." But then Merchant Ivory made *A Room with a View* and *Howards End,* and their movies stopped seeming so much like Cliffs Notes or something Martha Stewart might rent on video to get her through those lonely nights of creating dried pod arrangements in earthenware crocks. I know that Merchant produces and Ivory directs, but I like to imagine them as an artistic retailing team, like Lord & Taylor or Van Cleef & Arpels.

Howards End follows the story of two bohemian English sisters, played by Emma and Helena, as they search for love, social justice, and gorgeous country homes with gardens out of coffee-table books. In Merchant Ivory movies, the country homes are the equivalent of the state-of-the-art guns in the *Lethal Weapon* series; after seeing the movie, you desperately want to own one. Emma marries a rich old tycoon, and Helena gets pregnant out of wedlock, like Murphy Brown, only Helena doesn't yell all her lines the way Candice Bergen does. I wonder if Dan Quayle will go after *Howards End* as well; he probably thinks it's a gay porno movie. Everything in *Howards End* is romantic and tragic, and I just swooned; as a rule, I prefer the emotional problems of people with great clocks and wonderful paisley shawls. *Howards End* transported me, the way movies and catalogs are supposed to; I wanted to call up and order Emma's life, Helena's skin, and all the jewelry.

At most movies, I suspend disbelief, and at least for a while, I agree to accept that Tom Cruise is a race-car driver or a pool hustler or a person. *Far and Away* is very strange—it's like watching Tom in a $60 million school play, where you never forget that he's really the star quarterback and the class president. Tom plays a poor Irish tenant farmer who has to attend to his father's coffin shouting "Da! Da!" Nicole Kidman plays a feisty, spunky, ringlet-tossing rich girl; Nicole is very talented, but she should probably avoid any future roles that require her to be both headstrong and helpless, like a redheaded Shelley Long. Nicole stabs Tom with a pitchfork and peeks at his genitals when he's unconscious; then they run off together to America, packing only their clichés. They get to Boston and live together as brother and sister in a whorehouse; Nicole now peeks at Tom's semi-uncovered behind. Nicole and Tom barely even kiss in this movie; peeping and grinning must be the new safe sex. Nicole works as a chicken plucker, while Tom becomes a bare-knuckle boxer. Eventually, Tom loses a fight, and he and Nicole are tossed out of the whorehouse and are forced to wander for days through the worst fake snow and the phoniest Boston back lot I've ever seen; it's like Tom and Nicole are suddenly trapped in a cottage cheese blizzard during a musical number in *Newsies*.

Tom and Nicole never seem more like seven-figure movie stars than when they're supposed to be starving; they're like Farrah and Ryan wandering through Beverly Hills begging for a few pieces of radicchio. Tom and Nicole are married in real life, and *Far and Away* might be their *Shanghai Surprise;* costarring in a historical epic is grounds for divorce in Southern California. Nicole's lawyer could claim extreme mental anguish, because in *Far and Away,* Tom is forced to gaze at Nicole and refer to her as a "corker" in an accent on loan from an Irish Spring commercial. Eventually Tom and Nicole participate in the Oklahoma Land Rush, staking their claim to a photogenic piece of property. I kept expecting them to gallop just a bit farther and grab a few acres near Jessica Lange and Sam Shepard, or maybe a nice chunk of Aspen, as an investment.

Far and Away flunks the primary test of historical filmmaking: I didn't want to order anything I saw onscreen. Tom sports what appears to be a raw silk wardrobe of layered Matsuda peasant-wear, but it looks itchy, and even Nicole's Irish manor seemed chilly and underfurnished. *Far and Away* seems like a chapter from *Ronald Reagan's Golden Book of American History;* it's all about how attractive white people sailed over in first class and then received entire states because they were so well-mannered.

Far and Away proves once and for all that Americans are right to avoid historical subjects—we're better at phys ed. Tom, you're adorable, but your abs and dental work are circa 1992, if you ask me.

A MOVIE STAR
AMONG US
— — — —

I think it is very important for every one of us to explore cultures other than our own—provided those cultures have air conditioning, convenient and affordable parking, and duty-free shops. Hollywood clearly shares my feelings, because every so often it sends an all-American movie star off to visit a foreign land, tribe, or sect, as when Harrison Ford hid out in an Amish barn in *Witness,* or when Patrick Swayze played a Texas surgeon dropping by a Calcutta slum in *City of Joy.* Blond stars have horned in on American Indians, Creoles, convents, South Africa, and countless forbidden planets, and now, in *A Stranger Among Us,* Melanie Griffith ventures to Brooklyn to live among the Hasidim, a group of extremely orthodox Jews. Like her many platinum predecessors, Melanie experiences a love that cannot be, learns a lesson about brotherhood, and heads for home, maybe packing a souvenir beanie with the logo MY PARENTS VISITED THE JEWS AND ALL I GOT WAS THIS LOUSY YARMULKE.

Melanie plays a New York police detective assigned to investigate the murder of a young Hasid in the diamond district; murder is usually the event that introduces a star to a minority group, unless the movie's hero is simply a spoiled playboy who needs to see real life. To infiltrate the Hasidim, Melanie wears longer skirts and dowdy colors and dyes her hair brown; I hope her next assignment doesn't require her to pass in Harlem. Melanie moves into the household of a major rebbe; thank God no one saw *The Bonfire of the Vanities,* so she goes unrecognized. Every Hasidic location is bathed in golden yellow light, as if the Hasidim use special bulbs or live in one of those heartwarming AT&T ads; the Hasidim themselves are all wise and gentle and full of folk sayings, like Yiddish Charlie Chans or sidewalk Santas in an evening look. Melanie shares a bedroom with the rebbe's adopted daughter, and they stay up late swapping cross-cultural tips and giggling; I expected Melanie to say, "But don't you think Yitzhak Shamir is just *dreamy?*"

Melanie falls for Ariel, the rebbe's adopted son. Ariel's sister says that Ariel is a genius, that he is to Jewish learning "what Mozart was to music." This is the exact metaphor my mother-in-law uses when she describes her son's career in orthodontia. Ariel is one hunky Hasid, and pretty soon he and Melanie are sassing each other and exchanging steamy glances over the matzo balls. Probably the main trouble with *A Stranger Among Us* is that it's not a musical; Melanie and Ariel are like the star-crossed starlets in *West Side Story,* and every other line sounds like a song cue for "A Goy Like That," "Two Different Worlds," or "Not on Shabbes!" Melanie, as a career police officer, has been having doubts about her femininity, so she is drawn to the warmth and family traditions of her new friends; in this way, the film manages to offend both Jews and policewomen.

A Stranger Among Us, which I like to think of as *Debbie and the Rebbe,* is very careful to portray the Hasidim as cuddly, absent-minded bookworms, and no one ever asks if girls are allowed to study the Torah or become rebbes or even rent *Yentl.* At least in *City of Joy,* Patrick Swayze singlehandedly built a clinic, fought a monsoon, and brought feminism to India; I wish Melanie had charged into the shul and said, in her breathy American chirp, "Come on, you guys! Boys and girls—sit together!" Melanie keeps talking about what a tough life she's had as a cop, but it's hard to believe she'd ever really arrest anyone; she reminded me of Kathleen Turner or Madonna, because no matter what role they are assigned, they always seem to be playing red-hot call girls. Melanie nailing "perps" on a midtown stakeout is just a little hard to buy; would you stop hot-wiring a car if you heard Marilyn Monroe whisper "Freeze"?

I like all the visiting-blond movies because they show that you can sum up most foreign cultures in under two hours and still have room for a car chase and maybe a shower scene. And frankly, I really don't feel comfortable around people in native costumes unless there's a wholesome American star in the room to use slang and nibble the funny food. I prefer to treat ancient religions as if they were rides at EPCOT; I have this sneaking suspicion that Melanie and Patrick will soon find themselves in Russia, Tibet, or on a kibbutz, falling in love with whatever local actor has the most Hollywood-style facial features. Maybe it would be even better to do all of these movies as comedies; *A Stranger Among Us* might have been more fun if it had Goldie Hawn or Eddie Murphy disrupting a bar mitzvah in a fake beard and a long black coat. After *Top Gun* came out, Navy enlistments went way up, so I expect that after *A Stranger Among Us* hits cable, teenagers will line up outside their local yeshiva, since it looks so cool and all the chicks are so hot.

This month I also saw *Universal Soldier,* another film that deals successfully with cross-cultural issues. Jean-Claude Van Damme and Dolph Lundgren play American soldiers who are killed in Vietnam and are then brought back to life 35 years later as unstoppable androids. I wonder if Nobel scientists watch movies like *Universal Soldier* and *Terminator 2: Judgment Day* and then slap their foreheads and go, "Unstoppable androids! I gotta get to the lab!" Why are we spending so much money on space shuttles when we could be funding research on replicants, clones, and anything that sees through an infrared grid?

The cross-cultural issue in *Universal Soldier* is this: Jean-Claude is from Brussels and Dolph is Swedish, and they both have thick accents, so what were they doing in those rice paddies as American grunts? The film eventually declares Jean-Claude to be a Cajun from Louisiana and pretty much ignores the Dolph question; this makes far more sense than anything in *A Stranger Among Us.* The continuity in *Universal Soldier* is extremely innovative; whenever the movie can't figure out how to get Jean-Claude out of a motel room surrounded by unstoppable androids, it just cuts to the next scene, where Jean-Claude is driving a great old convertible. I'd love to see Jean-Claude and Dolph go undercover as Hasidim, in extra-large prayer shawls and bullet-proof *payess;* they could make wisecracks and go after Saddam Hussein. In *Universal Soldier*, there's a truly inspiring shot of Jean-Claude nude from behind. His rear looks like it's been polished with love and Lemon Pledge, and that's my idea of a universal language, if you ask me.

OH, HAPPY DAY!

— — —

First there was Fergie photographed topless with her "financial adviser," then Princess Di allegedly gabbing on the car phone, and now, as if England doesn't have enough scandal, there's me and Daniel Day-Lewis. I guess it all began when I went to see *The Last of the Mohicans,* in which Daniel plays Hawkeye, a Caucasian raised by Mohicans and taught to be a legendary woodsman who can listen very intently and hear danger miles away, just as my aunt Sylvia in Miami can sense trouble in Liz Taylor's marriages by concentrating on Mary Hart's necklines during *Entertainment Tonight.* In *The Last of the Mohicans,* Daniel has long black hair, which resembles Cher's wild mane in her "Gypsys, Tramps & Thieves" period, and he wears a loincloth, assorted feathers, and a sort of suede poncho, which would also look marvelous belted over one of my new longer-length skirts, the ones that make me look like Olive Oyl in bondage. Daniel carries several hatchets and knives and one very long rifle with him at all times so he can kill many evil people at once. In a way, Daniel is like the Terminator crossed with Walt Whitman; in another way, Daniel is my new love master, my harem king, my ultimate hug honey, and my latest spiritual fiancé.

I'm sorry, my husband, Josh, just entered the room, and if he sees what I am writing he will be crushed and might throw himself out the window and ruin the cute tin roof of our local Banana Republic; or even worse, he might ask me to go into couples counseling. I feel so much in common with Princess Di: here we are, both stunningly highlighted, dangerously thin wives and mothers, trapped in marriages to decent, honorable men who simply cannot fully satisfy our passionate natures, even if they can subsidize our sportswear. Of

course, Diana's husband is a prince and mine is a Park Avenue orthodontist, so Di has much more to worry about in terms of financial security and the respect of her peers. Sometimes I can feel
Diana reaching for her phone, desperate to dial me, to say, Libby, I
can't take it one more minute—I can't take his dowdy female
"friends," our bratty kids with the bowl haircuts and the accents,
and I certainly can't take my mother-in-law, who keeps hanging
onto that throne as if she were in the bathroom with the new
Harper's Bazaar; I need Daniel, but he says that I'm just a princess
while you, Libby, are a supreme goddess of desire with a B.A. in
marketing!

In *The Last of the Mohicans,* Daniel falls in love with Madeleine
Stowe, who, while beautiful and gifted, is obviously nothing but a
pathetic brunet substitute for me, a makeshift way station on the
journey to my Upper East Side address—which is in the *phone book,*
Daniel. The whole movie takes place during the French and Indian
Wars of the 1700s, so I never worried about not understanding a
thing that was going on. It looks incredible and it's very violent, but
all of this pales beside the images of Daniel striding through the
forest, or Daniel canoeing over a waterfall, or Daniel forcing himself with all his willpower not to stare directly into the camera and
murmur, Libby, come live with me in a charmingly rustic cabin I
will build for you with a disposal and no bugs; Libby, let me take
you in my arms and explain who the Hurons are; Libby, let me
challenge your husband's lawyers to a duel and win your heart and
the place in Amagansett or at least alternate weekends through
Labor Day!

Daniel makes American actors look like giggly junior high
school boys playing Nintendo during the prom; at one point,
Madeleine asks Daniel what he is looking at, and he says, I'm looking at *you,* Miss, and let me tell you, the usher had to conk me with
his flashlight to make me stop whimpering. Daniel embraces Madeleine and kills most of the thirteen colonies to defend her; while he
was doing this, I, frankly, experienced my first multiple orgasm
since Entenmann's came out with its fat-and-cholesterol-free Black
Forest Pastry. At one point, Madeleine is captured by the bad Indians, whose chief looks like my aunt Sylvia after a hokey-pokey

marathon. Daniel shows up and offers his own life in exchange for Madeleine's. Somehow Madeleine's prissy-if-well-meaning English fiancé gets burned alive by the tribe instead, and Daniel shoots him to put him out of his misery—that is what I call a really good date. I would not want Daniel to shoot Josh; maybe the bad Indians could just make Josh spend a little more time on the treadmill and then introduce him to a nice squaw who enjoys watching professional golf, while Daniel and I homestead in the Carlyle for the weekend.

Daniel, in his beads and buckskins, is the first really swoony leading dreamboat to hit the movies in ages. Daniel has played gay punks, Victorian fops, and Czechoslovakian surgeons; he's like Laurence Olivier with genitals. I read somewhere that he was having a tempestuous affair with the French actress Isabelle Adjani; many men turn to Isabelle once they hear that I am married. I have it on good authority that Isabelle even refers to herself as the French Libby, or La Libby. Daniel, I know that Isabelle has told you terrible things; I'm sure that she has said that I am a devoted, radiantly fulfilled wife and mother who could never be tempted into a squalid back-alley tryst with an English movie star. Lies! Cheap French lies!

And so here I sit, much like Diana, in my tub with the whirlpool attachment turned to the adultery setting, with my bayberry candles lit and the love theme from *My Left Foot* playing on my bathroom boombox. I have my chintz-covered diary open, and I've begun scribbling Libby Gelman-Day-Lewis inside little hearts. I am sure that an ocean away, Daniel is experiencing a similar melancholy as he slaps Isabelle's bony French hands away and scrawls countless poems in his journal, poems that all begin with To Libby in All Her Dewy Bounty and end with Now I Hath Made Libby Mine, See How She Doth Grin and Blither. I feel you, Daniel, more than I feel my own children scratching at the door for Oreo Minis, more than I feel my own husband yelling about where have I put his ratty tennis headband, more than I feel my own mother trying to get through on my cordless phone to remind me about chipping in for Aunt Sylvia's 90th-birthday nutria stole.

I hear your agony, Daniel, and I sense your enduring loneliness, your unspoken cries of Libby, Libby, Libby, this clutchy French tart with the rice-powdered moon face won't leave me alone. We will be together soon, my dearest, and please do not forget your loincloth—I have plans for it. I am yours, and you are mine, and even if you turn out to be not all that tall, I don't mind, because we won't be standing up much, and that's what pure timeless selfless epic love is all about, if you ask me.

FILM FAMINE

▬ ▬ ▬

This month I decided to cheer up my cousin Andrew, because both he and his lover, Robert, lost their jobs as art directors when the magazines they were working for folded. Andrew had been at *Metropolitan Pet*, a fashion magazine for animals; he says that because of the recession, most cats and dogs are sticking to classic flea collars and maybe a new leash once a year, so real couture is dead. Robert was at *Blank*, a downtown paper that printed the identical photograph of an opera glove on every page, in every issue, and had no articles; Robert says that *Blank* was ahead of its time and that advertisers never understood that it was a magazine directed at the modeling community. Andrew and Robert have started a consulting service called We Hate You, Inc.; they will come to your house while you're having a party and tell you which friends and family to eliminate from your Rolodex. Business has been slow, especially since Andrew advised one hostess to tell everyone that her mother-in-law was a hermaphrodite, just to give her some oomph. What Andrew needed was a day at the movies, so we went through *The New York Times*.

Right away we eliminated the two Christopher Columbus movies, since Andrew said he's shocked that anyone would claim to have discovered America, given the current state of the Broadway musical. We discussed how only Gérard Depardieu, who plays Columbus in *1492: Conquest of Paradise,* can still be sexy with a gut that big; as Andrew said, in America he'd be married to Roseanne. Andrew said that we really should be celebrating Ralph Lauren Day, since while Ralph didn't discover America, he styled it, allowing Navahos to buy back their own blankets as fabulous trench coats. I told Andrew that I deal with this whole multicultural thing by telling my children that America was discovered by Malcolm X, Geronimo, Betsy Ross, and their great-aunt Sylvia, who saw land and made everyone stop the boat so she could find a clean bathroom and a nosh.

Next I suggested the film adaptation of David Mamet's Pulitzer prize-winning play, *Glengarry Glen Ross*. Andrew said that he had seen the play on Broadway and that it was about a bunch of desperate real estate salesmen whose lives show the emptiness of the American Dream. He said that if we wanted to hear boring old guys talk about deals, we could just look at the videos of my wedding reception. I saw a picture of David Mamet's second wife in the paper; she's a twentysomething tootsie who's starring in his new off-Broadway play, so I felt that supporting his movie would be a direct slap at David's first, older wife, Lindsay Crouse. Andrew says that David Mamet is the Hulk Hogan of the American theater and that his word processor should be tested for steroids. I mentioned that Alec Baldwin was in the movie of *Glengarry*, but Andrew and I agreed that Alec's dreamboat status would be counteracted by the emotionally rending performance of Jack Lemmon.

Andrew and I had both already seen Robert Redford's film of the book *A River Runs Throught It*, and we declared a moment of silent orgasm in honor of Brad Pitt, who plays a freewheeling ne'er-do-well and whose smile can actually cause the onset of puberty. In real life Brad lives with Juliette Lewis, the nineteen-year-old actress from *Cape Fear*; Andrew says that Brad and Juliette are two of the only people in America who can make love while being discussed by Siskel and Ebert. Andrew and I both liked *A River Runs Through It*; it's a very restrained story about a Waspy family at the turn of the century, and all the men spend a lot of time fly-fishing. Craig Sheffer plays Brad's less roguish brother, and Tom Skerritt plays their minister dad; as Andrew said, the movie makes you want to go right out and buy a white person. Andrew and I almost went to see it again, but we decided to just think about Brad and have some lox later on; browsing at Zabar's is the Jewish equivalent of fly-fishing and could be turned into a film called *Some Liver Runs Through It*.

Andrew had also seen the latest movie version of *Of Mice and Men*, which he said was like a lovely brochure for the Depression, with lots of golden sunlight and distressed denim; he said he kept picturing Martha Stewart creating a dust-bowl centerpiece out of battered tin cups, wheat, and work boots for a picturesque picnic without food. John Malkovich stars in *Of Mice and Men* as Lennie, the mentally deficient giant; Andrew said that instead of playing with rabbits, John should have been stroking Dustin Hoffman's Oscar for *Rain Man*. I suggested we go see Steven Seagal in the action film *Under Siege* but Andrew made a face and explained that Steven is kind of lumpy and slicks his hair back the way Diana Ross used to; Steven himself must wonder how he became a movie star instead of a security guard at a small-town supermarket. Unlike Clint or Arnold or Dolph or Jean-Claude, Steven has never had a cute period; Andrew says he wants to see Steven stretch in his next film and play a character with lips.

We decided not to see *Sneakers* because we had heard that it was about computer hackers; I'm waiting for a fast-paced thriller about guys who can set the timer on their VCRs. We decided not to see either *Mr. Baseball* or *Mr. Saturday Night*; as Andrew said, they didn't call it *Mr. Grand Illusion. The Mighty Ducks* featured Emilio Estevez as a yuppie lawyer who coaches a kids' hockey team; Andrew said it sounded like a Judd Nelson film without the sparkle.

Finally, we settled on *Swoon*, an acclaimed film by a young gay director about the Leopold and Loeb murder trial. The whole movie was in grainy black and white, and as Andrew said, the lighting was far more important than the plot. It was sort of like watching a glossy coffee-table book, if the pages were being turned extremely slowly; Andrew said it was an art film, because it was like a painting, only less suspenseful. He said that most downtown art films are just Hollywood movies with the color, stars, story, and budget removed; all that's left is film stock and people sitting in a theater. I tried to cheer up Andrew by reminding him that at least we got to see the trailer for *Bram Stoker's Dracula*; Andrew said that God probably shows exciting trailers about life to babies to get them to come out of the womb but that once they're out, they realize that the feature attraction is directed by Leonard Nimoy. I took him to Rumpelmayer's for a sundae, which cheered us both up. As Andrew said, the NEA should fund banana splits instead of experimental filmmakers. I agree, because a nice parfait glass full of chocolate chocolate chip, with a wafer cookie, is always an enduring masterpiece, if you ask me.

A FEW GOOD STARS

I was thinking—if John Stamos and Ed Asner had starred in *A Few Good Men*, it would have been an ABC Movie-of-the-Week; if it had starred Treat Williams and Robert Duvall, it would have been an HBO Special Presentation. But *A Few Good Men* is actually a feature film with Tom Cruise and Jack Nicholson, even if it still feels like a two-hour pilot for a series called *Navy Law*. Tom plays a wayward but charming attorney; he drives an old beat-up car and never discusses fees, so you know it's a movie.

While *A Few Good Men* made me feel like my brain had been Scotchgarded, another Hollywood creation turned out to be just the thing to cheer me up—Whitney Houston and Kevin Costner in *The Bodyguard*. In this film, Whitney gets to live out one of my most cherished private fantasies—to be stalked by a killer as I accept the Academy Award for Best Actress, the same year I'm nominated for Best Song. *The Bodyguard* is Whitney's very first movie, and already she's playing a character who wins an Oscar—I have not experienced such bliss since Pia Zadora played a writer accepting a statuette for Best Screenplay in *The Lonely Lady*. Whitney wins for her role in something called *Queen of the Night*, and we don't even get to see a still from it, let alone a clip—something tells me it might even rival *Satan's Alley*, the Broadway musical in *Staying Alive* that made John Travolta a chorus-boy star.

Whitney plays Rachel Marron, a tempestuous pop star/actress with a lot of wigs, a small son whose father is never mentioned, and a jealous sister with whom she sings gospel duets. Just for starters—has there ever been a really big star named Rachel? Whitney seems like a genuinely nice, klutzy girl—sort of like Doris Day—which is not exactly dead-on casting for a diva. Whitney also has the most breathtakingly horrifying clothes I've ever seen; her Oscar-night ensemble includes a beaded jacket that doesn't fit, a mismatched halter, and a skirt with a huge knot of satin right at the crotch, as if she'd been wading through something wet and unpleasant, like the script of *The Bodyguard*. Kevin plays the film's stalwart title role, and he looks like he hasn't slept in about ten years. Kevin is troubled, because when he was in the Secret Service, he was off gadding about at his mom's funeral on the day Ronald Reagan was shot, and he's never forgiven himself. Kevin is playing a man seriously tormented over Ronald Reagan—maybe in his next film he'll save Dan Quayle from the media.

Kevin and Whitney fall in love, even though they never quite seem to have met: *The Bodyguard* may be the first computer-generated love story. Whitney is initially a touch spoiled, refusing Kevin's protection and whining, "I just want to have brunch with my friends!" Things heat up when she pokes Kevin with a samurai sword and they dance at a roadhouse where no one seems to recognize her, even though she's mobbed and shot at everywhere else. Eventually the couple go to visit Kevin's dad at his fabulous ski lodge. This is where Whitney's conniving sister is killed; the sister has taken out a contract on Whitney's life, hiring a killer from someone she knows only as "Armando." Whitney recovers sufficiently from her sister's death to attend the Oscars; when Kevin questions Whitney's decision, her publicist tells him, "You don't know a thing about show business!" As a rule, I love any film that tries to fake a real event, like the Super Bowl or the Olympics, especially when it's done with about fifty strategically placed extras. My favorite extra in *The Bodyguard* is the lonely person holding a sign that reads RACHEL—YOU'RE OUR QUEEN OF THE NIGHT!

Just as Whitney's about to give her acceptance speech, the assassin fires and Kevin takes the bullet, allowing Whitney to face the TV cameras and cry, "He's my bodyguard!"—which is right up there with Barbra Streisand accepting a Grammy in *A Star Is Born* from Tony Orlando and Crystal Gayle. The film ends as Whitney and Kevin part weeks later at an airport; Kevin's arm is in a sling, and Whitney strokes it rather cruelly. Then she sings "I Will Always Love You," and Kevin goes on to protect a congressman who presumably demanded, "Get me that guy from the Oscars!"

The Bodyguard made me proud to hail from the U.S.A.: what other country can spend millions to make a movie about how dangerous it is to win Best Actress? I just wish that while Whitney was on the floor, sobbing over Kevin and getting blood on her bugle beads, in the background we'd seen Sally Kirkland running onstage to heist the statuette. In fact, *The Bodyguard* could've achieved perfection if only Sally or Marsha Mason or Ellen Burstyn had actually been the stalker. A platinum single, an Oscar, and a dreamboat with my slug in his shoulder; it's all I've ever really wanted, if you ask me.

LETTERS TO LIBBY

I s it just me, or is everyone thrilled to pieces with the new administration? I can't tell you how good it feels to have women with highlights in the White House; I especially adore Hillary, because we're both smarter than our husbands but love them anyway. Bill is just like my Josh; they can balance a budget, but then they put on a Ninja headband and a pair of stinky old track shorts from college and jog right over to Dunkin' Donuts for a big greasy bag of Munchkins. I also love Chelsea, because I can use her as a role model to get my kids into braces. And Tipper and Al are adorable—I always picture them dropping by after a Save the Beavers rally and remembering to bring a nice bottle of Gallo's Chauvignon Blanc and a can of Ranch Flavor BBQ Pringles. I feel like the whole nation has gone Libby; at last, we've got some hot young people in charge, who'll invite the Venezuelan ambassador into the Oval Office for some Nick at Nite, some Michael Bolton classics, and a few rounds of Twister.

Of course, an issue still facing the Clintons is what I call Danielgate. Ever since my review of *The Last of the Mohicans*, in which I revealed my deep sensual bond with Daniel Day-Lewis, the letters have been pouring in. As one reader from Shreveport, Louisiana, writes, "Poor, poor Libby. Cling to your pathetic fantasy that he could somehow be attracted to you, if you must. I happen to know that it is I, Gwyn Stuart, seductive housewife and mother of two, whom Daniel Day-Lewis dreams about at night. Give it up, Libby!" Meanwhile, Jacqueline Denehy Vigue of Bristol, Connecticut, insists, "I will fight you tooth, nail, and vibrator, if I must! Just because my husband doesn't know Daniel Day-Lewis from Jerry Lewis does not restrain me from striving for my rightful place in his heart.

With my five-foot-nine-inch frame, my wild brunet hair, my shared Irish heritage—ah, well, need I say more? Sorry, Lib, he's mine!" Jacqueline goes on to write, "Did you know he smokes, Libby? *I* can live with that," and she concludes by proclaiming, "I don't care what you, my husband, my children, or even that dog, Isabelle, have to say. He's only going to be looking at *me*, Miss!"

Jamie Mann of Whittier, California, plans to arrange "for an airplane to fly over all of Europe with a banner that reads DANIEL DAY-LEWIS—CALL ME—I LOVE YOU—I WANT YOU!" Deb Englof of Mankato, Minnesota, says of my feelings for Daniel, "I hear you talking, girl!" while Mrs. William Vance of Bristol, Tennessee, perhaps says it best by stating flat out: "Daniel Day-Lewis is better than chocolate." Of course, there are dissenters, such as Janet Myles and Cheryl Laugherty of Fremont, Ohio, who, while admiring Daniel, claim Patrick Bergin as their "ultimate hug honey and love master" and note, "We've accumulated countless bills for damages committed at local movie theaters when, on occasion, we catapulted ourselves onto the screen, clinging with our custom-built suction cups to the object of our desire."

I look to Bill Clinton to settle this seething controversy in the most responsible manner possible: by inviting Daniel to the White House and presenting him with my nude, oiled, carefully lit body as a token of international goodwill. Hillary knows what I'm talking about—she knows what a warm and enduring marriage to a Pillsbury Doughboy can do to a woman. Bill might also look into the affairs of some of my other devoted fans, such as Mike Chapman of Dixon, Illinois, who writes, "I have always felt the column by Libby Gelman-Waxner was an embarrassment to *Premiere* and well beneath the standard set by the rest of the magazine. She must be related to someone high in the decision-making process to have access to such space. Her columns are always so much dribble, but her piece on Daniel Day-Lewis hit a new low in creative effort. The poor, star-struck woman could have just written, 'I would do anything to have this hunk notice me,' and saved you a lot of space and the reader a lot of pathetic mumbling." As an American, I feel that Mike is entitled to his opinion, and I'm sure that our new president will agree with me, and that he'll also create many new jobs for the workers on that new superhighway going right through Mike's living room.

I would also like to take a moment to answer Jodi Torpey of Denver, Colorado, a grad student in "liberal studies" who requests my opinion on "the connection between thinking and writing." This is a fascinating topic, Jodi, although, as Mike's letter proves, there is no connection. And, of course, there is even less connection between thinking and mailing. Thinking and moviegoing are also not directly related, as we can see in the sweet letter from Sylvia M. Brummett of Fort Worth, Texas, who writes that the Tom Cruise film *Far and Away* "comes within my boundaries of good entertainment: it had a good story line, clean romance, enough suspense and drama, a few good fights, hardly any profanity, no 'blood and guts,' no nude bodies or elusive bed scenes. . . . Moviegoers will pay their money and take time out of their busy lives to see a CLEAN and WHOLESOME movie." And, naturally, moviegoers will pay even more money to rent *9½ Weeks* for the fifth time and keep it over the weekend.

America is on the upswing, and I know that even Mike and Sylvia join me in wishing the Clintons well, unless of course they would enjoy being audited until they have to sell their patio furniture and all their Franklin Mint collectibles. I think the new American spirit is best summed up by George R. Clay of Manchester, Vermont, who writes, "I've just read five of your columns in back issues of *Premiere* and have concluded that if I weren't older than God and twice as ugly, I would love you. Oh, hell—I do anyway." And I love you, George, and I even love Mike and Sylvia, because a new American loves everyone; I even love George and Barbara Bush, who can now spend their days as happily retired Republicans, playing golf with their Secret Service men, drinking with abandon, and blaming Millie for everything. Of course, I do wish that in his final days, George had also pardoned Amy Fisher and Carolyn Warmus, but even a new American can't have everything, if you ask me.

SPECIAL ACADEMY AWARDS SECTION

Usually at this time, I take a column to hand out my annual Libby Awards, which are hotly desired in Hollywood by anyone who did not receive even a Golden Globe nomination for Best Actress in a Bad Year. The Libbys are awarded for cinematic achievements in good taste, and this year I have decided to give *all* the Libbys to Madonna. I take this unprecedented step because Madonna has worked so very hard this year, and because she has dared to be a commercial success by walking around naked in every possible medium. Like everyone else on earth, I feel I have become Madonna's lover, agent, chiropractor, and gynecologist; I am more familiar with her breasts and abdominals than I am with my children's curriculum. And after seeing Madonna's latest filmic venture, *Body of Evidence,* in which she tries to murder rich old men by having sex with them, I have no choice but to say, Madonna, take all my Libbys—please.

To properly honor Madonna, I tried to live her life for just one day. I woke up at 6 A.M. and thought to myself, I'm the most famous naked woman in the world, and then I charged my husband $60 to watch me floss. Next I pretended that my four-year-old, Mitchell Shawn, was my hunky personal trainer; he put me through a grueling two-hour workout while we watched Montel Williams and Sally Jessy Raphaël, both of whom were devoting their shows to the subject "Madonna: Why Hasn't All Her Hair Fallen Out?" Mitchell made me do crunches while I cursed Sandra Bernhard and Annette Bening; then he made me do extra leg raises and donkey kicks by reminding me that Sean Penn is having another baby with his twenty-seven-year-old girlfriend. We ended with three hours on the StairMaster, where I pretended I was climbing up to the stage of the Dorothy Chandler Pavilion to accept a Special Oscar for Lifetime Achievement in Upper-Arm Definition and Overall Chutzpah, as presented to me by a bitter yet gracious Jane Fonda.

Feeling toned and taut, I nibbled the paper cup off a bran muffin, performed oral sex on a bottle of Evian, and slipped into just a pair of marabou mules and a fun '50s handbag. The doorman was surprised to see so much of me as I went down to the lobby to get the mail, but I reminded him of my $60 million deal with Time Warner, and he said that my vagina was clearly more valuable than Prince's midriff or Michael Jackson's third nose. Back home, I wrote a new page for my next photo essay book, *Sex II: Another Look at My Butt;* this volume will feature pictures of me bringing famine relief to Somalia while wearing just sandals. Then I laid down a few tracks for my next album of techno dance music; the beat was supplied by a mix of the dishwasher, the juicer, and the disposal. The theme of the album is that even kitchen appliances need physical love; it will be titled *Front-Loading and Self-Cleaning* and will feature a retouched photo of me removing a dry baked potato and a pair of nipple clamps from my microwave.

After lunch, which consisted of licking the refrigerator sweat off of a single strawberry, I spent the afternoon with my adorable nine-year-old daughter, Jennifer, who I decided was really my devoted and haggard publicist who can't keep up with me. Together we tried to decide on which incredibly influential look I should assume for the next fifteen minutes: should I revive last month's crocheted vest/platform shoe/plucked eyebrow thing; should I go brunet, in case I want to be photographed reading; or should I simply tattoo new genitals on my forehead? Finally we decided that I should go for another moment of childlike innocence by wearing flipflops and just my bathing-suit bottom. I wondered about the effect of all this on children everywhere, but Jennifer assured me that kids understand that Madonna's body is like the violence on TV shows—it's meant to entertain, and it's not real.

After putting the kids to bed, I appeared at various downtown clubs with seedy, muscular male models, whom I treated like so much greasy-haired Kleenex. Then I mingled with transvestites, hustlers, and pierced lesbians; I assured all of them that they would be photographed in my next book, right after they cleaned my apartment. Then I was interviewed on *Nightline* by Ted Koppel, where I told him that if only more people would stare at my armpits, there would be no more war. Finally I went home to my husband, Josh, and we duplicated the sex scenes from *Body of Evidence*, perhaps the first truly arousing film set in Portland.

First I had Josh pretend he was an elderly millionaire; to get him in the mood, I straddled his nude body and whispered, We'll do it *my* way, Mr. Perot. Then I handcuffed him to the headboard; I made him hand over the remote, and I said that he could watch the Mary Tyler Moore marathon some other night. Then I smashed the light bulb in the bedside lamp and put the broken glass all over his back; he began to writhe and moan, but the only words I could make out were "tetanus" and "Bactine." Finally I lit a leftover bayberry candle from the Thanksgiving centerpiece, dripped the hot wax onto his chest, and then cooled the wax with diet Sprite—Madonna used champagne on William Dafoe, but she hasn't seen my inner thighs or Josh's neck rolls. I tried to lick the wax off Josh's chest, but it was clumped in his chest hair, so I used my old Epilady, with the rotating coils, and let me tell you, it's a good thing I'd remembered to gag Josh with that pair of torn panty hose. Before we actually made love, I dripped the rest of the hot wax, and a few crayons for good measure, right on Josh's crotch; I won't describe what happened next, but the internist says that Josh will be back playing squash sometime next month and that it's okay, since we already have two children. I tried to explain to Josh that I was Madonna and that the hot wax represented pleasure/pain; I assumed that being an orthodontist, he would be familiar with this concept. I was forced to punish him by reading aloud from *Sex*, especially the part about how "one time I was fucking this guy and every time he came he was so loud I finally had to smack him."

I am not just a fan, I am a citizen of Madonna. I feel just a little safer, knowing that somewhere, every minute of the day, she's working out, making out, or making up. Madonna is like God, or TV, or the Gap, because she's everywhere at once, and we should be grateful. My day as Madonna was exhausting; she's more than earned her Libbys, and maybe a few months off, if you ask me.

I'VE GOT A SECRET

Here is the difference between real life and the movies: in real life, things just happen, while in the movies there are surprise twists. In life, nothing adds up satisfyingly, but in movies everything is worked out so you go home happy and don't have stress over what would've happened if only all the characters had lost five pounds. This month, I saw two films that depend on surprise twists, and here is where I should say, Stop reading if you haven't seen *Sommersby* or *The Crying Game*! Of course, if you stop reading, my feelings will be hurt and my job here at the magazine might be in jeopardy and I do have two children who need accessories for their troll dolls, but you know what's best, so just go ahead and be selfish and stop reading, if you can live with that. I'll try not to reveal too much, but I may get overexcited and tell you that in *Sommersby*, Richard Gere turns out to be a KLINGON BENT ON DESTROYING THE ENTIRE STARFLEET! See, you were still reading, weren't you? You made the right choice, and bless you.

Sommersby is about how Richard Gere returns to his wife, Jodie Foster, in the South after the Civil War. Richard was away for six years, and when he comes back, he and Jodie have great, sharing, fun-loving sex, mostly in nightshirts, and Richard also organizes some sort of tobacco-growing co-op that even includes the local black people. Everything is very New Age, except, of course, the fact that everyone is pitching in to produce an addictive, cancer-causing substance; it's kind of like watching a calendar-art movie about the early days of Dow Chemical, when the colonists first began using butter churns to make napalm. Still, everything is fine until it's revealed that Richard may be an imposter; no one even discusses how unusual it would be for two guys to look like Richard Gere—there are plenty of, say, Robert Duvalls around, but Richard has based his entire career on being the cutest squinty-eyed movie star alive. I'd tell you how it all turns out, but I didn't quite follow the plot myself. I'll reveal instead that Richard wears a fabulous woven jacket with a contrasting leather collar—I'm surprised he didn't organize the villagers into licensing an Armani franchise. Richard is also getting a little paunchy, and at one point, he leaps around a tobacco field in ecstasy—Richard must never be allowed to exult onscreen, as filmgoers will recall from his diaper dance through Jerusalem in *King David*.

The trouble with *Sommersby* is that the plot twist is everything; afterward, the only thing I could think about was Okay, so what if my husband, Josh, went away to an orthodontists' convention in Tampa and came back a while later as Richard Gere? Naturally, I wouldn't say anything for a couple of nights, but then I'd start to wonder: Could Richard really haggle over a camcorder at Newmark and Lewis? Could Richard install a set of braces without telling a patient about his relationship with the Dalai Lama? Would Richard eventually start to compare me unfavorably with Cindy Crawford and suggest that I rent her workout tape, the one that involves rhythmic hair-tossing on a beach?

All of these questions puzzled me, but eventually I realized, Hey, don't worry, it's not gonna happen. Coping with a hunky husband-imposter is not exactly a universal theme; for dramatic resonance, it's right up there with What if a cyborg returned from the future and tried to prevent me from giving birth to the Messiah? *Sommersby* is beautifully made, but it's like watching a really expensive episode of *Bonanza* or a tasteful film version of a *National Enquirer* headline—HE LOOKED JUST LIKE MY HUSBAND—BUT HE WAS NICE! Jodie is gorgeous in the movie, with perfectly streaked blond tendrils drifting out from under her bonnets, and she and Richard actually work in the fields—I love to watch stars holding hoes while they try to figure out which end is the handle.

The Crying Game has a kinkier twist than *Sommersby*, even if it was blown by the Oscars. But if you don't know, here's the deal—about halfway through the movie, it's revealed that the beautiful black

hairdresser is really RICHARD GERE, AND HE'S COME TO SAVE THE TO-
BACCO CROP FROM MEALYBUGS! Ha ha, caught you again—you'll believe anything. *The Crying Game* is actually about an IRA terrorist
who takes a hostage and then moves to London, where all sorts of
things happen. It's a terrific movie, and not just because it doesn't
ask you to understand a thing about Irish politics. It's basically a
sort of bizarre thriller-love story, although it's still an art movie because everyone lives in grimy apartments and drinks from spotted
glassware and knows about despair—I kept wondering if there will
be an American remake in which the hero will have a tan and better
arms.

I am feeling very frustrated, because I can't tell you anything
else about *The Crying Game* without ruining it, so instead I'll just
give away the secret twists of movies I haven't seen. The twist in
Scent of a Woman is that the bitter, blind hero played by Al Pacino
also turns out to be autistic and deaf, and he has cerebral palsy, and
that all of these conditions can be traced to the backstage water
fountains at the Dorothy Chandler Pavilion. The twist in *Alive*, the
movie about plane-crash survivors who resort to cannibalism, is
that Jenny Craig was also on board, and she brought along her own
low-fat, skinless human flesh in a resealable pouch. And finally, the
plot twist in *Home Alone 2: Lost in New York* is that Macaulay Culkin's
parents never do find him, and his trust fund is split between Gary
Coleman, Dana Plato, and Danny Bonaduce.

Plot twists are fun, just like in *Oedipus Rex*, where the hero eventually finds out that he's killed his dad and married his mom—I
hear that Disney is preparing an action-comedy remake, starring
Dana Carvey, called *Oops!* I want my life to start having twists, so
this afternoon I just might grab myself some henna and a tight, se-
quined evening gown and tell my husband that I'm Ginger, back
from *Gilligan's Island*. I bet my life can become every bit as dumb
and exciting as a movie, if you ask me.

FALLING DOWNTOWN

████ ████

What a month it's been; I don't know if you saw it on the news, but my dear friend Stacy Schiff and I saw *Falling Down* and afterward Stacy went on quite a rampage. *Falling Down* is a pretty funny movie about being in a really bad mood; Michael Douglas plays a nerd who snaps—an unemployed defense worker with a brush cut, a short-sleeved white shirt, a briefcase, and a pocket protector. Michael is sitting in his car during a traffic jam in L.A.; the air conditioning breaks and a fly attacks him; and pretty soon, he's marching across the city, shooting up fast-food joints, bashing gang members, and detonating phone booths. The movie kind of hints that Michael has been betrayed by America, but mostly he's just cranky, which is a far more sympathetic justification for mayhem. I don't care about the moral barrenness of pop culture, but I sure understand about needing to make a call and having every pay phone on the street either out of order or charge only.

Of course, I'm nothing compared to Stacy, whose spree began as we left the theater. It was drizzling, and as an empty cab cruised by, the driver flicked on his OFF DUTY light. Inspired by Michael Douglas, Stacy ran into the street and leapt onto the hood of the cab. She took off one excruciatingly painful platform pump and broke the windshield, then accused the cabdriver of selfishness, deliberate cruelty, and the World Trade Center bombing and insisted that he take us home. At 57th Street, we encountered a Con Edison crew that had narrowed Madison Avenue to one lane; Stacy jumped out of the cab, kicked over all the barriers, and grabbed a particularly annoying panhandler and threw him into an open manhole. "Madison Avenue," Stacy declared, "belongs to the people who tip!"

By this point, a cheering mob had gathered, and Stacy led them into a nearby supermarket, where a customer was holding up the express lane by attempting to pay with a check; the cashier had left her register and was having the check approved by the teenage manager, who was smoking dope in that little elevated room with the time clock. The crowd grabbed the cashier, the customer, the manager, an elderly woman who was counting out pennies to buy a single plum, and another cashier who had run out of singles, and dumped all of these hostages into the dairy case, drenched them in products labeled FREE, LITE, and REDUCED CALORIES, and ignited them. By now, the crowd was singing jubilant show tunes, led by Stacy with her favorite numbers from *Evita* and *Les Miz*.

Hiking west, Stacy hit the Yale, Harvard, and Princeton clubs, where she broke off bottles of imported beer and demanded that all the available professional men be brought before her. She interrogated the bachelors, demanding to know exactly how many trusting women they had taken to a bed-and-breakfast in New Hampshire and then dumped for an anorexic assistant editor at Viking. Stacy then dragged a rabbi out of Temple Emanu-El and forced him to marry her to at least fifty men: "One for every Singles-Only New Soviet Film course at the New School!" she howled. Roping her new husbands together, she was borne aloft to Bed, Bath & Beyond, the housewares megabarn on Sixth Avenue, and using her husbands to barricade the exit, she declared a retailing coup and announced on the PA system that "Stacy Schiff now owns every item in this store, especially the wicker!"

By this time, the police had surrounded the building, trying to contain Stacy before she could also hit Pier One Imports, Victoria's Secret, and the Pottery Barn outlet. I begged Stacy to surrender, or at least to besiege more upscale stores, but she was in a frenzy. "Please," she scoffed, "I'm a thirty-four-year-old woman with hips and a going-nowhere job in marketing, and the last date I had was with a crack dealer in Washington Square who let me buy him coffee because it was snowing! All I have to look forward to are more Gail Sheehy articles on the enigma of menopause! For me, prison would be a step up—at least they have dances!" I had to agree, and then we heard Stacy's mother yelling through a megaphone, "Come out, Stacy! You have such a pretty face and a pleasant personality! Give yourself up—and bring me a shower curtain, a shampoo caddy, and anything on sale in bone!" Stacy began negotiating with the police via cordless phone; in exchange for releasing terrified customers, she demanded that Stedman finally set a date for marrying Oprah, that the *Today* show rehire Jane Pauley, even though Katie is very nice, and that Liam Neeson be rotated among all the women in America, not just Julia Roberts and Brooke Shields.

At last, Stacy broke down in my arms and began sobbing. "Please, Stacy," I said. "It's not so bad, and this is a brand new Mizrahi." "All I want is a life," she moaned, "and some quilted picture frames." I led her out of the store, and we faced the squad cars, the mayor, the TV news crews, and all of the agents who were getting nowhere with Katie Beers. Everyone began to rush at Stacy, but I held up a hand. "Leave her alone!" I insisted. "Can't you see she's single?" Everyone backed off, except for Valerie Bertinelli, who kept clawing at me and screaming, "But I *am* Stacy Schiff!" Finally, Jean Harris pulled up in a minivan; since her parole, Jean has been running an outreach program for women on the verge. She wrapped Stacy in a cozy cashmere throw, and as they drove off, I could smell the tea brewing and hear the nibbling of Pepperidge Farm Mint Milanos, all accompanied by the opening strains of Richard Simmons's latest *Sweatin' to the Oldies* tape.

I haven't heard from Stacy for a few weeks, but I know she's doing just fine. Of course, Michael Douglas dies at the end of *Falling Down*, but as Stacy says, everything is always easier for men. Sometimes, a violent crosstown crusade is just the thing to cure a loss of hope and to get you through that in-between season, where a blazer may not be enough but acrylic leopard is still a bit stifling. But as I said to Stacy: at least grunge is over—and that gives us all something to live for, if you ask me.

A DECENT PROPOSAL
– – – –

Hey, I'm Josh Waxner, and I'm filling in for Lib this month because, as she said, Josh, this is your story, so you tell it, but keep it NC-17. It all started when we went to see this flick *Indecent Proposal*. Usually Lib goes to movies with her girlfriends—excuse me, woman friends—or with her cousin Andrew, the unemployed art director (don't get me started), but hey, it was her birthday, so I took off from work early and picked up a bottle of sangria, some yellow flowers at the Korean deli, a new lens for my Nikon, and this really pretty scarf with gold stuff on it from a sidewalk guy who didn't have a box, but he threw in this pink satin thing with an elastic band for a ponytail, so I figure I got Lib two presents. Even though I know that what she really wants are tickets to see *Sunset Boulevard,* this new Andrew Lloyd Webber musical that doesn't even open till, like, next year, the tickets are, like, 65 bucks each, and that Webber guy is English, so I said, Lib, we gotta support our own economy and make some sacrifices, and I really need the lens for my series documenting the effects of leather protectants on the padded dash of my Lexus, and that's why I got stuck going to the movies and wearing this turquoise cotton sweater she gave me that Andrew said will look great with my Dockers, the khaki pants that make me look like a laundry bag (every time Andrew says the word "Dockers," he starts giggling, then swears he's thinking of a joke he heard on the subway).

Anyway, so we go to this movie, which is about this architect, Woody Harrelson (yeah, right), and his wife, Demi Moore. They're broke, and they go to Vegas, and then Bob Redford shows up as some kind of billionaire and offers a million big ones for one night with Demi (yeah, right; it could happen). The couple talk it over and decide to go for it; Demi comes back in the morning, and you expect Woody to yell, Yippee, we're rich! and for Demi to go, What do you mean, *we*? But instead, she and the Woodster start getting all wussy about, like, relationship issues, and I'm thinking, Yeah, I really needed to pay $7.50 for couples counseling with the bartender from *Cheers*, even if Demi does sometimes discuss commitment with one of her nipples hanging out, kind of like Shari Lewis letting Lamb Chop in on things. So Demi goes off with Bob again, and Libby starts cheering; but then Demi and Woody get back together and their marriage is stronger, even if the Woodman donates the million bucks to save the hippos at some zoo—I'm not kidding. Woody also gives a speech about how architecture can uplift the human spirit, and he holds up a brick and shows a slide of the cathedral at Chartres and says that even a brick can aspire to be more than a brick—which, I guess, explains what Woody's doing in a feature film.

So we get out of the theater, and I'm feeling all cramped and gassy from waiting so long to see if Demi's gonna take a shower to cleanse her sins, and then it happens: Demi Moore is standing right outside Loews Tower East, staring at me. (I mean, I swear it was Demi, or at least an incredible body double.) She comes over to Lib and says, How much? and Lib assumes it's like a Richard Simmons Deal-A-Meal and says, Ten pounds and five inches from my hips and thighs, and Demi says, No, how much for a night with your husband?

And I go, like, Excuse me? and Demi says, My husband, Bruce Willis, only has a career in action films, and I didn't get a nomination for *A Few Good Men*, and I need some excitement in my life—how much? And Lib says, Wait, you want to have sex with my husband? as if she's on the cellular with *Ripley's Believe It or Not*. Demi explains that she's tired of actors and billionaires and that she wants a professional man, and I go, like, Whoa, how did you know I was an orthodontist? That's major psychic network! And Demi says, You have this air of healing authority and incredibly sensuous hands, and you're wearing a white nylon smock with a little mirror sticking out of the pocket. And then she says, I will give you $170 for one night, and I start to go, No way!—I mean, I've got the Fiedler twins coming in with killer occlusions at 8 A.M.—but I hear Lib say, Demi, do you by any chance know Andrew Lloyd Webber, like, personally?

So I pull Lib aside, and I say, What will this do to our relationship? How can you put a price on our love, and do you want me to be a cheap whore? And Lib says, Afterward, ask her what she uses on her hair for shine, and I say, Lib, I'm not some stud-for-hire, and Lib says, Ask her how tall Patrick Swayze is, and I say, Come on, this is pure human evil, and she says, Make sure the seats are orchestra or at least front mezzanine.

So Demi brings me back to this incredible suite at the St. Regis, and she says that I can have anything I want, and pretty soon we're knee-deep in Amstel Light, Doritos Tortilla Thins, and this great video game called Sonic the Hedgehog 2. I wanted to shove the furniture around and play Wiffle ball, but Demi says, Josh, it's time. She says, I stared at you in the movie theater and thought, I want what Libby has; I want one glorious night with a pudgy orthodontist with a bald spot from Lexington Avenue. And I go, Well, excuse me, Little Miss Flash-the-Works-on-the-Cover-of-*Vanity Fair*—I mean, I saw your mondo dud, *The Butcher's Wife,* on video, like everyone else. And we both laugh, and I say, Okay, babe, it's your dime, and I go to the bathroom to get ready. When I come out, she's in bed wearing only these white cotton G-string panties and French high heels, and I'm in my track shorts, my ORTHODONTISTS DO IT IN YOUR MOUTH T-shirt, and my flip-flops, and she says, Don't worry, you might like it, and I say, Don't bet on it, and she starts kissing my neck and moans and says, You're wearing Kouros, aren't you? and I say, You bet, babe—ever since Father's Day.

So when I get home the next morning, Lib asks, How was it? and I say, Let's never discuss it, and she says that she has to know for her own peace of mind, and I say, Here you go, row E, two on the aisle. And I ask, Was it worth it? but she's already on the phone with her mom, choosing a restaurant for after the show. So I head for the La-Z-Boy and put my feet up and think, Will I ever be truly clean again? Then I find this note in my pocket that says, "Dear Josh, You will never look at me the way you looked at Sonic the Hedgehog. Libby is a saint." It was unsigned.

I told my partner, Marv Schlein, about my night with Demi, and he said, Right, like she really paid you for sex when she could get an oral surgeon. So I showed him one of the Polaroids I took that night, and he says, That's not Demi Moore, I say, It is too Demi, and he says, No way—that's Jaye Davidson. And suddenly, it dawns on me . . . Oh, my God! Oh, my God! But hey, at least I had sex with a movie star. And that's what counts, if you ask me.

—Josh Waxner

Remember that day a few months ago, when all the working women in America were supposed to bring their daughters to the office, to boost the daughters' self-esteem? And people like Cybill Shepherd and Joan Lunden dragged their kids to the set and explained, This is where Mommy makes millions for getting up early and being interviewed by *TV Guide* and demanding a bigger trailer. While I am proud of my status as an assistant buyer of juniors' activewear, I told my adorable nine-year-old daughter, Jennifer, that if she really wanted self-esteem, she should head off to work with Sharon Stone.

Sharon is truly a career sex symbol for the '90s; on her tax return, where it says "Profession," she can proudly have her accountant type in "Jezebel." Unlike Julia Roberts or Michelle Pfeiffer, Sharon really loves being a movie star, and you'll never catch her slouching in shades and a man's overcoat as she leaves a premiere; Sharon likes acting, but she knows that true creative fulfillment can come only from presenting minor-category Oscars, describing herself as shy and geeky on talk shows, and dating Dwight Yoakam. If Meryl had only followed Sharon's example, *Sophie's Choice* might have made some real money; where was Meryl's *Playboy* pictorial entitled "We Choose Sophie"?

During the shooting of her latest film, *Sliver*, Sharon fell in love with the movie's coproducer, Bill Macdonald, who had gotten married only a few months earlier. Bill has since left his new bride and is engaged to Sharon, who reportedly broke off her relationship with a twenty-four-year-old. As I told Jennifer, at last, a woman who takes Helen Gurley Brown seriously. In *Sliver* Sharon plays Carly Norris, an editor (as she puts it, a "book editor," so she won't be confused with Ben Bradlee or Tina Brown). Carly is currently editing a biography of James Dean; she has also just gotten out of a bad seven-year marriage and moved into a Midtown high-rise; being a serious career woman and also a vulnerable single gal, she wears berets like Madonna did in *Body of Evidence* and removes her panties at a restaurant and hands them to her date, which I assume is '90s etiquette for saying, "Thanks for dinner." I told Jennifer that both Jeane Kirkpatrick and Anita Hill have been known to do this, and sometimes, during a dull session, all the justices on the Supreme Court ditch their boxers under their robes and pass them down to Sandra Day O'Connor. Removing underwear has a proud history in women's films, from Jennifer Beals's Houdini action with her bra in *Flashdance* to Grace Jones flinging her panties at a perfumer in *Boomerang* as a scent suggestion; I heard that in an early cut, several saucy Resistance fighters hurled their briefs at the camera in *The Sorrow and the Pity*.

Sharon eventually falls for William Baldwin, who plays a rich computer genius who owns the high-rise and has installed video cameras in every room in the building so that he can spy on all the tenants and still not fix anything. William shows Sharon his control room, which is filled with video screens; she becomes very aroused at what looks like the main floor at Nobody Beats the Wiz. Sharon and William have sex all over the building; *Sliver* breaks a final cinematic taboo by showing intercourse with a landlord. All sorts of other tenants are getting killed, and this upsets Sharon; even Jennifer spotted this as a screenwriter's faux pas, since in Manhattan the death of a neighbor means that an apartment is available and everyone rushes to the phone.

Sharon has insisted in interviews that *Sliver* is not just a retread of her role in *Basic Instinct*; I agree completely, because in *Sliver* Sharon parts her hair in the middle and does not show her vagina. The most shocking scene in *Sliver* does not actually involve sex; it is a moment in Sharon's office where she is seen eating an eclair.

Feminists and gays protested Sharon's work in *Basic Instinct*, but where are they when a woman that thin is photographed nibbling that many calories? William also offers to take Sharon to the gym; Sharon hesitates, claiming that she's worried about all the mirrors; this is coming from a woman who can wear all white without looking like a movie screen and who's had cameras in places where most of us barely have husbands.

I hope that Sharon keeps making films in which she plays gorgeous women with great outfits who keep taking long, hot, soapy showers; I'd hate it if she became Jessica Lange and started playing farm wives and lawyers. It's good to have some career movie stars around; maybe Sharon and Demi Moore can host a "We Are the Babes" fund-raiser to help Kim Basinger with her breach-of-contract lawsuit. As I told Jennifer, careful lighting, Vaseline on the lens, and slightly parted lips are what self-esteem is all about, if you ask me.

FIFTH ANNIVERSARY
■ ■ ■ ■

Four years ago, when I first began my career as America's foremost auteurist critic, I was just like you. I was an average American filmgoer, leaving my charmingly eclectic home in search of naked movie stars, exploding squad cars, and a good look at Cher's latest surgical procedure. I was innocent, a naively gifted yet unformed cinematic amoeba. Today, I am a veteran—weary, savvy, perhaps a tad cynical, yet still possessing a knack for wearing bulky oversize sweaters with all the coltish allure of Julia Roberts. I think I am truly beginning to understand cinema, because for the past four years I have not only reviewed films for *Premiere*, I have actually *read* many issues of the magazine. And after thumbing through all the gossip columns with their frothy typefaces, the just-for-fun charts on popcorn sales in Taiwan, and the mini-interviews with the Hot Gaffer or Development-Girl-of-the-Month, I now feel that I truly understand how a film comes into being, from first frame to flammable Halloween costume.

I've learned that the birthplace of a film is the studio. Some films are actually made outside the studio system, but these films usually portray human beings in interesting situations, so they cannot really be considered American movies. The typical studio is a group of buildings in California filled with men and women who used to be agents, so their families have already learned to deal with shame. The studio executives I have seen in the pages of *Premiere* are mostly tiny hairless men, sort of like Chihuahuas with speakerphones. Studio executives are hired for one very specific reason: to make sure that American films resemble all other successful American products, such as I Can't Believe It's Not Butter!, Spam, and Vidal Sassoon's Ultracare. Today's studio execs spend most of their time trying to create films with the great scent of lemon.

The idea for a film, I now know, originates in one of the following places: a TV show, a song title, or another movie. Some people believe that films can come from books, but this is incorrect; the studio execs hire people to summarize books in a paragraph or less, so any resulting film is listed as "Based on the memo by." Before I came aboard at *Premiere*, I imagined that films might come from someone's imagination or perhaps their actual experience. I have asked *Premiere* staffers to come up with examples of such works; everyone thought for a while, and then someone asked if the USS *Enterprise* had ever been a real starship.

Most films begin when a studio exec thumbs through the week's *TV Guide*, which conveniently identifies programs as "comedy" or "drama" so the studio can avoid hiring someone just for this purpose. Any programs labeled "news" or "documentary" are of no interest to the exec, as they rarely have a three-act structure or anything for Eddie; the fish out of water in a documentary tends to be dead of mercury poisoning. Once the exec selects a program, he or she locates a person to "flesh out" the idea, to "open it up," and to make it interesting for two hours without the benefit of commercials. This person is called a "screenwriter." A screenwriter is someone who would never dream of writing a book or a play or even a personal letter; he or she knows that anyone can write a movie, because anyone can see one. The screenwriter is often a cabdriver, a manicurist, an English teacher, or anyone who hates their real job; screenwriting is the literary equivalent of Lotto. All you need is a word processor and a dream. Screenwriters often work in pairs, because one partner usually specializes in writing the phaser battles, while the other partner is good at lines like *"Hasta la vista,* baby," or "Lieutenant, what the hell is going on out there?" Screenwriters can make millions of dollars as long as they avoid writing characters, dialogue, or plots; such devices have become obsolete, as they require actors and movies require stars.

Premiere has taught me that writing for stars is very simple, if the screenwriters remember one primary rule: they're all Lassie. Lassie couldn't talk, act, or be in any way human and yet she became very popular by simulating these talents; Lassie is the role model for today's biggest box office idols. Whenever a star stops behaving like Lassie, that star will be in big trouble. Debra Winger, Meryl Streep, and Daniel Day-Lewis, for example, play complicated, challenging roles, and their films rarely open big; where would Lassie have been if she had called her agent and said, "I want to play a reptile," or even, "I want to play a troubled Belgian dog." Of course, Lassie could always make a comeback by playing a dog with a disease, such as mange or rabies, in the *Rain Man/Awakenings* tradition, or by playing the pet of a gorgeous, psychotic nanny. Movie stars also provide fine role models for youngsters; stars are the only people who make more money than drug dealers, and for less work. Now that we have assembled a greedy studio, an incoherent script pieced together from previous hits, and a bankable but talent-free star, we need only two more elements for a successful film: a director and marketing. The director is the most important figure in moviemaking, for one all-consuming reason: no one really knows what a director does. Everyone else on a film has a visible task; the director's job is to watch them do it. If I bake a cake, I buy the mix, I put it in the microwave, and I take it out when it beeps; my husband watches me do all this, which makes him the cake's director. The director is like God: no one knows if God really exists, but it's someone to blame. Some directors even went to film school, mostly to watch old movies; film school is a three-year version of a snow day.

Marketing is, of course, 99 percent of filmmaking, because it is the only part of the process that the execs, the writers, the stars, the director, and the audience really enjoy. In the TV ads, the movie is always the feel-good hit of the summer, the star looks great, and the audience gets to see the only thirty seconds of the movie that actually work.

My first four years at *Premiere* have taught me so much about the wonders of American filmmaking. In fact, I believe that the recent fall of Soviet Communism can be directly linked to the appearance of *Premiere* T-shirts in the Kremlin. I've also heard that a few *Premiere* baseball caps and mugs have been sighted in Beijing; it's a very good sign, if you ask me.